Hugo's Simplified System

Japanese Simplified

John Breen

Hugo's Language Books Ltd, London

Fifth impression 1992

Written by

John Breen M.A.(Cantab.)

Lecturer in Japanese at the
School of Oriental and African Studies,
University of London

Set in 10/12 Plantin by
Typesetters Limited, Stanstead Abbotts, Herts
Printed and bound in Great Britain by
Scotprint Ltd., Musselburgh.

Preface

For well over one hundred years the name of Hugo's has been synonymous with language tuition. In this, the emphasis has been on providing simplified courses in European languages – courses which the adult student can work at without need to attend classes, and throughout which he is able to monitor his progress. After three months or so, he will have a good practical grasp of the language he has chosen to learn; a working knowledge that will enable him to visit those countries where it's spoken, where he can speak it with confidence and understand what's said to him in reply.

When it was suggested that we should publish a Japanese course in our 'Three Months' series, the initial reaction was predictable: 'Huh! You mean three years, surely ... and what about those hundreds of characters in their so-called alphabet? It can't be possible.' But we felt certain that it *was* possible, and that in these times of a rapidly shrinking world where Eastern and Western cultures meet in anybody's high street there was undoubtedly a place for such a course – or something like it.

As the author says in his introduction, learning Japanese isn't as hard as it is so often made out to be. Flicking through these pages and noticing the lack of Japanese characters, maybe you've just had the same thought! This is a step in the right direction because your mind immediately takes on a more positive attitude. It's a fairly safe assumption that you'll be looking for a course with a lot of conversation because you need to speak Japanese more than you need to write it. You may be a business person who realizes that talking to Mr Tanaka in his own language will enhance your prospects, you may be planning a more leisurely visit to Japan, or you may be interested in learning more about the country, its people and its culture. This course will prove suitable for you.

John Breen graduated with a first class honours degree in Japanese Studies from St John's, Cambridge, before spending several years in Japan – where he won more linguistic prizes, and married a Japanese. He returned to Cambridge for his Ph.D., moving on to hold a lectureship in Japanese at the School of Oriental and African Studies, University of London. He wrote this course for us in 1986, before taking a one-year sabbatical from SOAS.

Contents

Introduction 7

Pronunciation 9

Lesson 1 13
Some useful expressions

Lesson 2 16
Statements
Questions: *is/isn't ...?*
Answering questions
Possession
Exercise & conversations

Lesson 3 23
Questions: *who/where/what ...?* etc.
Location expressions
Some particles: *to/from/with*, etc.
Exercise & conversations

Lesson 4 31
Verbs and subjects (*wa* and *ga*)
Verbs and objects (*wa, o* and *ni*)
The past tense
Exercise & conversations

Lesson 5 40
Numbers
Time
Dates
Numeral expressions
Exercise & conversations

Lesson 6 51
Adjectives
Adverbs
Exercise & conversations

Lesson 7 59
The *te* form of verbs and adjectives:
  its formation and applications
Exercise & conversations

Lesson 8 67
Is/are, was/were doing
Has/have, had done
Has/have, had been doing
Duration of time
Exercise & conversations

Lesson 9 74
Verbs: formation of plain forms
Some idiomatic usages of these
'Why ...?' 'Because ...'
Idiomatic expressions: *probably,*
  I wonder, may(be), intend to,
  should
Exercise & conversations

Lesson 10 82
Verbs of giving and receiving
Doing things for people
Having things done
Exercise and conversations

Lesson 11 89
Indirect speech: statements, questions,
  commands
Miscellaneous expressions
Exercise & conversations

Lesson 12 96
Like/dislike
Want (someone) to do
More on *wa/ga*
More on *naru/narimasu*
More on *yō ni*
Exercise & conversations

Lesson 13 104
Appearance: *appears to be/looks*
  like
Feel, sense, taste, smell, etc.
Exercise & conversations

6

Lesson 14   109
Relative clauses, simple and
  complex
Someone/something
Nobody/nothing
Anybody/anything
Exercise & conversations

Lesson 15   115
Must (not)/may (not)/can (not)
Some uses of *koto* and *no* with
  verbs
Exercise & conversations

Lesson 16   123
Comparing things
Superlatives
Exercise & conversations

Lesson 17   129
Some expressions of time:
  before, after, while, when, etc.
Exercise & conversations

Lesson 18   136
If ... clauses
Some related expressions
Exercise & conversations

Lesson 19   142
The passive, the causative and the passive
  causative
Exercise & conversations

Lesson 20   149
Summary of informal and honorific
  language
Conversations

Key to Exercises   155

Key to Conversations   161

Vocabulary: English–Japanese   175

Vocabulary: Japanese–English   188

Appendix 1   203

Appendix 2   206

Introduction

Japanese has a reputation as an extremely difficult language to learn, if not an impossible one. Yet there is no doubt that the difficulties are greatly overstated. For example, in studying the language you'll encounter few problems with the pronunciation. Individual Japanese sounds are easy to master. Moreover, Japanese, unlike Chinese (with which it shares no common roots) does not have awkward sound combinations, nor does it have tricky tonal variations. Japanese is also without the stress accents found in English. It is spoken rather in a monotone. Grammatically, Japanese is altogether different from English and other European languages (and indeed from Chinese), but the simple explanations and the abundant examples that have been provided will enable you to grasp with the minimum of effort the special grammatical features of the language. By the end of the course, you will be able to understand – and to be understood – in a wide variety of situations, and you will also have some thousand items of useful vocabulary under your belt.

In this book, all the Japanese is given for convenience in romanized form. While the Japanese are, of course, able to read their own language in this romanized form (*romaji* they call it), they do in fact use three quite different writing systems: *hiragana*, *katakana* and *kanji*. Appendix 1 gives an introduction to *hiragana*, while Appendix 2 contains a selection of the more common *katakana* and *kanji* which the visitor is likely to see in the streets of Japan.

Something needs to be said about the format of the course. The examples used to illustrate grammatical points are given for the most part with the English first and the Japanese second. Experiments suggest that the traditional method, where the language being learnt comes before the translation in English, slows down the learning process. The method adopted here, however, will enable you to learn quickly what can and what cannot be said in Japanese. Where possible, related grammatical items are grouped together, and at the end of each group you will find a translation exercise. There is another type of exercise too: occasionally you will be asked to 'check that you can form ...' (say, the past tense of a selection of verbs). This exercise requires you to cover up the answers, which are provided in the right-hand column of the page, and to form the past tense unaided. Then check your answers against those printed. Each lesson closes with a conversational dialogue together with notes that relate to particular points arising within this. The conversations cover grammatical items recently explained, while the notes amplify those explanations where necessary and provide translations of 'difficult' words or phrases. Occasionally they may shed some light on Japanese customs and culture, which helps you understand the make-up of the language. For a lesson to be considered completed, go over all the examples and exercises a second time, covering up the appropriate columns to make sure that you can translate confidently from and into both languages. All the vocabulary is placed for convenience at the end of the book, but it may be a useful exercise to compile your own vocabulary lists for each individual lesson and commit the new words to memory.

The final thing to say is that the single greatest problem in learning the language is in overcoming the 'culture gap'. Japanese is spoken by people from a social and cultural background entirely different from our own, and you will undoubtedly find that the learning process is made much easier if you take the trouble to read some introductory books on Japanese society and culture. Edwin Reischauer's *The Japanese* (published by Belknap Press, Harvard University, USA, in 1982) is recommended as a standard and readily obtainable work. It contains chapters on a variety of subjects, including one on the language.

Abbreviations

In the vocabulary lists and occasionally in the lessons you will see the following conventional abbreviations:

adj.	adjective
adv.	adverb
lit.	literally
n.	noun
vt.	transitive verb (one that takes a direct object)
vi.	intransitive verb (one that does not)

J: Throughout the lessons, where model sentences are given in English and Japanese, the English sentence will sometimes contain within parentheses a letter *J*: followed by more English. This *J*: means 'the Japanese treat this in the following way' – the phrase or word formation that comes after it will show you how.

<u>A</u> ... <u>B</u>: Where these letters appear underlined, they stand for a noun and/or an adjective, etc. which for simplicity's sake has been omitted from the construction being explained.

A and B (in small capitals) will be found against the English model sentences that represent a 'question and answer' routine or where the Japanese for B is constructed in a way that is dependent on A.

In the conversations, initial letters indicate who is speaking.

Pronunciation

Japanese sounds, unlike those in English, are best thought of as being composed of syllables rather than of vowels and consonants. The table below gives you all the possible individual syllables in Japanese. You will see, however, that these syllables may combine to give a number of other sounds. As a first exercise, practise the sounds in the table – after you've read notes 1–10 (and listened to the pronunciation tape if you've got our Cassette Course):

Column:	1	2	3	4	5
Row 1	a	i	u	e	o
2	ka	ki	ku	ke	ko
3	ga	gi	gu	ge	go
4	sa	shi	su	se	so
5	za	ji	zu	ze	zo
6	ta	chi	tsu	te	to
7	da	ji	zu	de	do
8	na	ni	nu	ne	no
9	ha	hi	fu	he	ho
10	ba	bi	bu	be	bo
11	pa	pi	pu	pe	po
12	ma	mi	mu	me	mo
13	ya	–	yu	–	yo
14	ra	ri	ru	re	ro
15	wa	–	–	–	n

1) The 'a' sound of the syllables in column 1 (**a, ka, ga, sa** etc.) is pronounced much the same as the vowel sound in the French word *chat*, somewhere between the 'a' in *cat* and the 'u' in *cut*.

2) The 'i' sound of the syllables in column 2 (**i, ki, gi, shi** etc.) is pronounced rather similar to the vowel sound in *wit*.

3) The 'u' sound of the syllables in column 3 (**u, ku, gu, su** etc.) is pronounced similar to the vowel sound in *could*.

4) The 'e' sound of the syllables in column 4 (**e, ke, ge, se** etc.) is pronounced similar to the vowel sound in *get*.

5) The 'o' sound of the syllables in column 5 (**o, ko, go, so** etc.) is pronounced similar to the vowel sound in *cot*.

6) The 'g' sound of the syllables of row 3 is generally pronounced hard as in *get*, but sometimes soft as in *sing*.

7) The 'n' sound of the syllables of row 8 is pronounced as in *no*.

8) The one consonant in Japanese, **n**, comes only at the end of a syllable; here it is pronounced 'ng' as in *sing*.

9) The 'f' sound in the syllable **fu** (row 9, column 3) is not hard like the English 'f' in *flip*. It is much lighter and is made by blowing gently through slightly parted lips.

10) The 'r' sound in the syllables of row 14 is not heard in English. It is a sound which lies somewhere between the English 'r' and 'l', and is often rather close to a 'd' sound. It is made by tapping with the tip of the tongue against the gum behind the top front teeth.

Vowel combinations and other points

More sounds can be created in Japanese by combining certain syllables:

a) By combining syllables in column 1 (**a, ka, ga** etc.) with **i** (column 2, row 1) you get **ai** (and **kai, gai** etc.), which is pronounced similar to the English *eye*.

b) By combining syllables in column 4 (**e, ke, ge** etc.) with **i** you get **ei** (and **kei, gei** etc.), which is pronounced similar to the vowel sound in *wait*.

c) By combining syllables of column 2 (**ki, gi, shi** etc.) with those of row 13 (**ya, yu, yo**) you get **k'ya, g'ya, sh'ya** etc.; **k'yu, g'yu, sh'yu** etc.; **k'yo, g'yo, sh'yo** etc. For convenience, these sounds will be written without the apostrophe: **kya, kyu, kyo** etc.

d) Syllables of any column may combine with row 1 of the *same* column to make a 'long syllable': e.g. **a, ka, ga** plus **a** gives **aa, kaa, gaa**. Conventionally, such long syllables are transcribed with what is known as a macron: **ā, kā, gā** etc.; **ī, kī, gī** etc.; **ō, kō, gō** etc. They are pronounced as a single unbroken sound twice the length of the corresponding short syllable. N.B.: It is very common for foreign speakers of Japanese to make the mistake of not heeding long vowel sounds when they occur. This can often totally alter the meaning of the word – for example, **o-ba-san** means 'aunt' whereas **o-bā-san** means 'grandmother'.

e) Something needs to be said about what appear from the romanized Japanese to be double consonants, as in **katta** ('bought'). Strictly speaking, these are not double consonants – as we have pointed out, Japanese has neither consonants nor vowels. They are in fact a type of combined syllable (see Appendix 1, page 204). However, here it has been thought sensible to follow the conventional romanization and render them as 'double consonants'. As far as pronunciation is concerned, where the 'consonant' is doubled it must be held for an extra beat. This is not dissimilar to the effect created in English words like *home-made* or *Ben-Nevis*. Failure to observe the pronunciation of these 'double consonants' is another common error made by the non-native speaker, and can again totally alter the meaning of a word – for example, **katta** means 'bought' whereas **kata** means 'shoulder'.

f) Finally, a word on devoicing. The 'i' sound in the syllable **shi** is devoiced, so that **shita** ('below', 'under') is pronounced 'shta'. Also, the 'u' sound is often devoiced in the syllables of column 3, such as **ku** and **gu**, but particularly **su**: the style of Japanese wrestling known as **sumō** is pronounced 'smō', and **desu** (the verb 'to be') is generally pronounced 'dess'.

Pronunciation practice (1)

Practise the following words (with the aid of the cassettes if you have them), not forgetting the few rules given above, and taking care not to impose English rhythm on the words – particularly those with which you may be familiar:

Ikeda (family name)
karate
sake (rice wine)
Tanaka (family name)
Nagasaki
Hitachi
Hiroshima
yama (mountain)
shita (beneath, below)
Matsushita
kudasai (please)
geisha
samurai
hai (yes)
rei (example)
kyonen (last year)

shashin (photo)
shujutsu (operation)
shūkan (custom)
o-ba-san (aunt)
o-bā-san (grandmother)
Kyōto
shōgun
sumō
sukiyaki (meat dish)
Kyūshū
Tōkyo
dōjo (martial arts hall)
ana (hole)
anna (that sort of)
kata (shoulder)
katta (bought)

Pronunciation practice (2)

In Japanese there exist quite a few words of foreign origin, and it is essential that you should pronounce these in the Japanese way. Below is a selection of the more common imported words:

apāto (apartment)
uisukī (whisky)
karēraisu (curry rice)
kōhī (coffee)
koppu (cup)
sakkā (soccer)
shatsu (shirt)
takushī (taxi)
naifu (knife)

tabako (cigarettes)
tēburu (table)
depāto (department store)
sunakku bā (bar)
hoteru (hotel)
fuirumu (film for camera)
miruku (milk)
basu (bus)
fuōku (fork)

Lesson 1

In this lesson, you will be consolidating your understanding of the pronunciation points while learning some basic greetings and conversational phrases. Read the following out loud, listen to the cassette if you have it, and refer back to the previous pages if you still have doubts about pronunciation.

A: *What is your name?*   **O-namae wa nan to osshaimasu ka.**
B: *My name's Tanaka.*   **Tanaka to mōshimasu.**

A: *Hello, Yumiko!*   **Konnichi wa, Yumiko-san[1]!**
B: *Hello!*   **Konnichi wa.**

A: *Good morning, Mr Tanaka!*   **O-hayō gozaimasu, Tanaka-san!**
B: *Good morning, Mrs Brown!*   **O-hayō gozaimasu, Buraun-san!**

A: *Good evening, Sir!*   **Sensei[2], konban wa.**
B: *Good evening.*   **Konban wa.**

A: *Good night, Kunio.*   **O-yasumi nasai, Kunio-kun[3].**
B: *Good night.*   **O-yasumi nasai.**

A: *Goodbye!*   **Sayōnara.**
B: *Goodbye!*   **Sayōnara.**

A: *Excuse me (but I must be off).*   **Shitsurei shimasu.**
B: *Goodbye!*   **Sayōnara.**

A: *Pleased to meet you.*   **Hajimemashite.**
B: *Pleased to meet you too.*   **Hajimemashite, dōzo yoroshiku[4].**

A: *How are you?*   **Go-kigen ikaga desu ka.**
B: *Very well thank you.*   **O-kagesama de.**

A: *How are you?*   **Genki[5]?**
B: *Fine.*   **Genki yo.**

A: *It's been a long time, hasn't it[6]?*   **O-hisashiburi desu ne.**
B: *Yes, it's been a long time.*   **O-hisashiburi desu ne.**

A: *Thank you very much.*   **Dōmo arigatō gozaimasu (gozaimashita).**
B: *It's a pleasure.*   **Dō itashimashite.**

A: *Thank you.*   **Arigatō gozaimasu (gozaimashita).**
B: *No, thank <u>you</u>.*   **Kochira koso.**

14

A: *Thanks.*	**Dōmo.**
B: *Not at all.*	**Īe.**
A: *I'm sorry.*	**Gomen nasai.**
B: *That's all right.*	**Ii desu.**
A: *Here you are!*	**Hai, dōzo.**
B: *Thank you very much.*	**Arigatō gozaimasu.**
A: *After you.*	**O-saki e dōzo.**
B: *Thank you.*	**Sumimasen.**
A: *Come in!*	**O-hairi kudasai**[7].
B: *Thank you.*	**O-jama shimasu**[8].
A: *I'm off now.*	**Itte kimasu.**
B: *See you later.*	**Itte (i)rasshai**[9].
A: *I'm back.*	**Tadaima**[10].
B: *Hello.*	**O-kaeri nasai.**
A: *Excuse me, is anyone there?*	**Gomen kudasai**[11].
B: *Yes, just a minute, please.*	**Hai, chotto matte kudasai.**
A: *Cheers!*	**Kanpai!**
B: *Cheers!*	**Kanpai!**

Notes:

1. **-san** may be added to family names to mean Mr, Mrs, Miss or Ms. It is also added, as here, to first names to show some respect. It is never used of oneself (see the first conversation). N.B. Often, as here, girls' names end in **-ko**. Boys' names never do!

2. Male and female teachers (of anything) and, for example, doctors will be addressed as **sensei**. Sensei is also attached to family names and sometimes first names (e.g. **Tanaka-sensei; Jon-sensei**) when addressing or referring to a teacher.

3. **-kun** is added to boys' first and family names by superiors as a sign of affection.

4. **Dōzo yoroshiku** is really untranslatable. It is a word used to request favourable consideration from another person (see Lesson 2, Conversations 2a and 2b).

5. This is a much more informal version of the previous greeting.

6. Alternatively, 'I haven't seen you for ages!'

7. **O-hairi kudasai** is used for 'come into a room or a Western-style house'. 'Come into a Japanese house' is usually **O-agari kudasai**.

8. **O-jama shimasu** means literally 'I'm going to make a nuisance of myself'.

9. A family member (or guest) will say **Itte kimasu** either in the morning when he/she goes off to work or when he/she leaves the house to go shopping, etc. **Itte (i)rasshai** is the stock response of anyone left in the house.

10. **Tadaima** is what the same person will say upon returning from work or shopping, and **O-kaeri nasai** is the stock reply.

11. **Gomen kudasai** would, for example, be said by a customer on entering a shop when there appears to be no shop assistant.

Lesson 2

MAIN POINTS: Statements – _A_ is/isn't _B_; questions – _is/isn't A, B?;_ answering questions; possession.
CONVERSATIONS: (a) Introductions; (b) Are you American? (c) A business meeting.

1 Nouns

Japanese nouns do not have masculine, feminine or neuter forms, nor do they have singular or plural forms. Also, in Japanese there are no direct equivalents of _a, an, some_ or _the_. So, 'a bullet train', 'the bullet train', 'bullet trains', 'some bullet trains' and 'the bullet trains' are all translated by **shinkansen**. The context in which this is placed – the rest of the sentence – will usually make clear if it is singular or plural.

2 Pronouns

Pronouns are used in Japanese much less frequently than in English. Again, the context is relied upon to make clear who or what is being referred to. The most common pronouns are the following:

I, me	**watashi**
you (sing.)	**anata**
he, him	**kare**
she, her	**kanojo**
we, us	**watashi-tachi**
you (pl.)	**anata-tachi**
they	**ano hito-tachi**

The words 'this' and 'that' serve for 'it':

this or it	**kore**
that or it (near speaker and not far from hearer)	**sore**
that or it (near neither speaker nor hearer	**are**

Learn also the following words:

here (this place)	**koko** or **kochira**
there (near speaker and not far from hearer)	**soko** or **sochira**
there (near neither speaker nor hearer)	**asoko** or **achira**

3 The particle 'wa'

The particle is a most important element of basic grammar. Different particles are placed after words to indicate, for example, the subject and object of the verb. The particle **wa**, whose literal meaning is 'as for', may denote the subject and is needed to compose the basic sentence pattern 'A is B' (lit. 'as for A, it is B'. When placed after a word and said with rising intonation A **wa** means, in a very broad sense, 'What about A?' (Where is A? Will A do? What happened to A? etc.)

Study the following:

What about me?	**Watashi wa?**
What about here?	**Koko wa?**
What about this?	**Kore wa?**
What about there?	**Asoko wa?**
What about the bullet train?	**Shinkansen wa?**
What about the beer?	**Bīru wa?**

4 Verbs (i)

Main verbs come at the end of a sentence. They have no 1st, 2nd or 3rd person forms, and no singular or plural forms: '(I) am ...', '(You) are ...', '(He/she/it) is ...', '(We) are ...' and so on are translated by the one word **desu** (*be*).

De wa arimasen (or more colloquially **ja arimasen**) is the negative of **desu**.

'A is/is not B' is **A wa B desu/ja arimasen**; *literally* this translates as 'As for A, it is/is not B':

That's the bullet train (J: As for that, it's the bullet train).	**Are wa shinkansen desu.**
I'm not American (J: As for me...).	**Watashi wa Amerikajin ja arimasen.**
He's a businessman.	**Kare wa sararīman desu.**
They're not students.	**Ano hitotachi wa gakusei ja arimasen.**

When the context makes clear who or what the subject is, then it (and the following **wa**) are very often omitted:

She's Korean.	**Kankokujin desu.**

Watch out for the many examples hereafter in which the subject is left unexpressed.

5 Questions

Questions are formed by placing the question particle **ka** after the verb. 'Is A, B?' and 'Isn't A, B?' are **A wa B desu ka** and **A wa B ja arimasen ka,** respectively.

Is that the bullet train? (J: As for that, is it the ...?)	**Are wa shinkansen desu ka.**
Isn't she Japanese?	**Kanojo wa Nihonjin ja arimasen ka.**

Note the effect of putting two interrogatives together:

Is this Kobe or (is it) Osaka?	**Koko wa Kōbe desu ka Ōsaka desu ka.**
Is she Korean or (is she) Chinese?	**Kanojo wa Kankokujin desu ka Chūgokujin desu ka.**

6 Answering questions

'That's right', 'that's so', 'I agree' is **sō desu**; 'that's not so', 'that's wrong', 'I disagree' is **chigaimasu**:

A: *Is she Korean?*	**Kanojo wa Kankokujin desu ka.**
B: *Yes, that's right. She's Korean.*	**Hai, sō desu. Kankokujin desu.**
A: *Is he Japanese?*	**Kare wa Nihonjin desu ka.**
B: *No, he's not. He's Chinese.*	**Īe, chigaimasu. Chūgokujin desu.**

'I'm not sure' is **chotto wakarimasen**:

A: *Is she Japanese or Chinese?*	**Kanojo wa Nihonjin desu ka Chūgokujin desu ka.**
B: *I'm not sure.*	**Chotto wakarimasen.**

'Umm...' is **sō desu ne,** or **etto**:

A: *Is that the bullet train?*	**Are wa shinkansen desu ka.**
B: *Umm, I'm not sure.*	**Sō desu ne. Chotto wakarimasen.**

Note the use of **sō desu ka** (lit. 'is that so?'):

A: *She's a housewife.*   **Kanojo wa shufu desu.**
B: *Oh, is she?*   **A, sō desu ka.**
A: *He isn't a businessman.*   **Kare wa sararīman ja arimasen.**
B: *Oh, isn't he?*   **A, sō desu ka.**

Exercise 1
Put into Japanese:

1 'I'm not a student. What about you?'
2 'Is that the bullet train?' 'No, it's not.'
3 'Is she Japanese or Chinese?' 'Umm ...'
4 'This is my wife.' 'Pleased to meet you.'
5 'She's Korean.' 'Oh, is she?'

7 Two final particles – 'you know', 'isn't it?'

Yo after the main verb adds emphasis, often with the force of 'you know':

A: *This isn't the Dai Ichi hotel, you know.*   **Koko wa Dai Ichi hoteru ja arimasen yo.**
B: *Oh, isn't it?*   **E, sō desu ka.**
A: *This is the Hilton.*   **Koko wa Hiruton desu yo.**
B: *Oh, is it?*   **A, sō desu ka.**

Ne after the main verb is similar to the French 'n'est-ce pas?', so:

A: *That's the bullet train, isn't it?*   **Are wa shinkansen desu ne.**
B: *That's right.*   **Sō desu yo.**
A: *He isn't Japanese, is he?*   **Kare wa Nihonjin ja arimasen ne.**
B: *No, he isn't.*   **Hai, sō desu yo*.**

*Be careful! The Japanese use 'Yes' (**Hai**) to mean 'What you say is correct'.

8 Possessive 's – the particle *'no'* (i)

No is a particle indicating possession in a very broad sense. **B no A** can mean, for example, 'B's A', 'A of B', 'A which is B', 'A who is B', 'A which is from B', 'A which is in B'. Study these examples:

Tokyo is Japan's capital.	**Tōkyō wa Nihon no shuto desu.**
This is a map of Tokyo, isn't it?	**Kore wa Tōkyō no chizu desu ne.**
This is Chieko (who is) my wife.	**Kanai no Chieko desu.**
What about the car (which is) over there?	**Asoko no kuruma wa?**
This is Mr Tanaka (who is) from Mitsui.	**Mitsui no Tanaka-san desu.**
What about the cost of living in Japan?	**Nihon no bukka wa?**

'My', 'your', 'his', 'her', 'our' and 'their' are expressed by the relevant pronoun followed by **no**:

It's my money.	**(Sore wa) watashi no o-kane desu yo.**
That's his house, isn't it?	**(Are wa) kare no ie desu ne.**

'Mine' or 'my one', 'yours' or 'your one', 'his' or 'his one', 'hers' or 'her one' and so forth are expressed by the pronoun plus **no** alone, as in:

What about mine?	**Watashi no wa?**
What about the one over there?	**Asoko no wa?**
That isn't Mr Tanaka's, you know.	**Are wa Tanaka-san no ja arimasen yo.**

No turns certain nouns, and some colours, into adjectives. For example:

real	**hontō no**
present	**ima no**
brown	**cha-iro no**
yellow	**ki-iro no**
green	**midori-iro no**

Is this real coffee?	**Hontō no kōhī desu ka.**
Is yours the brown bag?	**Anata no wa cha-iro no kaban desu ka.**
Yes, my bag is brown.	**Hai, watashi no kaban wa cha-iro desu*.**

***No** is used with these adjectives only when they come before a noun.

Exercise 2

Put into Japanese:

1 'That's real coffee, isn't it?' 'No, it's instant.'
2 'Is the yellow car yours?' 'No, it's not. My car is green.'
3 'What about some coffee?' 'Yes, please.'
4 That person over there isn't Japanese.
5 This isn't today's paper, you know.

CONVERSATION 2a: Introductions

At the airport, Mr Brown (B) introduces to his wife Chieko (C) and his son David (D) his friend Professor Emura (E):

B: Chieko, kochira[1] wa Tōkyō Daigaku no Emura-sensei desu. Emura-sensei, kanai no Chieko desu.
C: Hajimemashite. Dōzo yoroshiku o-negai shimasu.
B: Kanai wa Eigo no sensei desu.
E: A, sō desu ka. Dōzo yoroshiku.
B: Sensei, kore[1] wa musuko no Dēbiddo desu. Dēbiddo wa shōgakusei desu.
E: A, sō desu ka. Hajimemashite.
D: Hajimemashite.

CONVERSATION 2b: Are you American?

A young Japanese businessman (A) starts a conversation with a foreign student (B):

A: Sumimasen, Amerikajin desu ka[2, 3].
B: Īe, chigaimasu. Igirisujin desu.
A: A, sō desu ka. Gakusei desu ka.
B: Hai, sō desu. Rondon daigaku no Nihon gakubu no gakusei desu.
A: Naruhodo[4]. Watashi wa kaishain desu yo. Shitsurei desu ga[5], o-namae[6] wa?
B: Maiku desu.
A: Ya, Maiku-san desu ka. Watashi wa Kunio desu. Satō Kunio[7]. Dōzo yoroshiku.
B: Dōzo yoroshiku.

CONVERSATION 2c: A meeting

Mr Brown (B) has arranged to meet a Mr Ikeda (I) from the Mitsui company in the lobby of the Dai Ichi hotel in Tokyo. He first inquires of a passer-by (P) if he's at the right hotel:

B: Sumimasen. Koko wa Dai Ichi hoteru desu ka.
P: Īe, chigaimasu yo. Dai Ichi wa asoko no hoteru desu yo.
B: A, asoko desu ka. Arigatō gozaimasu.
P: Dō itashimashite.

Mr Brown enters the lobby of the hotel:

I: Shitsurei desu ga, ICI (ai-shi-ai) no Buraun-san de irasshaimasu[8] ka.
B: Hai, sō desu.
I: Hajimemashite. Mitsui no Ikeda to mōshimasu. Dōzo yoroshiku.
B: Dōzo yoroshiku.
I: Watashi no meishi desu.
B: A, dōmo arigatō gozaimasu. Watashi no mo[9] dōzo.

Notes:

1. **kochira wa, kore wa: kochira wa** is more respectful than **kore**, hence the former is used for Prof. Emura and the latter for members of Brown's family.

2. **Amerikajin desu ka:** the Japanese tend to avoid using the pronoun 'you' as much as possible. (The context makes clear who is being referred to here.)

3. **Amerikajin: -jin** placed after the name of a country gives a national of that country ... *America,* **Amerika**; *an American,* **Amerikajin**. *England,* **Igirisu**; *an English person,* **Igirisujin**. *Japan,* **Nihon**; *a Japanese,* **Nihonjin**.

4. **Naruhodo:** *I see.*

5. **shitsurei desu ga:** 'Excuse me for asking but ...'

6. **O-namae:** (lit. 'What about your name?'); the **o-** is honorific. **O-** may be attached to certain nouns out of respect for the listener. **O-** is also attached to certain nouns as a matter of course with no particular respect involved e.g. **o-mizu** – *drinking water*; **o-tearai** – *the toilet*; **o-cha** – *Japanese tea.*

7. **Satō Kunio:** In Japan, family names come first and first names second.

8. **de irasshaimasu:** the 'honorific' equivalent of **desu**; it is never used of oneself, only of others to whom one wishes to show respect for whatever reason (e.g. strangers of similar or superior status; acquaintances of superior status).

9. **watashi no mo:** 'here's mine too'. Consider the following in the positive with **mo**:
He's a businessman too. **Kare mo sararīman desu.**
Both he and she are students. **Kare mo kanojo mo gakusei desu.**

And in the negative:
Neither he nor I are businessmen. **Kare mo watashi mo sararīman ja arimasen.**

In order to consider this and later lessons completed you should now go over all the examples once again, covering up one side at a time, to ensure you can translate confidently into and from both languages.

Lesson 3

MAIN POINTS: Questions – *Who/where/what* etc. *is A*; locational expressions – *A is in front of/behind* etc. *B*; some particles – *to, from, with*, etc.
CONVERSATIONS: (a) Asking for someone; (b) 'Where are we?' (c) A chance meeting.

9 'Who', 'where', 'what', 'when', etc.

Learn the following:

who	**dare** (or **dochira-sama** in more polite speech)
where	**doko** (or **dochira**)
what	**nani** (but often **nan** before syllables of rows 6, 7 and 8 in the table on page 9)
which one (= of two)	**dochira**
which one (= of three and more)	**dore**
when	**itsu**
what's ... like	**dō**
how about	**dō** (or **ikaga** in more polite speech)

'Who is *A*?' is **A wa dare desu ka** (literally: 'As for *A*, who is it?'). Study the following examples, noting those where the subject is not expressed:

A: *Who is she (J: as for her, who is she?)*	**Kanojo wa dare desu ka.**
B: *She's a singer.*	**Kashu desu.**
A: *Who are you?*	**Dochira-sama de irasshaimasu ka.**
B: *I'm Tanaka from Mitsui.*	**Mitsui no Tanaka desu.**
A: *Excuse me, where is the exit?*	**Sumimasen, deguchi wa doko desu ka.**
B: *It's over there.*	**Asoko desu.**
A: *Where is the toilet?*	**O-tearai wa dochira desu ka.**
B: *It's that way.*	**Achira desu.**
A: *What is that?*	**Sore wa nan desu ka.**
B: *This is an alien registration card*	**Kore wa gaijintōrokushō desu.**
A: *Which one (of the two) is his?*	**Kare no wa dochira desu ka.**
B: *His is that one over there.*	**Kare no wa achira no desu yo.**
A: *Which (of three or more) is yours, Yumiko?*	**Yumiko-san no wa dore desu ka.**
B: *That one.*	**Are desu.**
A: *When is the baseball match?*	**Yakyū no shiai wa itsu desu ka.**
B: *It's tomorrow.*	**Ashita desu.**

23

A: *What's today's weather like?*   Kyō no tenki wa dō desu ka.
B: *It's all right.*   Māmā desu.
A: *How about tomorrow?*   Ashita wa dō desu ka.
B: *Tomorrow's no good.*   Ashita wa dame desu.
A: *How about some tea?*   O-cha wa ikaga desu ka.
B: *Yes, please.*   O-negai shimasu.

10 The particle *no* (ii)

No may be used with **dare, doko, nan** and **itsu**:

A: *Whose money is it?*   Dare no o-kane desu ka.
B: *It's mine.*   Watashi no desu.
A: *Where's he from (J: a person of where)?*   Doko no hito desu ka.
B: *He's from America.*   Amerika no hito desu.
A: *What's the book about (J: a book of what)?*   Nan no hon desu ka.
B: *It's about karate.*   Karate no hon desu.
A: *Which newpaper is it (J: a newspaper of when)?*   Itsu no shinbun desu ka.
B: *It's today's.*   Kyō no desu.

11 'This', 'that', 'which', etc.

The adjectives 'this', 'this sort of', 'what', 'what sort of' are:

this	**kono**
that (= near speaker and hearer)	**sono**
that (= not near speaker or hearer)	**ano**
which, what	**dono**

this sort of	**konna**
that sort of	**sonna**
that sort of	**anna**
which/what sort of	**donna**

Consider the examples below:

A: *That car is a Toyota.*   Ano kuruma wa Toyota desu yo.
B: *Which car do you mean? (lit. 'is it?')*   Dono kuruma desu ka.
A: *That brown car.*   Ano chairo no kuruma desu.
B: *Oh, is it?*   A, sō desu ka.
A: *What sort of person is he?*   Donna hito desu ka.
B: *He's an ordinary person.*   Futsū no hito desu yo.

12 'In front of', 'behind', etc.

Note the following locational words:

front (= in front of)	**mae**
before (= this side of)	**temae**
back (= behind)	**ushiro**
inside	**naka**
outside	**soto**
top (= on top of)	**ue**
bottom (= under)	**shita**
near	**chikaku**
beside	**tonari**
beyond	**mukō**
opposite	**mukai**

The particle **no** is used to join these words to others. Note the word order:

in front of the coffee shop	**kissaten no mae**
behind the door	**doa no ushiro**
this side of the department store	**depāto no temae**
beyond the police box	**kōban no mukō**
beside the station	**eki no tonari**
under the chair	**isu no shita**
on (top of) the table	**tēburu no ue**

Consider the 'expanded' examples below:

the coffee shop in front of the station	**eki no mae no kissaten**
the person behind the door	**doa no ushiro no hito**

Locational words may fit into the basic **A** wa **B** desu (de wa arimasen) structure:

The coffee shop is (J: as for the coffee shop, it is) in front of the station.	**Kissaten wa eki no mae desu.**
The police box is beside the bar.	**Kōban wa sunakku no tonari desu.**

Locational words followed by **no** act as adjectives:

the person in front	**mae no hito**
the back door	**ushiro no doa**
the top drawer	**ue no hikidashi**
the shop opposite	**mukai no o-mise**

Exercise 3

Put into Japanese:

1 'Who is the man over there?' '(Do you mean) the man in front of the window?'
2 Is this paper today's or yesterday's?
3 'Excuse me, but where is the toilet?' 'It's over there.'
4 'What's that?' 'That's my ticket, you know.'
5 'What's the sashimi like?' 'It's all right.'

13 Verbs: plain and polite

All verbs have a plain form (the form found in a dictionary) and also a polite form. In every case except one the latter ends in **masu**, and is usually called the **masu** form. In the vocabularies, verbs are given in both forms: e.g. **suru/shimasu** ('do'). The difference is one of politeness alone. **Shimasu** is more polite than the plain **suru**. Consequently, the **masu** form is taught throughout most of this book, and you are advised to stick to the **masu** form yourself.

The one verb which has no **masu** form is **desu** ('be'). **Desu**, however, corresponds in politeness to a **masu** form. **Da** is its plain form.

14 'Be' – *Aru/arimasu, iru/imasu*

Aru/arimasu and **iru/imasu** mean 'be' (not in the sense of '$\underline{A}$ equals $\underline{B}$', for which **da/desu** is used). These verbs mean 'be (in a place)', '(there) is/are', 'exist'. For inanimate subjects, **aru/arimasu** is used, and for animate subjects **iru/imasu** is generally used.

The <u>negative</u> of **masu** is **masen**. Consider carefully the following:

A: *Is there (have you got) any coffee?*	**Kōhi wa arimasu ka.**
B: *Yes, there is (I have).*	**Hai, arimasu yo.**
A: *Haven't you got the passports?*	**Pasupōto wa arimasen ka.**
B: *(No,) I haven't.*	**Arimasen.**
A: *Yumiko isn't here.*	**Yumiko wa imasen yo.**
B: *Isn't she?*	**Sō desu ka.**

The future is also translated by the plain **masu** form:

A: *Will you be in tomorrow, Kunio?*	**Kunio-san, ashita imasu ka.**
B: *No, I shan't.*	**Imasen yo.**

15 'Be' – *Irassharu/irasshaimasu, oru/orimasu*

Two other verbs for 'be (in a place)' are needed:

(a) **Irassharu/irasshaimasu,** an 'honorific' verb used to exalt the position of the subject of the verb. It is never used of oneself, nor when referring to members of one's family or intimates. It would be used, for example, to <u>address</u> someone of superior status, or someone of similar status to whom, for whatever reason, one wished to show respect. It may also be used when <u>referring</u> to someone of superior status or someone of similar status to whom one wished to show respect.

(b) **Oru/orimasu** is a humble verb, used to lower the status of the speaker, his family and those associated with him out of deference for others.

Study carefully the examples below, taking particular note that (i) Mr Murata is visiting Mr Habu (who works for a travel agent) and (ii) Professor Tanaka is a colleague of Professor Inoue:

Mr Murata: *Is Mr Habu in?*	**Habu-san wa irasshaimasu ka.**
Habu's colleague: *Yes, he is.*	**Hai, orimasu.**
Student: *Is Professor Tanaka in?*	**Tanaka-sensei wa irasshaimasu ka.**
Professor Inoue: *He's not in now.*	**Ima imasen.**
Student: *Tanaka-sensei! Are you there?*	**Tanaka-sensei! Irasshaimasu ka.**
Professor Tanaka: *Yes, I'm here.*	**Hai, orimasu yo.**

If two students are talking together, then they are unlikely to use 'honorifics' when referring to the Professor, and may well use the plain **iru**:

Student: *Is Prof. Tanaka in?*	**Tanaka-sensei wa imasu ka.**
Student: *Yes, he is.*	**Hai, imasu yo.**
Student: *Is Prof. Tanaka in?*	**Tanaka-sensei iru?**
Student: *Yes, he's in.*	**Iru yo.**

N.B. There is a good deal of flexibility in these honorific forms. They are by no means used consistently, and the forms given above are intended as a guide only.

16 'In', 'of', 'to': the particle *ni*

Location is commonly expressed by the particle **ni** ('in') plus **aru/arimasu, iru/masu** (or one of its other forms):

A: *Where (J: in where) is the professor?*	**Sensei wa dochira ni irasshaimasu ka.**
B: *He's in his room.*	**Heya ni irasshaimasu yo.**

A: *Where's the dictionary?*   Jisho wa doko ni arimasu ka.
B: *Isn't it on the table?*   Tēburu no ue ni arimasen ka.

'To' and 'towards' (always expressed in Japanese) are also translated by **ni**, or by **e**:

A: *Where (J: to where) are you going?*   Doko ni (e) ikimasu ka.
B: *I'm going to the shops.*   O-mise ni (e) ikimasu.
A: *Are you going home?*   Uchi ni (e) kaerimasu ka.
B: *No, I'm going to a friend's place.*   Īe, tomodachi no tokoro ni (e) ikimasu.

17 'From' and some other particles

Note here that word order is fairly free in Japanese. As a rule the item followed by **wa** comes first.

'From' is **kara**. It can be used of place or time:

I'll walk from the station.   Eki kara arukimasu.
The holidays start from today.   Yasumi wa kyō kara hajimarimasu.

In 'from <u>A</u> to (until) <u>B</u>' the 'to' or 'until' is **made**:

I walk from the station to the office.   Eki kara kaisha made arukimasu.
She'll be at home from morning until   Kanojo wa asa kara ban made uchi ni
evening.   imasu.

'In' or 'at', in the sense of 'performing an action in/at (a place)' is **de** (**ni** only being used for 'static' verbs such as 'be', 'stand', 'sit', 'live'):

A: *Where will you wait?*   Doko de machimasu ka.
B: *I'll wait in front of the exit.*   Deguchi no mae de machimasu.

'On, by (a train)', 'with (chopsticks)', 'in (English)' are also translated by **de**:

I go by bus to work.   Basu de kaisha e ikimasu.
I'll eat with chopsticks too.   Watashi mo hashi de tabemasu yo.
I'll speak in English.   Eigo de hanashimasu.

All particles can be followed by **wa** or **mo**. With **wa**, a contrast is often implied, as in:

In Tokyo there aren't any (but, e.g., there   Tōkyō ni wa arimasen.
   are in Kyoto).
I won't go by bus (but, e.g., by bike).   Basu de wa ikimasen.

Followed by **mo**, the meaning may be '...both ... and ...', or in the negative '... neither ... nor...':

Guests are coming from both Korea and Hong Kong.	**O-kyaku-san wa Kankoku kara mo Honkon kara mo kimasu.**
He won't tell either me or you, will he?	**Watashi ni mo anata ni mo iimasen ne.**

Exercise 4
Put into Japanese:

1 Have you got any coffee?
2 Will you go by bus to the airport?
3 The passports are over there.
4 I'm going to speak in Japanese.
5 Mr Ikeda will not be in tomorrow.

CONVERSATION 3a: Asking for someone

Mr Brown (B) goes to the travel agent's and speaks to a colleague (C) of Tanaka's:

B: Sumimasen. Buraun to mōshimasu ga[1] Tanaka-san wa irasshaimasu ka.
C: Tanaka wa ima orimasen[2] ga ...
B: Sō desu ka. Sore de wa nochi hodo ukagaimasu[3].

CONVERSATION 3b: 'Where are we?'

Mr Brown (B) is on a subway train stopped at a station; he talks to another passenger (X):

B: Sumimasen. Koko wa doko desu ka. Shinjuku desu ka.
X: Īe, Shinjuku ja arimasen yo. Etto, Shibuya desu.
B: Sō desu ka. Shinjuku made ikimasu ka.
X: Etto, chotto matte kudasai. Hai, Shinjuku ni ikimasu yo.
B: Kono tsugi[4] desu ka.
X: Chigaimasu. Tsugi no tsugi desu.
B: Dōmo arigatō.

CONVERSATION 3c: A chance meeting

Mr Brown (B) bumps into Mr Katayama (K), whom he hasn't seen for a while:

B: Katayama-san, konnichi wa!
K: Buraun-san desu ka. O-hisashiburi desu ne. O-genki desu ka.

B: O-kagesama de genki desu. Katayama-san wa?

K: Genki desu.

B: Dō desu ka[3], Katayama-san. O-cha demo[6] nomimasen ka[7].

K: Sō desu ne[8]. Nomi ni[9] ikimashō[10]. Etto, eki no tonari no kissaten wa dō desu ka.

B: Kadota desu ne. Asoko ni shimashō[11].

K: Kuruma[12] de ikimasu ka soretomo[13] arukimasu ka.

B: Arukimashō.

Notes:

1. **ga:** a conjunction meaning 'but', but often (as here) it has no adversative force at all. See Lesson 4.

2. **orimasu:** the humble verb is used by the speaker, who is humbling himself and Tanaka out of respect for the customer, Mr Brown.

3. **ukagaimasu: ukagau/ukagaimasu** is a humble verb meaning here 'visit'.

4. **kono tsugi:** 'the one after this'.

5. **dō desu ka:** 'how about it?'

6. **o-cha demo:** 'tea or something similar'.

7. **nomimasen ka:** 'would(n't) you like to drink?'; the negative **masu** form is used often in invitations.

8. **sō desu ne:** depending on the intonation **sō desu ne** can be either a posititive-sounding 'umm' as here, or a negative-sounding one.

9. **nomi ni:** remove **masu** from any verb, add **ni** and the verb **iku/ikimasu** (go) or **kuru/kimasu** (come) to make 'go/come and do'.

10. **ikimashō:** change **masu** to **mashō** to make 'Let's ...'; add **ka** to make 'Shall I/we ...'. Consider the following:

A: Let's go to a pub.	**Pabu ni ikimashō.**
B: Yes, let's.	**Ikimashō.**
A: Shall we eat in that coffee shop?	**Ano kissaten de tabemashō ka.**
B: Yes, let's (*J*: let's do sc).	**Sō shimashō.**

11. **ni shimashō:** 'Let's decide/settle on ...', 'let's make it ...'

12. **kuruma:** here, the word for 'car' is used to mean 'taxi'.

13. **soretomo:** 'or'.

Lesson 4

MAIN POINTS: Verbs and their subjects (*wa* and *ga*); verbs and their objects (*wa*, *o* and *ni*); the past tense.
CONVERSATIONS: (a) In a coffee shop; (b) In a taxi.

18 Verbs and their subjects ...
The differences between *wa* and *ga*

The subject of a verb is followed by the particle **ga**:

There is a book (a book is) on the table.	**Tēburu no ue ni hon ga arimasu.**
Mr Brown uses chopsticks.	**Buraun-san ga hashi o tsukaimasu.**

But, as you know, **wa** can also follow a word which is the subject of the sentence, so something must be said on the difference between the two particles. The difference is one of emphasis.

Ga often implies that the word it follows is new to the conversation, therefore it often corresponds to the English 'a (book)', 'some (books)' as opposed to 'the (book which you're reading)'; **ga** emphasizes the word it follows, rather than the rest of the sentence; **ga** and only **ga** is used after question words (e.g. **dare ga ...; doko ga ...**), and in reply to such sentences **ga** and only **ga** is used (e.g. **watashi ga ...; asoko ga ...**).

Wa follows what is the general topic of the sentence ('the topic' may in fact be the object or some other part of speech, and not exclusively the subject), and A **wa** has the meaning of 'as for A, the following is important', or 'we're discussing A, this is what I want to say about it/him etc.'; **wa** is also used to provide a contrast, so A **wa** can mean 'A in contrast to others, ...'; **wa** is generally used more in negative sentences.

Study the following and then refer back to the explanation:

A: *There is a passport on the table.*	**Tēburu no ue ni pasupōto ga arimasu.**
B: *The passport is on the table.*	**Pasupōto wa* tēburu no ue ni arimasu.**
A: *There's a coffee shop over there.*	**Asoko ni kissaten ga arimasu.**
B: *The coffee shop is over there.*	**Kissaten wa* asoko ni arimasu.**

(* the item followed by **wa** generally comes first in the sentence)

A: *I'm going.*	**Watashi ga ikimasu.**
	(in answer to 'Who's going?')

31

B: *I'm going.*   **Watashi wa ikimasu.**
(in answer to 'What about you?')

A: *He's coming.*   **Kare ga kimasu.**
(in answer to 'Who's coming?')

B: *He's coming.*   **Kare wa kimasu.**
(in answer to 'What about him?')

A: *I'm going but my wife isn't.*   **Watashi wa ikimasu ga kanai wa ikimasen.**

B: *He's a teacher, but she isn't.*   **Kare wa sensei desu ga kanojo wa chigaimasu.**

19 Verbs and their objects (i)

Direct objects of verbs are followed by the particle **o**:

I'm going to watch the television.   **Terebi o mimasu.**
Let's have a(n alcoholic) drink.   **O-sake o nomimashō.**

Where the object is a question word such as **nani** or **dare**, it too will be followed by **o** (NEVER by **wa**):

A: *What do the Japanese eat for breakfast?*   **Nihonjin wa asa-gohan ni nani o tabemasu ka.**

B: *They eat toast.*   **Tōsuto o tabemasu.**

A: *Who(m) are you going to invite?*   **Dare o yobimasu ka.**

B: *Let's invite Professor Tanaka.*   **Tanaka-sensei o yobimashō.**

The emphasis here is on the word followed by **o**.

Sometimes **mo** and **wa** are more appropriate for the direct object: **Mo** ('also', 'both … and …' or 'even') will replace **o** in sentences such as the following:

Today I'm going to eat both sashimi and natto.   **Kyō wa sashimi mo nattō mo tabemasu.**

He doesn't even eat rice.   **Kare wa gohan mo tabemasen.**

Wa will often replace **o** in negative sentences:

I shan't buy the Mainichi (newspaper).   **Mainichi wa kaimasen.**
Aren't you going to watch the news?   **Nyūsu wa mimasen ka.**

when making a contrast:

I'll buy the paper, but I won't get the bread.   **Shinbun wa kaimasu ga pan wa kaimasen.**

in answer to a question containing **wa**:

A: *What about the Ryoanji temple? Are you going to see that?* **Ryōanji wa mimasu ka.**

B: *Yes, I'm going to see the Ryoanji.* **Hai, Ryōanji wa mimasu.**

Finally, note that in less formal conversation **wa, ga** and **o** are all very frequently dropped!

20 Verbs and their objects (ii)

Some verbs take the object particle **o**, where English may require 'over', 'along', 'around' or 'at' or nothing at all. Consider:

Let's cross (over) the road at the traffic lights. **Shingō de michi o watarimashō.**

We'll go straight along this road. **Kono michi o massugu ikimasu yo.**

Let's turn (to the) left at (round) this corner. **Kono kado o hidari e magarimashō.**

'... please', ... **kudasai** or, more politely, **o-negai shimasu**, 'Here you are, here's ...', **dōzo**, and 'Thank you for ...', **arigatō gozaimasu**, require **o**:

(May I have) the Mainichi, please. **Mainichi o kudasai.**

A coffee, please. **Kōhī o o-negai shimasu.**

Here's your coffee. **Kōhī o dōzo.**

Thank you for the flowers. **Hana o arigatō gozaimasu.**

21 Verbs and their objects (iii)

The *indirect* objects of verbs must be followed by **ni**:

I'll phone him (J: to him). **Kare ni denwa o kakemasu.**

Are you going to write a letter to your teacher? **Sensei ni tegami o kakimasu ka.**

Exercise 5
Put into Japanese:

1 There is some money in my purse.
2 'The money is not in the drawer.' 'Where is it?'
3 'He speaks both Japanese and Chinese.' 'Does he?'
4 'Who's going to post the letter?' 'I'll post it.'
5 I shan't go today. I'll go tomorrow.

22 'And', 'or', 'with'

When 'and' joins nouns, **to** may be used:

My wife and I are having a party.	**Watashi to kanai (to) ga pātei* o hirakimasu.**
A hamburger and chips, please.	**Hanbāgā to furaido poteto o o-negai shimasu.**

*Pronounce as in English 'party'.

Ya conveys the idea of '<u>A</u> and <u>B</u> amongst other things':

We bought wine and beer and cola (amongst other things).	**Wain ya bĭru ya kōra o kaimashita.**

Equally common is **... toka ... toka ... nado.** The **nado** corresponds, in some cases, to 'etcetera', 'and all sorts of things':

There are books and newspapers and letters and all sorts of things on the floor.	**Yuka no ue ni hon toka shinbun toka tegami nado ga arimasu.**

With just one item either **toka** or **nado** may be used:

There were magazines (and things).	**Zasshi toka arimashita.** or **Zasshi nado arimashita.**

'Or' is **ka** or **mata wa**:

The Japanese eat (either) rice or toast for breakfast.	**Nihonjin wa gohan mata wa tōsuto o chōshoku ni tabemasu.**

'With' is **to**, and sometimes **to issho ni**:

I'll go with him.	**Kare to ikimasu.**
Who are you going with?	**Dare to (issho ni) ikimasu ka.**

Note how you say the following:

Let's do it together.	**Issho ni shimashō.**
Are you coming (with us)?	**Issho ni kimasu ka.**

23 'But', 'and'

'But' may be **ga** or **keredomo**:

Excuse me, but where is the toilet?	**Sumimasen ga o-tearai wa dochira desu ka.**
I'm not going tomorrow, but what about you (are you going)?	**Watashi wa ashita ikimasen ga anata wa?**
The passport is mine but the wallet isn't.	**Pasupōto wa watashi no desu ga saifu wa watashi no ja arimasen.**

Ga often ends a sentence, indicating hesitation:

A: *Have you got any tea?*	**O-cha wa arimasu ka.**
B: *We have (why, would you like some? etc.).*	**Arimasu ga ...**
A: *Are you Mr Tanaka?*	**Tanaka-san de irasshaimasu ka.**
B: *Yes, I'm Tanaka (why do you ask?; what do you want? etc.).*	**Hai, Tanaka desu ga ...**

'And (then)' can be expressed by **sore kara** (or **soshite**):

Let's go and see a film and then have a meal.	**Eiga o mi ni ikimashō. Sore kara gohan o tabe ni ikimashō.**

24 The past tense (i)

The past tense of **desu** is **deshita**:

A: *Who was it?*	**Dare deshita ka.**
B: *It was Mr Ikeda.*	**Ikeda-san deshita yo.**
A: *What was the film like?*	**Eiga wa dō deshita ka.**
B: *It was all right.*	**Māmā deshita.**

The past tense of **masu** is **mashita**:

A: *Who came last night?*	**Yūbe dare ga kimashita ka.**
B: *I did.*	**Watashi desu.**

The past <u>negative</u> of **desu** is formed by adding **deshita** to **de wa (ja) arimasen**:

It wasn't me.	**Watashi ja arimasen deshita.**
Wasn't it her?	**Kanojo ja arimasen deshita ka.**

The past negative of other verbs is made by adding **deshita** to **masen**:

I didn't read yesterday's paper.	**Kino no shinbun wa yomimasen deshita.**
Didn't you eat the sushi?	**Sushi wa tabemasen deshita ka.**

N.B. The perfect tense, e.g. 'Have you (finished?)', 'I've (eaten)', etc., may also be expressed by the **mashita** form:

A:	Have you finished?	**Owarimashita ka.**
B:	Yes, I have.	**Hai, owarimashita.**
A:	I've eaten.	**Tabemashita.**
B:	Have you?	**So desu ka.**

The negative past (**masen deshita**), however, is <u>not</u> used for the negative perfect (i.e. 'have not done', etc.). The entirely different construction required for this will be introduced in Lesson 8.

25 'Now', 'already', 'not yet' – *Ima, mo, mada*

Ima, mo and **mada** are three adverbs easily confused. **Ima** is used for 'now' with a verb in the **masu** or **masho** form, and 'just now' with a verb in the past tense:

I'm going out now.	**Ima dekakemasu yo.**
Let's eat now.	**Ima tabemasho.**
There was a phone call just now.	**Ima denwa ga arimashita.**

Mo means both 'already' and 'now':

Are you going to bed already (now)?	**Mo nemasu ka.**
Have you finished already (now)?	**Mo owarimashita ka.**

Mada with a negative means 'not yet':

It won't be finished yet.	**Mada owarimasen.**
We're not going out yet.	**Mada dekakemasen yo.**

Mada desu alone is very commonly used to mean 'not yet':

A:	Have you read it yet?	**Mo yomimashita ka.**
B:	Not yet.	**Mada desu.**

Sugu (ni), 'immediately', 'straight away', combines with **ima** to give 'at this very moment'; and with **mo** to give 'soon', 'in a minute':

I can't do it at this very moment.	**Ima sugu dekimasen.**
We'll be having dinner in a minute.	**Mo sugu gohan o tabemasu yo.**

Exercise 6

Put into Japanese:

1 We didn't go out for a drink last night.
2 She went straight home.
3 I didn't eat the sashimi.
4 The soya sauce and the sashimi are over there.
5 I'll finish in a minute.
6 A hamburger and a coffee, please.
7 Didn't you speak to her in Japanese?

CONVERSATION 4a: In a coffee shop

Mr Brown (B) orders breakfast from the waitress (W):

W: Irasshaimase[1].

(She brings water and a hot towel to Mr Brown, who takes a seat)

W: Nani ni itashimashō[2] ka.
B: Sō desu ne. Kyō no mōningu[3] wa nan desu ka.
W: Tamago to tōsuto de gozaimasu[4] ga.
B: Sore ja[5], mōningu (o)[6] o-negai shimasu.
W: Kōhī no mōningu de gozaimasu ka. Kōcha no mōningu de gozaimasu ka.
B: Kōhī (o) o-negai shimasu. A, yappari kōcha ni shimasu yo.
W: Miruku-tei* ga yoroshii desu ka[7].
B: Hai.
W: Sore de wa miruku-tei no mōningu de gozaimasu ne. Kashikomarimashita[8]. Shōshō o-machi-kudasai[9].

B: Sumimasen. Kyō no shinbun (wa) arimasu ka.
W: Hai, sochira ni gozaimasu[10]. Asahi to Mainichi wa gozaimasu ga Eiji-shinbun wa gozaimasen.

W: Miruku-tei no mōningu o-matase shimashita[11].
B: Dōmo.

(Some time later)

B: O-kanjō (o) o-negai shimasu.
W: Hai, kashikomarimashita.

* Pronounce as in English 'tea'.

CONVERSATION 4b: In a taxi

Mr Brown (B) asks a passer-by (P) if there's a taxi rank:

B: Sumimasen. Chikaku ni takushī noriba wa arimasen ka.
P: Takushī noriba desu ka. Etto, chotto matte kudasai. Asoko no depāto no mae no basu tei no chikaku ni arimashita yo.
B: Arigatō.

He finds a taxi:

B: Tarumi eki made o-negai shimasu.
D (Driver): Eki no dono hen desu ka.
B: Eki-mae o-negai shimasu.
D: Hai, wakarimashita.

Ten minutes later:

B: Untenshu-san, mō sugu tsukimasu ka.
D: Hai, mō sugu desu yo ... Hai, eki-mae desu.
B: Kono hen de oroshite kudasai[12].

The passenger pays:

B: O-tsuri wa kekkō desu[13].
D: Āa, dōmo.

Notes:

1. **Irasshaimase:** a stock greeting made by shop assistants, waiters, etc., when one enters shops, cafés, restaurants. No reply is necessary.

2. **itashimashō:** itasu/itashimasu is a humble form of **suru/shimasu**.

3. **mōningu:** an abbreviation of **mōningu sābisu**, which is a cheap and light breakfast available at most Japanese coffee shops.

4. **de gozaimasu:** de gozaru/de gozaimasu is a politer, humbler form of **da/desu**.

5. **sore ja:** an abbreviation of **sore de wa,** 'well, then'.

6. **(o) o-negai shimasu:** as mentioned on page 33, the object particle **o** and other particles are frequently omitted in conversation.

7. **... ga yoroshii desu ka:** a polite form of **... ga ii desu ka,** literally 'is it good?' (for adjectives ending in **i**, see Lesson 6).

8. **kashikomarimashita:** a polite word meaning 'very well'. The past tense implies 'I have understood'.

9. **shōshō o-machi kudasai:** a politer form of **chotto matte kudasai.**

10. **gozaimasu: gozaru/gozaimasu** is a politer, humbler form of **aru/arimasu.**

11. **... o-matase shimashita:** 'I'm sorry to have kept you waiting for ...'. A polite expression.

12. **oroshite kudasai:** '(Please) let me off here'.

13. **kekkō desu:** here '... is unnecessary'. Tipping is not commonplace in Japan, except in the form of a few coins to a taxi driver.

Lesson 5

MAIN POINTS: Numbers; time; dates; *only*; miscellaneous numeral expressions.
CONVERSATIONS: (a) Birthdays; (b) At the post office; (c) At the station ticket office.

26 Numbers (Chinese)

There are two counting systems, both in daily use. One is of Chinese origin, the other Japanese. Chinese numbers can be used alone or in combination with various 'counters'.

Alone, the Chinese numbers will be used for: counting from 1 onwards, without reference to specific concrete objects; in mathematics; and for saying telephone numbers.

Learn the numbers from 0–10, and then from 11–20 – noticing how the latter are formed logically, by saying 'ten-one', 'ten-two' and so on up to 'two-ten':

0	**rei (zero)**		
1	**ichi**	11	**jūichi**
2	**ni**	12	**jūni**
3	**san**	13	**jūsan**
4	**shi (yon)**	14	**jūshi (jūyon)**
5	**go**	15	**jūgo**
6	**roku**	16	**jūroku**
7	**shichi (nana)**	17	**jūshichi (jūnana)**
8	**hachi**	18	**jūhachi**
9	**kyū (ku)**	19	**jūkyū (jūku)**
10	**jū**	20	**nijū**

From 20 to 100 there are some irregularities: 40 is **yonjū** (not shijū); 70 is **nanajū** (not shichijū); 90 is **kyūjū** (not kujū).

In the Chinese system, then, there are variants for certain numbers: 4 is either **shi** or **yon** (the latter being in practice so much more common that you may may use it unless otherwise advised), 7 is **shichi** or **nana,** 9 is **ku** or **kyū.**

100 is **hyaku,** 1,000 is **sen.** Learn the following, and note the phonetic changes in those with an asterisk*:

100	hyaku	1,000	sen
200	nihyaku	2,000	nisen
300	sanbyaku*	3,000	sansen
400	yonhyaku	4,000	yonsen
500	gohyaku	5,000	gosen
600	roppyaku*	6,000	rokusen
700	nanahyaku	7,000	nanasen
800	happyaku*	8,000	hassen*
900	kyūhyaku	9,000	kyūsen

10,000 is **ichiman**; 100,000 is **jūman** and 1,000,000 is **hyakuman**.

You can now form any number:

28	**nijū hachi**
376	**sanbyaku nanajū roku**
5,211	**gosen nihyaku jūichi**
199,805	**jūkyūman kyūsen happyaku go**

27 Telling the time

'O'clock' requires the time counter **ji**. Learn the following:

1 o'clock	**ichiji**
2 o'clock	**niji**
3 o'clock	**sanji**
4 o'clock	**yoji** (not yonji)
5 o'clock	**goji**
6 o'clock	**rokuji**
7 o'clock	**shichiji**
8 o'clock	**hachiji**
9 o'clock	**kuji**
10 o'clock	**jūji**
11 o'clock	**jūichiji**
12 o'clock	**jūniji**

'Half past' is expressed by **han** placed after the hour, so that 'half past one' becomes 'one o'clock, half': **ichiji han**. Similarly, 'half past twelve' is **jūniji han**, and so on.

'Minute' is **fun**, but again there are some phonetic changes evident from the spelling below:

1 minute	**ippun**
2 minutes	**nifun**
3 minutes	**sanpun**
4 minutes	**yonpun**
5 minutes	**gofun**
6 minutes	**roppun**
7 minutes	**nanafun**
8 minutes	**hachifun** (or **happun**)
9 minutes	**kyūfun**
10 minutes	**juppun**
20 minutes	**nijuppun**
etc.	

To express minutes past the hour, you must again change the conventional English order:

Three minutes past one (J: one o'clock, three minutes).	**Ichiji sanpun.**
A quarter past six (J: six o'clock, fifteen minutes).	**Rokuji jūgofun.**
Nine minutes past nine.	**Kuji kyūfun.**

Minutes before the hour maintain this same order, with the addition of **mae** ('before'):

Five minutes to four (J: four o'clock, five minutes before).	**Yoji gofun mae.**
A quarter to eleven.	**Jūichiji jūgofun mae.**
Four minutes to four.	**Yoji yonpun mae.**

Ni expresses 'at':

She came at a quarter past three.	**Sanji jūgofun ni kimashita.**
We boarded the plane at half past four.	**Yoji han ni hikōki ni norimashita.**

'What time ...' is **nanji**:

A: *What time is it?*	**Nanji desu ka.**
B: *It's 9.45 a.m. (p.m.)*	**Gozen (gogo) kuji yonjū gofun desu.**
A: *At what time in the morning do you leave?*	**Asa no nanji ni dekakemasu ka.**
B: *Normally at seven o'clock.*	**Futsū wa shichiji desu.**

28 Some other counters

(i) Money counters:

1 yen	**ichien**
5 yen	**goen**
10 yen	**jūen**
50 yen	**gojūen**
100 yen	**hyakuen**
500 yen	**gohyakuen**
1,000 yen	**sen'en***
5,000 yen	**gosen'en***
10,000 yen	**ichiman'en***

'How much?' is **ikura**:

A: *How much is it to Osaka?*   **Ōsaka made wa ikura desu ka.**
B: *It's 2,000 yen.*   **Nisen'en* desu.**
A: *How much did the ticket cost?*   **Kippu wa ikura kakarimashita ka.**
B: *10,000 yen.*   **Ichiman'en* desu.**

*The apostrophe here and elsewhere indicates that the pronunciation should be senyen, gosenyen, ichimanyen, etc.

(ii) People counters:

'One person' is **hitori**; 'two people' is **futari,** but from three people onwards the counter **nin** is used ('four people' is **yonin**). 'How many people' is **nannin**:

A: *How many came?*   **Nannin kimashita ka.**
B: *Four friends came.*   **Tomodachi ga yonin kimashita.**

(iii) Cylindrical things (e.g. bottles, pencils, legs):

Note the phonetic changes for **hon: ippon, nihon, sanbon, yonhon, gohon, roppon, nanahon, hachihon** (or **happon**), **kyūhon, juppon, jūippon** etc. 'How many?' is **nanbon**:

A: *Have you got any pencils?*   **Enpitsu wa arimasu ka.**
B: *Yes, there are two here.*   **Koko ni wa nihon* arimasu yo.**
A: *How many bottles of beer did you buy?*   **Bīru wa nanbon* kaimashita ka.**
B: *Six.*   **Roppon* desu.**

(*When counters are used alone no particle is required.)

(iv) Cupfuls, spoonfuls:

The phonetic changes for **hai** are the same as for **hon**. 'How many (spoonfuls/cupfuls)?' is **nanbai**:

A: *How many spoons of sugar shall I put in?* Satō wa nanbai iremashō ka.
B: *Two spoons for me, please.* Nihai kudasai.

(v) Flat things (e.g. sheets of paper, stamps, slices of bread):

The counter is **mai**. 'How many?' is **nanmai**:

A: *How many pieces of paper?* Kami wa nanmai desu ka.
B: *Seven please.* Nanamai kudasai.

(vi) Books, magazines:

The counter is **satsu**. Note the phonetic changes with 1, 11, etc. (**issatsu, jūissatsu**), and 10, 20, etc. (**jussatsu, nijussatsu**). 'How many books?' is **nansatsu**:

A: *I borrowed seven books.* Hon o nanasatsu karimashita.
B: *How many?* Nansatsu desu ka.

(vii) Times; floors (of a building):

The counter is **kai**. Note the phonetic changes in 1 floor/time (**ikkai**), 6 floors/times (**rokkai**), and 10 floors/times (**jukkai**). 'How many floors/times?' is **nankai**:

A: *How many times have you seen that film?* Ano eiga o nankai mimashita ka.
B: *Twice.* Nikai mimashita.
A: *Excuse me, what floor is the toy department?* Sumimasen. O-mocha uriba wa nankai desu ka.
B: *It's the sixth floor.* Rokkai de gozaimasu.

Other counters will be introduced later. For things which don't have their own counter you'll need the Japanese number system.

Exercise 7
Put into Japanese:

1 'How many went with you?' 'I went alone.'
2 Ten 60-yen stamps please.
3 'How much is it to Nagasaki from here?' '20,000 yen.'
4 I phoned him ten times.
5 My telephone number is 654 2908*.

(* This would read **roku go yon** *no* **ni kyū zero hachi**.)

29 Numbers (Japanese)

You need to know Japanese numbers up to 10 (thereafter the Chinese system is used). Japanese numbers are used for counting tables, chairs, boxes, fruit and vegetables and other things which don't have counters of their own. (You may well hear the Japanese system used for items which do have counters as well!)

Learn the numbers, all of which, except for 10, are almost always found with the suffix **tsu**:

1	**hitotsu**	7	**nanatsu**
2	**futatsu**	8	**yattsu**
3	**mittsu**	9	**kokonotsu**
4	**yottsu**	10	**tō**
5	**itsutsu**	11	**jūichi**
6	**muttsu**	12	**jūni**

'How many' is **ikutsu**:

I bought three chairs and a table in the sale.	**Isu o mittsu to tēburu o hitotsu bāgen sēru de kaimashita.**
A: *How many suitcases have you got?*	**Sūtsukēsu wa ikutsu arimasu ka.**
B: *Three.*	**Mittsu arimasu.**

Japanese numbers are also used for counting age (20 is **hatachi**). 'How old' is **(o-) ikutsu**:

A: *How old is he?*	**Ikutsu desu ka.**
B: *He's eight.*	**Yattsu desu.**

Sai with the Chinese system is also used for age. Note phonetic changes with 1 (**issai**), 8 (**hassai**), 10 (**jussai**). 'How old' is **nansai**:

A: *How old are you?*	**Nansai desu ka.**
B: *I'm five.*	**Gosai desu.**

30 Ordinal numbers

Ordinal numbers (1st, 2nd, etc., except dates) are made by adding **me** to any of the counters. Consider the following:

A: *Let's take (J: turn) the second turning to the right.*	**Futatsume no kado o migi e magarimashō.**
B: *Let's make it the third.*	**Mittsume ni shimashō.**

31 Dates (i)

The days of the month from 1st to 10th are based on the Japanese system. Learn the following:

1st	**tsuitachi**	6th	**muika**
2nd	**futsuka**	7th	**nanoka**
3rd	**mikka**	8th	**yōka**
4th	**yokka**	9th	**kokonoka**
5th	**itsuka**	10th	**tōka**

From the 11th to the 31st, the Chinese system with the counter **nichi** is used (**jūichinichi, jūninichi,** etc.) with the following exceptions: 14th, 24th are **jūyokka, nijūyokka;** (17th, 27th are **jūshichi, nijūshichinichi** and not jūnana, nijūnana); 20th is **hatsuka.** 'What day/date' is **nannichi:**

A: *What's the date today?*   Kyō wa nannichi desu ka.
B: *Umm, isn't it the 20th?*   Etto, hatsuka ja arimasen ka.
A: *What day shall we go back on?*   Nannichi ni kaerimashō ka.
B: *Umm, let's go back on the 10th.*   Sō desu ne. Tōka ni kaerimashō.

32 Dates (ii)

Days of the week are:

Monday	**getsuyōbi**
Tuesday	**kayōbi**
Wednesday	**suiyōbi**
Thursday	**mokuyōbi**
Friday	**kinyōbi**
Saturday	**doyōbi**
Sunday	**nichiyōbi**

'What day (of the week)' is **nanyōbi**.

For months of the year use the counter **gatsu** (notice how this is added to a Chinese number, 1 for January, 2 for February, and so on):

January	**ichigatsu**
February	**nigatsu**
March	**sangatsu**
April	**shigatsu**
May	**gogatsu**

June	rokugatsu
July	shichigatsu
August	hachigatsu
September	kugatsu
October	jūgatsu
November	jūichigatsu
December	jūnigatsu

'What month' is **nangatsu**.

Years use the counter **nen**:

1868	**senhappyaku rokujūhachinen**
1956	**senkyūhyaku gojūrokunen**
1984	**senkyūhyaku hachijūyonen**

'What year' is **nannen**.

Consider the following:

A: *In what year were you born?*
Nannen ni umaremashita ka.

B: *I was born on the 13th of March 1956.*
Senkyūhyaku gojūrokunen sangatsu (no) jūsannichi ni umaremashita.

A: *What day of the week is the 4th of April this year?*
Kotoshi no shigatsu yokka wa nanyōbi desu ka.

B: *It's a Thursday.*
Mokuyōbi desu yo.

33 'Only'

There are two expressions for 'only' in Japanese: **shika** and **dake**. **Shika,** always used with a <u>negative</u> verb, is the more common. The particles **wa, ga** and **o** are omitted:

I'm the only one here.
Watashi shika imasen.

I've only got one 10,000-yen note.
Ichiman'en satsu wa ichimai shika arimasen.

We're only going to Nara.
Nara ni shika ikimasen.

Dake, like **shika**, follows the word concerned. It does not take the negative:

I only went there once.
Ikkai dake ikimashita.

Is that all?
Sore dake desu ka.

48

The two words together are emphatic:

I'm only going to be here for a year.   **Ichinen dake shika imasen.**

34 Miscellaneous numeral expressions

(i) 'About' – **goro** (used of time only), **gurai**:

A: *At about what time shall we go?*   **Nanji goro (ni) dekakemashō ka.**
B: *Let's leave at about six o'clock.*   **Rokuji goro (ni) dekakemashō.**
A: *About how much does it cost?*   **Ikura gurai kakarimasu ka.**
B: *It's only about 10,000 yen.*   **Ichiman'en gurai shika kakarimasen.**

(ii) 'A little' and 'a lot' – **sukoshi, chotto** and **takusan, amari**:

Shall we have just a little sashimi?   **Sashimi o sukoshi dake tabemashō ka.**
I ate a lot (of food) today.   **Kyō wa gohan o takusan tabemashita.**
I didn't eat a lot today.   **Kyō wa amari (takusan)* tabemasen deshita.**

***Amari (takusan)** is used with a negative to mean 'not much'.

(iii) 'Some more', 'a little more' – **mō**:

A: *Would you like some more beer?*   **Bīru wa mō sukoshi nomimasu ka.**
B: *Yes, I'll have just a little bit more.*   **Hai, mō sukoshi dake itadakimasu.**
A: *One more orange, please.*   **Mikan o mō hitotsu kudasai.**
B: *Just (only) one?*   **Hitotsu dake desu ka.**

Exercise 8
Put into Japanese:

1 'How many people came to your party?' 'Only three (came).'
2 I'll have just one more glass of beer.
3 Roughly (about) when will you be going?
4 How many pieces of paper did you use for (**ni**) that?
5 This is my sixth glass of beer.

CONVERSATION 5a: Birthdays

A friend (A) asks John (J) about his birthday:

A: Jon-san no tanjōbi wa itsu desu ka.
J: Raishū desu yo.
A: Sō desu ka. Watashi no tanjōbi mo raishū desu.
J: Ē! Raishū no nanyōbi desu ka.
A: Kayōbi desu. Jūshichinichi no kayōbi desu yo.
J: Ē! Watashi wa hatsuka desu[1].
A: Jon-san wa nannen umare[2] desu ka. Watashi wa rokujūnen desu.
J: Onaji desu.

CONVERSATION 5b: At the post office

Mrs Brown (C) asks the counter clerk (X) for stamps and postcards:

C: Nanajūen no kitte o nimai ni[3] hagaki o yonmai kudasai. Sore kara kono tegami
   o Furansu made o-negai shimasu.
X: Kōkūbin desu ka funabin desu ka.
C: Kōkūbin de[4] o-negai shimasu. Sore ni earogramu o ichimai kudasai.
X: Sore de yoroshii desu ka[5].
C: Hai, sore dake desu.
X: Zenbu de[6] nana hyakuen desu ... Hai, chōdo nana hyakuen (o) o-azukari shimasu.
   Arigatō gozaimasu.

CONVERSATION 5c: At the station ticket office

Mr Brown (B) asks about trains to Kyoto:

B: Tsugi no Kyōto-yuki[7] wa nanji nanpun-hatsu[8] desu ka.
X: Kuji juppun desu. Ato[9] jūgofun arimasu.
B: Sore ja Kyōto made otona nimai[10] o-negai shimasu.
X: Katamichi desu ka ōfuku desu ka.
B: Ōfuku desu. Ikura desu ka.
X: Kyūsen'en desu. Hai, ichiman'en (o) o-azukari shimasu. Sen'en no o-kaeshi desu.
   Arigatō gozaimashita.
B: Nanbansen[11] desu ka.
X: Gobansen desu.

(On the train, the conductor (C) comes round):

C: Jōshaken o haiken itashimasu[12]... Kore wa Kyōto-yuki ja arimasen yo. Nagoya-yuki desu.

B: Shimatta! Densha o machigaemashita!

Notes:

1. **watashi wa hatsuka desu:** lit. 'as for me, it's the twentieth'.

2. **nannen umare:** set phrase for 'What year were you born in?'

3. **ni:** 'and'.

4. **kōkūbin de:** 'by (air)'.

5. **sore de yoroshii desu ka:** 'Will that be all?'

6. **zenbu de:** 'all together'.

7. **Kyōto-yuki:** '(the train) heading for Kyoto'; **... yuki** means 'destination ...'.

8. **nanjinanpun-hatsu:** 'at how many minutes past what hour does it leave?'

9. **ato:** 'there are 15 minutes left'; **ato** followed by counter often means '... left'.

10. **otona nimai:** it is unnecessary to use the word for ticket. The counter alone makes it clear what is meant.

11. **nanbansen:** **bansen** is the counter for platforms.

12. **haiken itashimasu:** 'I shall look at your tickets'; **haiken itasu/itashimasu** is a humble form of **miru/mimasu**. See Lesson 20.

Lesson 6

MAIN POINTS: Adjectives; adverbs.
CONVERSATIONS: (a) 'Your Japanese is good'; (b) A packed lunch.

35 'Adjectives' A (i)

There are two basic but quite different types of adjective. One is the **i** adjective (all adjectives of this type end in **i**). It is <u>essential</u> from the first to understand that **i** adjectives are quite unlike adjectives in English. Strictly speaking, they are <u>verbs</u>.

Take the sentence 'the car is fast'. In Japanese, the 'is fast' part is translated by the single word **hayai**. **Hayai**, then, means not just 'fast' but '<u>is</u> fast'. These **i** adjectives, being strictly verbs, do not have singular or plural forms, nor any 1st, 2nd or 3rd person forms, so 'I am/you are/she, he, it is/we are etc. fast' may all be translated by the one word **hayai**. Study these examples:

I'm young.	**(Watashi wa) wakai.**
You're clever.	**(Anata wa) kashikoi.**
That is tasty.	**(Sore wa) oishii.**

It follows that to say 'it isn't fast', 'it was fast' or 'it wasn't fast', the present negative, the past or the past negative forms of **hayai** are needed.

36 'Adjectives' A (ii)

The present negative of an **i** adjective is made by changing the final **i** to **ku** and then adding **nai: hayai→hayaku→hayaku nai.** Cover up the right-hand side to check you can form the present negative of the following adjectives:

takai (high/expensive)	→	**takaku nai**
hikui (low)		**hikuku nai**
yasui (cheap)		**yasuku nai**
ōkii (big)		**ōkiku nai**
chīsai (small)		**chīsaku nai**
nagai (long)		**nagaku nai**
mijikai (short)		**mijikaku nai**
hayai (fast/early)		**hayaku nai**
osoi (slow/late)		**osoku nai**

omoshiroi (interesting/funny)   **omoshiroku nai**
tsumaranai (boring/tiresome)   **tsumaranaku nai**

The past (positive) of the **i** adjective is made by replacing the final **i** with **katta**: **hayai→haya→hayakatta**.

The past <u>negative</u> is made from the present negative by changing **nai** to **nakatta**: **hayaku nai** (present negative)→**hayaku nakatta**.

Check you can form the past, positive and negative, of the following:

yasashii (easy/kind)	→	**yasashikatta; yasashiku nakatta**
muzukashii (difficult)		**muzukashikatta; muzukashiku nakatta**
kitsui (tight)		**kitsukatta; kitsuku nakatta**
yurui (loose)		**yurukatta; yuruku nakatta**
katai (hard)		**katakatta; kataku nakatta**
yawarakai (soft)		**yawarakakatta; yawarakaku nakatta**
amai (sweet)		**amakatta; amaku nakatta**
karai (spicy/hot)		**karakatta; karaku nakatta**
samui (cold (weather))		**samukatta; samuku nakatta**
atsui (hot)		**atsukatta; atsuku nakatta**
warui (bad)		**warukatta; waruku nakatta**
ii (good/nice)		**yokatta; yoku nakatta***

(***Yokatta** and **yoku nakatta** come from **yoi**, the old form of **ii**.)

N.B. All the adjectival forms above are similar, in terms of <u>politeness</u>, to the plain form of verbs. To make them polite it is necessary to add **desu**. Here **desu** has <u>no meaning whatsoever</u>, it simply makes the adjective more polite.

N.B. **Nai** in the negative examples is, in fact, the plain form of **arimasen**. It follows then that **hayaku arimasen** and **hayaku arimasen deshita** will be alternatives for **hayaku nai desu** and **hayaku nakatta desu**. Note here also that **de wa (ja) arimasen** and **de wa (ja) arimasen deshita** have rather more common forms in **de wa (ja) nai desu** and **de wa (ja) nakatta desu** respectively. Study the following:

A: *What was it like? Was it interesting?*   **Dō deshita ka. Omoshirokatta desu ka.**
B: *It was very interesting.*   **Totemo[1] omoshirokatta desu yo.**
A: *Was the meal tasty?*   **Gohan wa oishikatta desu ka.**
B: *No, it wasn't very tasty.*   **Amari[2] oishiku nakatta desu yo.**

(1. **totemo** – 'very' in positive sentences; 2. **amari** – 'very' in negative sentences)

37 'Adjectives' A (iii)

The **i** adjectives are used before nouns. (Even in polite speech, **desu** is not added to the **i** adjective in the pre-noun position):

an interesting place	**omoshiroi tokoro**
hot days	**atsui hi**
a nice person	**ii hito**

If you recall that **i** adjectives are really verbs, it is easy to understand that the above are probably more precisely translated as 'a place <u>which is</u> interesting'; 'days <u>which are</u> hot', and 'a person <u>who is</u> nice'. Bear in mind, then, that no such word as the English 'which', 'who', etc. is necessary:

They've only got fish which isn't very tasty.	**Amari oishiku nai sakana shika nai desu.**
He's a very kind person.	**Totemo yasashii hito desu.**

Exercise 9
Put into polite Japanese:

1 Today was very hot, wasn't it?
2 We went to buy some lacquerware, but they didn't have any.
3 This tea wasn't very tasty, was it?
4 The tall man is my father. The short man is his friend.
5 He's very kind.

38 Adjectives B (i)

The second major group of adjectives are grammatically a lot closer to English adjectives, since the verb 'to be' must be supplied. Below is a list of some common adjectives of this type:

simple	**kantan**	rude	**shitsurei**
disliked	**kirai**	ill, sick	**byōki**
famous	**yūmei**	strange	**hen**
liked	**suki**	stupid	**baka**
necessary	**hitsuyō**	unpleasant	**iya**
polite	**teinei**	useless	**dame**
pretty	**kirei**	various	**iroiro**

39 Adjectives B (ii)

The present positive plain form of these adjectives is made by adding **da**. The present negative, the past and the past negative plain forms are made with the appropriate plain forms of **da/desu**:

Present negative – **de wa (ja) nai**
Past – **datta**
Past negative – **de wa (ja) nakatta**

The present positive <u>polite</u> form requires **desu**, and the past positive <u>polite</u> form **deshita**. The present and past negative polite forms are made usually by the addition of **desu** to the plain form, i.e. **de wa (ja) nai desu; de wa (ja) nakatta desu**. Consider the following:

It's simple.	**Kantan desu yo.**
Isn't she famous?	**Kanojo wa yūmei ja nai desu ka.**
He was very rude.	**Kare wa totemo shitsurei deshita.**
It wasn't very quiet, was it?	**Amari shizuka ja nakatta desu ne.**

40 Adjectives B (iii)

This second group is known as **na** adjectives because when placed before a noun in the <u>present positive</u> tense <u>only</u>, they take the particle **na**:

a strange person	**hen na hito**
necessary things	**hitsuyō na mono**
a pretty face	**kirei na kao**

Na represents the verb 'to be', and so the above can equally well be translated as 'a person <u>who is</u> strange'; 'things <u>which are</u> necessary'; 'a face <u>which is</u> pretty'.

When the adjective comes before the noun in all <u>but</u> the present positive, the appropriate plain forms of **da/desu** are used. Consider the following:

He's not a very kind person.	**Amari shinsetsu ja nai hito desu.**
She's a very rude person.	**Kanojo wa totemo shitsurei na hito desu yo.**

Note that three **i** adjectives function also as **na** adjectives. They are 'big' – **ōkii** or **ōki na**; 'small' – **chīsai/chīsa** or **chīsa na**; 'funny' (amusing or strange) – **okashii** or **okashi na**:

He's a big man, isn't he?	**Kare wa ōkii (or ōki na) hito desu ne.**
That's a small dictionary.	**Chīsai (or chīsa na) jisho desu ne.**
That's a funny story.	**Okashii (or okashi na) hanashi desu yo.**

(In the final position, however, they all appear only as **i** adjectives.)

'Same (as)' – **(to) onaji** – is irregular. Before nouns, it does not take **na,** but in other ways it functions as a **na** adjective:

It's the same camera.	**Onaji kamera desu.**
It wasn't the same as mine.	**Watashi no to onaji ja nakatta desu yo.**

41 'Too ...'

'Too ...': remove the final **i** and add the verb **sugiru/sugimasu;** with **na** adjectives add **sugiru/sugimasu** to the adjective without **na. Amari (ni mo)** may precede the adjective:

It's too tight, isn't it?	**Kitsusugimasu ne.**
Isn't it too expensive?	**Amari takasugimasen ka.**
Isn't this too easy?	**Kore wa kantansugimasen ka.**

42 Adverbs (i)

Two types of adverb are made from the two main types of adjective. With **i** adjectives, the final **i** syllable is replaced by **ku:**

hayai (quick/early) → **hayaku** (quickly/early)
ii (good) → **yoku** (well)*

*****yoku** has the additional meaning of 'often'.

With **na** adjectives, add **ni:**

kirei (pretty/clean) → **kirei ni** (prettily/cleanly)
shinsetsu (kind) → **shinsetsu ni** (kindly)

Consider the following examples:

I bought it cheaply.	**Yasuku kaimashita.**
She taught in a kind way.	**Shinsetsu ni oshiemashita.**

'Become (get) ...' are made by adverbs and the verb **naru/narimasu** (become):

It's going to get cold(er).	**Samuku narimasu yo.**
She's become pretty.	**Kirei ni narimashita.**

Adverbs are used with **suru/shimasu** too:

Let's tidy up (J: make tidy) the room.	**Heya o kirei ni shimashō ka.**
I'll turn (J: make) the sound down (up).	**Oto o chīsaku (ōkiku) shimasu.**

43 Adverbs (ii)

There is another group of very common adverbs, many of which are followed by
to. Here is a small selection:

Did you do it properly?	**Chan to shimashita ka.**
I explained it clearly.	**Hakkiri setsumei shimashita.**
Let's have a leisurely cup of tea (lit. Let's drink slowly).	**Yukkuri o-cha demo nomimashō.**
I slammed the window (lit. shut it bang!).	**Batan to mado o shimemashita.**

Finally note the following sets of adverb-related words:

How?	**Dō**	or	**Dō yatte**
In this way	**Kō**	or	**Kō yatte**
In that way	**Sō**	or	**Sō yatte**
In that way	**Ā**	or	**Ā yatte**

A: *How do you write it? Do you write it like this?* — **Dō yatte kakimasu ka. Kō kakimasu ka.**

B: *No, you don't write it like that. You write it like this.* — **Ie, sō kakimasen. Kō kakimasu yo.**

Exercise 10
Put into Japanese:

1 'How do you go to school?' 'Me, I go by bus.'
2 She speaks very well, doesn't she?
3 'What about the size?' 'The size is just right.'
4 That Toyota is the same as my friend's.
5 Do you often go skiing?

CONVERSATION 6a: 'Your Japanese is good'

Mr Brown's friend (A) congratulates him on his accent:

A: Nihongo ga o-jōzu[1] desu ne.
B: Ya, sonna koto wa arimasen yo. Mada mada[2] desu.
A: Hontō desu yo. Hatsuon ga totemo kirei desu. Nihonjin to kawarimasen. Hontō ni kirei ni hanashimasu yo.
B: Sō desu ka. Arigatō gozaimasu.
A: Yappari muzukashii desu ka Nihongo wa[3].
B: Totemo muzukashii desu. Taihen kurō shimashita. Hatsuon wa wari to yasashii desu ga bunpō wa yayakoshii desu. Sore kara yomikaki mo taihen desu. Katakana mo hiragana mo kanji mo arimasu shi[4]. Hijō ni oboenikui desu[5].
A: Sore wa sō desu[6] ne. Kioku no mondai dake desu. Shikashi erai[7] desu ne.

CONVERSATION 6b: A packed lunch

Mr Brown (B) and Mr Tanaka (T) buy a packed lunch on the train to Kyoto:

Salesgirl (S): Maku-no-uchi, Sabazushi, Unagibentō ni O-cha, O-bīru wa ikaga desu ka.
T: Maku-no-uchi (o) futatsu kudasai.
S: Hai, Maku-no-uchi o-futatsu desu ne. Hai dōzo. O-nomimono wa?
T: Watashi wa tsumetai mono ga ii desu ne ... Bīru (o) kudasai. Buraun-san wa?
B: Watashi wa atsui o-cha ga ii desu ne.
S: Hai, dozo sen nihyakuen de gozaimasu. Hai, chōdo sen nihyakuen itadakimasu[8]. Arigatō gozaimashita.
T: Maku-no-uchi wa hajimete[9] desu ka Buraun-san?
B: Hajimete desu yo. Demo oishisō[10] desu ne. Dō iu mono ga haitte imasu[11] ka.
T: Mazu gohan desu ne. Sore kara kono ki-iroppoi[12] no wa takuwan desu. Tsukemono desu yo.
B: Ironna[13] mono ga arimasu ne. Kono akai no wa?
T: Sore wa ebi desu. Hontō wa akaku arimasen. Akaku iro o tsuketa dake[14] desu. Ma, tabemashō. Itadakimasu.
B: Itadakimasu. Kono hosonagai no wa ebi furai desu ne. Oishii desu. Kono sōsu o kakemasu ka.
T: Sō desu. Chotto karai desu yo. Hoka ni wa[15], kono kuroppoi no wa konbu desu. Omoshiroi aji desu yo.
B: Mō onaka ga ippai desu. Takusan tabesugimashita[16]. Demo totemo oishikatta desu yo.
T: Kore o tabete mite kudasai[17]. Umeboshi desu. Totemo suppai desu ga shōkafuryō ni saikō desu.

Notes:

1. **O-jōzu:** 'you're good at ...'; **o** is added out of respect for the person addressed. **Jōzu** is dealt with in Lesson 12.

2. **mada mada:** here it means 'that's a long way off'.

3. **... desu ka, Nihongo wa:** 'Is it difficult, Japanese?'; the inverted order is common in spoken Japanese.

4. **shi:** 'and also'.

5. **oboenikui:** 'difficult to remember'; replace **masu** with the adjective **nikui** to make 'difficult to ...'; **yasui** makes 'easy to ...'. For example: *Is Osaka dialect hard to understand?* **Ōsaka-ben wa wakarinikui desu ka.** And, *That man's Japanese is easy to understand.* **Sono hito no Nihongo wa wakariyasui desu.**

6. **sore wa sō desu:** 'it is as you say', 'you're right there'.

7. **erai desu:** here it means 'good for you'; elsewhere it means 'great', 'outstanding'.

8. **chōdo ... itadakimasu:** lit. 'I take from you just the right sum'.

9. **hajimete desu ka:** 'is it the first time you've had ...'; **hajimete** is a very useful word, e.g. *Is this the first time you've been to Japan?* **Nihon wa hajimete desu ka.**

10. **oishisō desu:** 'it looks tasty', see Lesson 13.

11. **haitte imasu ka:** 'What sort of things are in it?'; for the **te imasu** construction see Lesson 8.

12. **ki-iroppoi:** 'yellowish'; several adjectives have **-ppoi** added to them, but the meaning varies depending on the adjective used. One of the most common is **yasuppoi**, 'cheapo'.

13. **ironna:** 'various'; a very common abbreviated form of **iroiro na**.

14. **akaku iro o tsuketa dake desu:** 'they've simply coloured it red'.

15. **Hoka ni wa:** 'in addition', 'apart from that'.

16. **takusan tabesugimashita:** 'I've eaten too much'; just as **sugiru/sugimasu** can be added to adjectives, so it can to verbs, often with **takusan**, 'much'.

17. **tabete mite kudasai:** 'eat and see', 'try this'.

Lesson 7

MAIN POINTS: Formation of the *te* form of verbs and adjectives; applications of the *te* form.

CONVERSATIONS: (a) Using the telephone; (b) On the telephone.

44 Verbs and the *te* form (i)

In order to make the **te** form, which has many applications, you will need first to distinguish three different types of verb: Group 1 verbs; Group 2 verbs and (thirdly) verbs whose **te** form is irregular.

(a) A Group 1 verb is a verb whose plain form ends in the syllable **ru** and whose **masu** form is made by taking off the **ru** and putting **masu** in its place: e.g. **taberu → tabe → tabemasu; miru → mi → mimasu; iru → i → imasu.**

The **te** form of these verbs is made by replacing **ru** with **te**. Check the following:

taberu (eat)	→	**tabete**
miru (see/watch/look at)		**mite**
iru (be)		**ite**
deru (go out)		**dete**
dekakeru (depart)		**dekakete**

(b) Group 2 verbs include all other verbs (except a small number of irregular verbs), i.e. verbs whose plain form ends in the syllables **u; ku; gu; su; tsu; nu; bu; mu.** Group 2 verbs also include some verbs which end in **ru**. There need be no confusion, however, since Group 2 **ru** verbs in the **masu** form become **-rimasu.** (All verbs are given in the vocabularies in both plain and **masu** forms, so you will know immediately which group the verb belongs to.) Compare the following:

iru → imasu (be, exist) – Group 1
iru → irimasu (be necessary) – Group 2

Below is a list of all possible types of Group 2 verbs and their corresponding **te** forms:

Plain form	*te form*	*Meaning*
ka*u* (kaimasu)	**ka*tte***	buy *vt.*
ka*ku* (kakimasu)	**kai*te***	write *vt.*
oyo*gu* (oyogimasu)	**oyo*ide***	swim *vi.*
da*su* (dashimasu)	**da*shite***	take out *vt.*

59

matsu (machimasu)	matre	wait for vt.
shinu (shinimasu)	shinde	die vi.
yobu (yobimasu)	yonde	call, invite vt.
yamu (yamimasu)	yande	stop vi.
kiru (kirimasu)	kitte	cut vt.

(c) Verbs whose **te** forms are irregular:

Plain form	te form	Meaning
da (desu)	de	be
iku (ikimasu)	itte*	go vi.
kuru (kimasu)	kite	come vi.
suru (shimasu)	shite	do vt.

*__Iku/ikimasu__ is irregular only in its **te** and **ta** forms (see Lesson 9).

Check you can form the **te** forms of the following assortment of Group 1, Group 2 and irregular verbs:

neru/nemasu	(sleep)	→	nete
kaeru/kaerimasu	(go home)		kaette
kaeru/kaemasu	(change vt.)		kaete
arau/araimasu	(wash)		aratte
isogu/isogimasu	(hurry vi.)		isoide
tatsu/tachimasu	(stand vi.)		tatte
tateru/tatemasu	(stand ... up vt.)		tatete
suru/shimasu	(do/make)		shite

45 Verbs and the *te* form (ii)

There are two <u>negative</u> **te** forms, both made from the negative plain forms. The negative plain forms and the first of the **te** forms are as follows:

Group 1 verbs:

Positive plain form	Negative plain form	Negative te form
taberu (tabemasu)	tabenai	tabenakute
miru (mimasu)	minai	minakute

Group 2 verbs:

Positive plain form	Negative plain form	Negative te form
kau (kaimasu)	kawanai	kawanakute
kaku (kakimasu)	kakanai	kakanakute
matsu (machimasu)	matanai	matanakute

Irregular verbs:

Positive plain form	Negative plain form	Negative te form
da (desu)	**de wa (ja) nai**	**de wa (ja) nakute**
suru (shimasu)	**shinai**	**shinakute**
kuru (kimasu)	**konai**	**konakute**

Check you can form the negative **te** forms of the following selection:

suru/shimasu	→	**shinakute**
kaeru/kaerimasu		**kaeranakute**
kaeru/kaemasu		**kaenakute**
dasu/dashimasu		**dasanakute**
iru/imasu		**inakute**
kau/kaimasu		**kawanakute**

The second negative **te** form is made by adding **de** to the negative plain form:

kawanai → kawanaide
shinai → shinaide

N.B. This second form exists for all verbs except **nai** and **de wa (ja) nai**.

46 Verbs and the *te* form (iii)

Usages of the **te** form:

(i) 'Please ...' – **te** form plus **kudasai**; 'Would you be kind enough to ...?' **te** form plus **itadakemasen ka** (lit. can't I get you to ...?):

Please come with me.	**Issho ni kite kudasai.**
Would you be kind enough to speak slowly?	**Yukkuri hanashite itadakemasen ka.**
Would you be kind enough to wait there (for me) for a minute?	**Asoko de sukoshi dake matte itadakemasen ka.**

In the negative, only the **naide** form can be used:

Please don't talk.	**Hanasanaide kudasai.**
Please don't tell him.	**Kare ni iwanaide kudasai.**

(ii) The **te** form is used to join two clauses together where English would often use 'and (then)'. Whatever the tense of the English verb which precedes the 'and', the **te** form stays the same. Its tense is supplied by the final verb. Study the following:

This is my wife Chieko and this is my son Thomas.	**Kore wa kanai no Chieko de kore wa musuko no Tomasu desu.**
I went back home and watched the TV.	**Uchi e kaette terebi o mimashita.**
Let's go to a film and then have some sushi.	**Eiga ni itte sushi o tabe ni ikimashō.**
She went out for a drink and I stayed behind at home.	**Kanojo wa nomi ni itte watashi wa uchi ni nokorimashita.**
Go straight along this street and turn right at the end.	**Kono michi o massugu itte tsukiatari o migi e magatte kudasai.**

The **te** form may also mean 'and so':

He caught a cold and (so) didn't come.	**Kare wa kaze o hiite kimasen deshita.**
There were all sorts of problems so I gave up.	**Ironna mondai ga atte akiramemashita.**

(iii) 'After doing ...' may be expressed by **... te kara**:

What are you going to do after writing the letter?	**Tegami o kaite kara dō shimasu ka.**
What are you going to do after you get home?	**Ie ni tsuite kara dō shimasu ka.**

(iv) The **te** form is used adverbially:

We went on foot (J: walking).	**Aruite ikimashita.**
Let's hurry there (J: Let's go there hurrying).	**Isoide ikimashō.**
I ran here from the station.	**Eki kara koko made hashitte kimashita.**
(By) listening to the radio every day her English became good.	**Kanojo wa mainichi rajio o kiite Eigo ga umaku narimashita.**

47 Verbs and the *te* form (iv)

Many idiomatic expressions are made by adding **te** forms to **kuru/kimasu** and **iku/ikimasu**. Study the following carefully:

i) -te kuru/kimasu

Let's go and see (J: having seen, come).	**Mite kimashō.**
I'll go and buy some beer (J: having bought, I'll come).	**Biru o katte kimasu.**
I'll be straight back (J: having been, I'll come).	**Sugu itte kimasu.**
Let's go and get our coats.	**Kōto o totte kimashō.**
Bring me the paper, please.	**Shinbun o motte kite kudasai*.**

| *I've brought my father.* | **Chichi o tsurete kimashita*.** |
| *What time are you coming back?* | **Nanji ni kaette kimasu ka.** |

*Note that **motte kuru/kimasu** is used of inanimate objects, **tsurete kuru/kimasu** of people.

(ii) -te iku/ikimasu

Shall we eat first (J: having eaten, shall we go)?	**Tabete ikimashō ka.**
I'll buy some wine on the way (J: having bought, I'll go).	**Wain o katte ikimasu yo.**
Please take your umbrella.	**Kasa o motte itte kudasai*.**
I'll take him to the bus stop.	**Basu-tei made tsurete ikimasu*.**

*Again, note that **motte iku/ikimasu** is used of inanimate objects, **tsurete iku/ikimasu** of people.

Exercise 11
Put into Japanese:

1 I'm going to go and buy two postcards and six stamps.
2 Please sit there and wait.
3 They went to Kyoto, saw the Ryoanji temple and then came back.
4 'How many minutes does it take to walk?' 'I'm not sure. It takes about twenty minutes by bus.'
5 Will you go and get (J: call) your father, please.

48 Verbs and the *te* form (v)

The uses of the negative **te** form are similar to those of the positive **te** form. With **nakute**, often the sense is 'not ... instead', 'not ... and so':

I didn't have any time so I came straight back home.	**Jikan ga nakute sugu kaette kimashita.**
He's lonely as he hasn't got any friends.	**Tomodachi ga inakute samishii desu.**
It isn't today, it's tomorrow.	**Kyō ja nakute ashita desu.**
It wasn't me, it was him.	**Watashi ja nakute kara deshita.**

With **naide** the sense is often 'not ... instead' or 'without ...ing', but the subject of the main verb and the **naide** clause must be the same:

Yesterday I went straight to bed without having a bath.	**Kinō o-furo ni hairanaide sugu nemashita.**
He left the shop without paying.	**O-kane o harawanaide o-mise o demashita.**

49 Adjectival *te* forms

Adjectival **te** forms are used to mean 'and' or 'and so' (see the examples below, to understand the sort of context these words might appear in). The positive and negative **te** forms of **i** adjectives are formed respectively as follows:

takai → takakute
takaku nai → takaku nakute

The positive/negative **te** forms of **na** adjectives are:

kantan → kantan de/
kantan de wa (ja) nakute

Something tasty and cheap would be nice.	**Oishikute yasui mono ga ii desu ne.**
This is a nice big room.	**Hirokute ii* heya desu ne.**

*kute/de ii is 'nice and ...'

It's a nice and simple story.	**Kantan de ii hanashi desu.**
It was interesting so I watched it from start to finish.	**Omoshirokute saisho kara saigo made mimashita.**

CONVERSATION 7a: Using the telephone

Mr Brown (B) asks how to use a public call box:

B: Sumimasen, denwa no tsukaikata[1] o oshiete itadakemasen ka.
A: Tsukaikata desu ka. Ii desu yo. Jūen dama wa takusan arimasu ka.
B: Etto, komakai no wa amari arimasen. Warui desu ga[2], chotto kore o kuzushite itadakemasen ka.
A: Ii desu yo. Sore ja, mazu juwaki o totte, jūen dama o sanko gurai irete, bangō o mawashite kudasai.
B: Arigatō gozaimashita. Etto, mazu juwaki o totte, o-kane o irete, sore kara bangō o mawashite – 06 678 no 9809 desu ne – sore dake desu ne.
A: Sō desu.
B: Arigatō gozaimashita.
A: Dō itashimashite.
B: A, yappari hanashichū[3] desu. Mō sukoshi matte mata kakete mimashō[4].

CONVERSATION 7b: On the telephone

When he gets through to the Katayamas' house, Mrs K answers:

Mrs K: Moshimoshi[5].
B: Yabun osoku mōshiwake gozaimasen ga[6], Katayama-san no o-taku deshō ka.
Mrs K: Hai, sō desu.
B: Kunio-san wa irasshaimasu ka.
Mrs K: Hai, chotto matte kudasai, yonde kimasu.
B: Sumimasen.

Then his friend Kunio (K) comes to the phone:

K: Moshimoshi, Kunio desu ga.
B: Kunio-san? Jon desu.
K: A, Jon-san. O-hisashiburi desu ne. Genki deshita ka.
B: Okage-sama de. Kunio wa?
K: Un, watashi mo genki deshita yo.
B: Tokoro de, Kunio, asatte wa hima desu ka.
K: Asatte wa doyōbi desu ne. Hima desu yo.
B: Sore ja, issho ni Kyōto made ikimasen ka.
K: Kyōto wa hisashiburi desu ne. Ii desu yo. Issho ni ikimashō.
B: A, yokatta desu. Kyōto no doko o[7] mawarimashō ka.
K: Mazu machiawase no jikan to basho o kimemashō.
B: Sō desu ne.
K: Osaka eki no chūo guchi de hachiji goro ni machiawase shite[8] 8ji han no densha ni notte ikimashō.
B: Hai, wakarimashita.
K: Sore de wa asatte no asa no hachiji ni[9].
B: Hai, tanoshimi ni shite imasu[10].
K: Sore ja, o-yasumi nasai.
B: O-yasumi nasai.

Notes:

1. **tsukaikata:** 'the way (how) to use'; replace **masu** with **kata** to say 'the way to/ of ...' cf. **hanashikata,** 'way of speaking'; **hashirikata,** 'way of running'.

2. **warui desu ga:** 'I'm sorry, but ...'.

3. **hanashichū:** 'engaged'. There are a great number of uses of **chū (jū)**. Some are time expressions: **kaigichū,** 'at a conference'; **shigotochū,** 'in the middle of work'; **ichinichijū,** 'all day long'; **hitobanjū,** 'all night long'; **ichinenjū,** 'all year long'. Some are place expressions: **karadajū ga itai desu,** 'all over my body hurts'; **iejū**

ga kitanai desu, 'the whole house is dirty'.

4. **kakete mimashō:** 'I'll try phoning again later'; **te miru/mimasu** means 'try doing', 'do and see'.

5. **moshimoshi:** 'Hello', used mostly over the phone.

6. **yabun osoku ...;** set phrase meaning 'I apologize for phoning late at night'.

7. **doko o mawarimashō:** 'Where shall we go round?'; **mawaru/mawarimasu** is a motion verb which takes **o**.

8. **machiawase suru/shimasu:** 'arrange to meet'. There is a large group of verbs formed by the addition of a noun (here **machiawase**) to **suru/shimasu**, e.g. **benkyō** 'study' → **benkyō suru/shimasu** 'to study'.

9. **hachiji ni:** 'See you at 8', informal.

10. **tanoshimi ni shite imasu:** 'I'm looking forward to it'. For **te** form plus **iru/imasu** see Lesson 8.

Lesson 8

MAIN POINTS: *Is/are doing, was/were doing; has/have done, had done; has/have been doing, had been doing;* duration of time.
CONVERSATIONS: (a) Asking a policeman; (b) 'What's on television?'

50 'Is/are doing'

'Is/are doing' is translated by the **te** form plus **iru/imasu, irassharu/ irasshaimasu,** or **oru/orimasu:**

A: *Are you listening?*	Kiite imasu ka.
B: *No, I'm not.*	Īe, kiite imasen.
A: *What's the Professor doing?*	Sensei wa nani o shite irasshaimasu ka.
B: *He's talking to a visitor.*	O-kyaku-san to hanashite irasshaimasu yo.

'Was/were doing' involves changing **masu** to **mashita:**

A: *What were you doing?*	Nani o shite imashita ka.
B: *I was reading the paper.*	Shinbun o yonde imashita.
A: *Who were you talking to?*	Dare to hanashite imashita ka.
B: *I was talking to my teacher.*	Sensei to hanashite imashita.

In English, we don't necessarily use an 'ing' form to describe a continuing state of affairs: we say 'I love you' and not 'I'm loving you', and we may say 'I live here' as well as 'I'm living here'. In Japanese, however, if the state is continuing at the time of speaking, a **te imasu** form is generally used. Study some examples of this:

I love you very much.	Totemo aishite imasu.
I lived (was living) in Kobe.	Watashi wa Kōbe ni sunde imashita.
He works (is working) in Osaka.	Ōsaka de hataraite imasu.
I remember that too.	Watashi mo oboete imasu.
My children go to that school.	Kodomo wa ano gakkō ni itte imasu.
Is that writer still alive?	Ano sakka wa mada ikite imasu ka.
Do you know him?	Kare o shitte imasu ka.

Shitte imasu is unique – its negative form is not **shitte imasen,** but **shirimasen:**

A: *Do you know Kyoto well?*	Kyōto o yoku shitte imasu ka.
B: *No, I don't know it at all.*	Īe, zenzen shirimasen.

Motte imasu is very common as 'have got':

A: *Have you got any stamps?*   **Kitte o motte imasu ka.**
B: *No, I haven't.*   **Īe, motte imasen.**

There is a selection of intransitive verbs whose **te iru/imasu** form translates the idea of 'passive state': e.g. 'be closed', 'be open', 'be hungry', 'be thirsty', 'be crowded', 'be empty', 'be tired':

A: *Are the shops closed on Sunday?*   **Nichiyōbi wa o-mise ga shimatte imasu ka.**

B: *No, in Japan, they're open every day.*   **Īe, Nihon de wa mainichi aite imasu.**
A: *Are you hungry?*   **Onaka ga suite imasu ka.**
B: *No, I'm thirsty.*   **Īe, chigaimasu. Nodo ga kawaite imasu.**
A: *The trains are empty today, aren't they?*   **Kyō wa densha ga suite imasu ne.**
B: *Yes they are. But they're usually crowded, aren't they?*   **Sō desu ne. Futsū wa konde imasu yo ne.**

51 'Has/have, had done'

You know that both 'I bought a ticket' and 'I have bought a ticket' can be translated by **kippu o kaimashita.** A number of intransitive verbs, however, require the **te iru/imasu** form for their perfect tense. Below are some common verbs whose perfect form generally requires **te iru/imasu**:

iku/ikimasu   (go)
kuru/kimasu   (come)
deru/demasu   (come/go out)
hairu/hairimasu   (come/go in, enter)
dekakeru/dekakemasu   (depart, set off)
tsuku/tsukimasu   (arrive)
kaeru/kaerimasu   (return)
neru/nemasu   (go to sleep, go to bed)
okiru/okimasu   (get up)

So, 'he's gone to (and is in) Nagasaki' is **Nagasaki e itte imasu.** (If, however, by 'he's gone to Nagasaki' you mean 'he's left for Nagasaki', then **ikimashita** will do!)

Study the following, noting that in some cases there are two English senses:

A parcel has come (is here).   **Kozutsumi ga kite imasu yo.**
She's gone into (she's in) the garden.   **Niwa ni dete imasu.**
She's gone back to (she's back in) America.   **Amerika ni kaette imasu.**
Have you got (are you) up yet?   **Mō okite imasu ka.**
She's been on TV. a lot recently.   **Saikin yoku terebi ni dete imasu.**

The most common way to say 'is in ...' is **... (no naka) ni haitte imasu** (lit.: having entered, is in):

A: *My passport was in my pocket.* **Pasupōto wa poketto no naka ni haitte imashita yo.**

B: *Isn't it in your bag?* **Kaban no naka ni haitte imasen ka.**

The negative perfect of all verbs is translated by the **te iru/imasu** form, often with **mada**, 'not yet':

A: *Haven't you seen Kurosawa's new film?* **Kurosawa no atarashii eiga wa mite imasen ka.**

B: *No, I haven't seen it yet.* **Mada mite imasen yo.**

Exercise 12
Put into Japanese:

1 'Don't you remember that song by Nakajima Miyuki?' 'No, I don't.'
2 'Which university do you go to?' 'I don't go to university, I'm working.'
3 'Excuse me, but from what time to what time is the Post Office open?' 'I don't know.'
4 'Do you know the coffee shop next to the fish shop?' 'No, I don't.'
5 'He's gone back to his parents' place.' 'When did he go?'

52 Duration of time

(i) Years. Duration of years can be expressed with **nen** or with **nenkan**:

A: *How many years were you there?* **Nannen(kan) imashita ka.**
B: *I was there for five years.* **Gonen(kan) imashita.**

(ii) Months. For duration of months the Chinese system is used with the counter **ka** plus **getsu** (not **gatsu**):

1 month	**ikkagetsu**
2 months	**nikagetsu**
3 months	**sankagetsu**
4 months	**yonkagetsu**
5 months	**gokagetsu**
6 months	**rokkagetsu**
7 months	**nanakagetsu**
8 months	**hachikagetsu** (or **hakkagetsu**)

9 months	kyūkagetsu
10 months	jukkagetsu
11 months	jūikkagetsu
12 months	jūnikagetsu

A: *About how many months did it take?*　Nankagetsu gurai kakarimashita ka.
B: *It took about ten altogether.*　Zenbu de jukkagetsu kakarimashita.

(iii) Weeks. Duration of weeks is expressed by **shūkan**. Note the phonetic changes affecting '1 week' (**isshūkan**), '8 weeks' (**hasshūkan**) and '10 weeks' (**jusshūkan**). The interrogative form is **nanshūkan**.

A: *How many weeks will it continue?*　Nanshūkan tsuzukimasu ka.
B: *About four.*　Yonshūkan gurai.

(iv) Days. For duration of days the system is that for naming the days of the month, except that 'one day' is not tsuitachi but **ichinichi**. So, both 'the 2nd', 'the 3rd', 'the 4th' etc. and 'two days', 'three days', 'four days' etc. are translated by **futsuka, mikka, yokka** etc.

'How many days?' is **nannichi**:

A: *How many days did you spend there?*　Asoko de nannichi sugoshimashita ka.
B: *We spent only three days (there).*　Mikka shika sugoshimasen deshita.

(v) Hours and minutes. For duration of hours the suffix **kan** is attached to the o'clock times, while for minutes this suffix is not generally used:

One o'clock	ichiji
One hour	ichijikan
Half past two	nijihan
Two and a half hours	nijikanhan

A: *How many hours did it take?*　Nanjikan kakarimashita ka.
B: *It only took about ten minutes.*　Juppun gurai shika kakarimasen deshita.

'Ago' is translated by a duration expression followed by **mae**, 'before':

A: *How many hours ago did it close?*　Nanjikan mae ni shimarimashita ka.
B: *It closed about four hours ago.*　Yojikan gurai mae ni shimarimashita.
A: *About how many months ago did you come to Japan?*　Nankagetsu gurai mae ni Nihon ni kimashita ka.
B: *Umm, I came about three months ago.*　Etto, sankagetsu gurai mae ni kimashita.

53 'Has/have been doing'

'I have been studying Japanese for three months' may be expressed in two ways, either with **sankagetsu** or **sankagetsu mae kara**. 'How long ...' is **dore gurai**, or **itsu kara**. Study the following:

A: *How long have you been studying Japanese?*   **Dore gurai Nihongo o benkyō shite imasu ka.**

B: *I've only been studying for three months.*   **Sankagetsu shika benkyō shite imasen yo.**

A: *How long has the Professor been married?*   **Sensei wa itsu kara kekkon shite irasshaimasu ka.**

B: *He's been married for about five years.*   **Gonen gurai mae kara kekkon shite irasshaimasu.**

For 'had been doing' change **masu** to **mashita**:

I had been (was) waiting for six hours.   **Rokujikan mo matte imashita.**

In 'I've been living here since April', 'since' is **kara**:

A: *Since when (how long) have you been living in Japan?*   **Itsu kara Nihon ni sunde imasu ka.**

B: *I've been living here since April.*   **Shigatsu kara koko ni sunde imasu.**

Da/desu and **iru/imasu** do not have **te imasu** forms, so:

A: *How long have you been ill?*   **Itsu kara byōki desu ka.**

B: *For about ten days.*   **Tōka gurai (mae kara) desu.**

Such expressions as 'have you <u>ever</u> been (to Nagasaki)?' require a different construction altogether and will be dealt with later.

Exercise 13

Put into Japanese:

1 'How long have you been practising calligraphy?' 'For about six years.'
2 We go on holiday in June (of) every year for three weeks.
3 How long have you been in this beautiful country?
4 Being busy, I haven't read it yet.
5 They've been married for forty-five years.

CONVERSATION 8a: Asking a policeman

Mr Brown (B) asks first a passer-by (P), then a policeman (K: keisatsukan) how to find a bank:

B: Sumimasen, ginkō o sagashite imasu ga kono hen ni nai desu ka.
P: Kono hen wa yoku shirimasen ga. Ano keisatsukan ni kiite mite[1] kudasai.
B: Arigatō gozaimasu. Chotto ukagaimasu ga[2] ginkō wa chikaku ni arimasu ka.
K: Sochira ni Dai Ichi Kangin[3] ga arimasu ga mō shimatte imasu yo. Nihon no ginkō wa gozen kuji kara gogo sanji made desu.
B: Ā sō desu ka. Dō shimashō? Komarimashita[4] ne.
K: Nihongo[5] ga o-jōzu desu ne ... O-kuni wa dochira desu ka.
B: Kanada desu ga ...
K: Itsu kara Nihon ni irassharu n'desu ka[6].
B: Etto, yonkagetsu gurai mae kara desu.
K: Gaijin tōrokushō[7] o chotto misete kudasai.
B: Chotto matte kudasai. Kaban no naka ni haitte imasu. Ā. Arimashita. Hai dōzo.
K: Arigatō. Gakusei-san desu ne.
B: Hai, sengetsu kara Hitotsubashi Daigaku de kenkyū shite imasu.
K: Sō desu ka. O-sumai wa Kunitachi desu ne.
B: Hai, sō desu. Ima no tokoro wa ryō ni sunde imasu ga apāto o sagashite imasu.
K: Naruhodo. Hai, kekkō desu.

CONVERSATION 8b: 'What's on television?'

Mr Brown asks Mr Inoue if there's anything worth watching:

B: Terebi de nani o yatte imasu[8] ka.
I: Mite mimashō[9]. Kuizu to ka dokyumentarī to ka. Omoshiroku nai bangumi bakari[10] desu.
B: Kyō eiga wa yatte imasen ka.
I: Etto, chotto matte kudasai. Yatte imasen ne. Ā, jidaigeki wa yatte imasu yo.
B: Amari kyōmi (wa) nai desu[11] ne.
I: Eigakan de wa Kurosawa no 'Shichinin no Samurai' o yatte imasu yo. Shitte imasu ka.
B: Namae dake wa shitte imasu. Dare ga dete iru n'desu ka.
I: Oboete imasen. Mifune ja nai desu ka.
B: Sō desu ka. Sore ja dō shimashō. Mi ni ikimasu ka.
I: Ima sugu desu ka. Gohan mo tabenaide?[12].
B: Ikimashō. Sore de eiga ga owatte kara dokoka[13] e oishii mono de mo tabe ni ikimashō.

Notes:

1. **kiite mite kudasai:** 'ask and see', 'try asking'. See note 17, Lesson 6.

2. **chotto ukagaimasu ga:** 'I'd just like to ask you ...'; **ukagau/ukagaimasu** is a humble word meaning 'ask', 'visit', 'call on'.

3. **Dai Ichi Kangin:** abbreviation of **Dai Ichi Kangyō Ginkō,** the largest street bank in Japan.

4. **komarimashita:** 'That's a nuisance'; **komaru/komarimasu** = 'be stuck', 'be awkward'.

5. **Nihongo:** 'Japanese'. **-go** placed after the name of a country gives the language of that country, e.g. **Chūgoku** (China), **Chūgokugo** (Chinese). But 'English' is **Eigo**.

6. **irassharu n'desu ka:** the plain form with **n'desu** is a common alternative for **masu**, particularly in questions. See Lesson 9.

7. **Gaijin tōrokushō:** 'Alien registration card'; full name is **Gaikokujin Tōroku Shōmeishō**. The law requires that all non-naturalized foreigners in Japan for longer than 90 days must have and always carry one.

8. **yatte imasu: yaru/yarimasu** is a very common, if somewhat colloquial, alternative to **suru/shimasu**.

9. **mite mimasu:** 'I'll have a look and see'.

10. **bakari:** 'nothing but'.

11. **kyōmi wa nai desu:** 'I'm not interested', lit. 'as for interest, there isn't any'.

12. **Gohan mo tabenaide:** 'without even having a meal'; **mo** here means 'even'.

13. **dokoka e:** 'somewhere'; other indefinite expressions are studied in Lesson 14.

Lesson 9

MAIN POINTS: Formation of the plain forms; some idiomatic usages of the plain forms: *why ... because/probably/I wonder/may(be)/intend to/should.*
CONVERSATIONS: (a) Talking to Mrs Inoue; (b) 'My family'.

54 The plain form – Present

While in polite speech the <u>main</u> verb is best put in the **masu** form, the plain form does feature, for example, in subordinate clauses, in indirect speech and in a good number of idioms.

For such purposes, we must consider the formation of the various plain forms of Group 1, Group 2 and Irregular verbs. The present positive plain forms of all verbs are listed in the vocabularies together with the **masu** form. The present negative plain form you have already come across (refer to Lesson 7).

55 Plain form – Past positive (the *ta* form)

All verbs (with the one exception given below) have their past positive plain form (the so-called **ta** form) made by changing the **te** (or **de**) of the **te** form to **ta** (or **da**).

Plain form (present)	te form	ta form
taberu (tabemasu)	**tabete**	**tabeta**
miru (mimasu)	**mite**	**mita**
kau (kaimasu)	**katte**	**katta**
kuru (kimasu)	**kite**	**kita**

The one verb whose **ta** form is irregular is **da/desu**. Its plain form (present) is **da (desu)**, its **te** form is **de** and its **ta** form is **datta**.

Check you can form the **ta** forms of the following:

taberu (tabemasu) →	**tabeta**
yobu (yobimasu)	**yonda**
kaku (kakimasu)	**kaita**
arau (araimasu)	**aratta**
tatsu (tachimasu)	**tatta**
da (desu)	**datta**
iku (ikimasu)	**itta**

kaeru (kaerimasu)	**kaetta**
kaeru (kaemasu)	**kaeta**

55a Plain form – Past negative

This is made from the present negative. To form the plain past negative, change **nai** to **nakatta: inai → inakatta; konai → konakatta.**

Check you can form the past negative plain forms of the following:

shinai	→	**shinakatta**
matanai		**matanakatta**
kawanai		**kawanakatta**
kiranai		**kiranakatta**
kaeranai		**kaeranakatta**
ikanai		**ikanakatta**

N.B. The **te iru/imasu** forms are changed into the plain form, as one would expect, by the appropriate plain forms of **iru/imasu**. Check the plain forms of the following:

tabete imasu	→	**tabete iru**
owatte imasen		**owatte inai**
yasunde imashita		**yasunde ita**
nete imasen deshita		**nete inakatta**

The remainder of this lesson is given over to considering some of the idiomatic uses of the plain forms.

56 'Why ...?' 'Because ...' (i)

In questions, especially 'why' questions, the plain form of a verb or adjective followed by **n'desu** (or **no desu** in its less common unabbreviated form) is best. 'Why' is either **naze** or **dōshite**. **N'desu** has the literal meaning 'it is because', 'the thing is':

A: *Why don't you go abroad?*	**Dōshite kaigai e ikanai n'desu ka.**
B: *(Because) I don't have any money.*	**Okane ga nai n'desu.**
A: *Why are you crying?*	**Naze naite iru n'desu ka.**
B: *(Because) my leg really hurts.*	**Ashi ga sugoku itai n'desu.**

The plain forms of verbs and adjectives are used with **n'desu** not only in questions and answers. Generally **n'desu** has an explanatory or emphatic role, although sometimes it may simply serve to relieve the monotony of too many **masu** forms:

| *(The thing is) I've got work to do.* | **Shigoto ga aru n'desu.** |
| *(You see) he's got no money.* | **O-kane ga nai n'desu.** |

If the verb before **n'desu** is **da/desu** or a **na** adjective, then, in the present positive, **na** (not **da**) must come before **n'desu**:

| *The fact is, it's no good.* | **Dame nan'desu.** |
| *He's a friend of mine, you see.* | **Tomodachi nan'desu.** |

57 'Why ...?' 'Because...' (ii)

'Because' or 'so' may be either **kara** or **no de** (the **te** form of **no desu**), the only difference being that even in polite speech **no de** is often preceded by a plain form, while in polite speech **kara** is generally preceded by the **masu** form:

| *It's got late so I'm going to take my leave of you in a minute.* | **Osoku natta no de mō sorosoro kaerimasu.** |
| *It was my wife's birthday last week so we ate out.* | **Senshū wa kanai no tanjōbi deshita kara gaishoku shimashita.** |

Note, however:

| *As it's no good I'm going to throw it away.* | **Dame na no de sutemasu.** |
| *I invited her because she's a friend of mine.* | **Tomodachi na no de shōtai shita n'desu.** |

Exercise 14
Put into Japanese:

1 'Why did you buy two new suitcases?' 'Because I'm going abroad next week.'
2 'The thing is we got back late.' 'Why's that?'
3 I've given up Japanese, you see.
4 Why didn't you come?
5 She's crying because her boyfriend has gone back to America.

58 Idiomatic expressions (i)

Deshō (plain form **darō**) means 'probably', and is often found with adverbs like **tabun** (perhaps) and **osoraku** (presumably):

| *He presumably won't come tomorrow.* | **Osoraku ashita konai deshō.** |

They've probably finished now.	**Tabun mō owatta deshō.**
He's probably asleep.	**Tabun nete iru deshō.**

With rising intonation **deshō** has a meaning almost identical to **ne**:

You'll be going too, won't you?	**Anata mo iku deshō.**
There aren't any more, are there?	**Mō nai deshō.**

Deshō cannot be preceded by **da**:

He's probably a policeman.	**Ano hito wa keisatsukan deshō.**
It's tomorrow, isn't it?	**Ashita deshō.**

Deshō ka (ne) means 'I wonder if/whether':

I wonder if they'll come.	**Kuru deshō ka ne.**
I wonder whether they're up.	**Okite iru deshō ka.**

With a question word such as 'who', the meaning is 'I wonder who ...':

I wonder who wrote it?	**Dare ga kaita deshō ka ne.**
I wonder where they bought it?	**Doko de katta deshō ka ne.**

59 Idiomatic expressions (ii)

Ka mo shiremasen attached to a plain form or to a noun translates 'may possibly be'. It is often used with adverbs like **hyotto suru to** or **moshi ka suru to** ('maybe'):

They may not sell it in this shop.	**Kono o-mise de utte inai ka mo shiremasen.**
She may be pretty but she's not my cup of tea.	**Kanojo wa kirei ka mo shiremasen ga watashi no shumi ja nai desu.**
She may possibly be Japanese.	**Hyotto suru to Nihonjin ka mo shiremasen.**

60 Idiomatic expressions (iii)

Tsumori da/desu translates 'intend to' or 'mean to', and **yotei da/desu** translates 'plan to'. The negatives of both forms are **tsumori wa nai/arimasen** and **yotei wa nai/arimasen**:

A: *When do you intend to go to Japan?*	**Itsu Nihon e iku tsumori desu ka.**
B: *I don't intend going this year.*	**Kotoshi wa iku tsumori wa nai desu.**
I meant to phone but I forgot!	**Denwa suru tsumori deshita ga wasureta n'desu.**

When do you plan to publish it? Itsu shuppan suru yotei desu ka.

61 Idiomatic expressions (iv)

In English 'should' and 'ought' may either suggest an obligation or they can simply suggest expectation, as in 'It's gone nine o'clock, so the shop ought to be open by now'. **Beki (ja nai)** is used for the former:

You shouldn't say that.	Sonna koto, o iu beki ja nai desu.
I should have written it in Japanese.	Nihongo de kaku beki deshita.

Hazu is used in the second of the meanings. It may also translate 'expected to', 'due to' and 'supposed to':

It's gone nine o'clock so the shop ought to be open now.	Kuji ni natta no de o-mise ga aite iru hazu desu.
The plane is due to arrive at about six o'clock.	Hikōki wa rokuji goro tsuku hazu desu.
We were supposed to go too but the car broke down.	Watashitachi mo iku hazu deshita ga kuruma ga koshō shita n'desu.

Compare the following:

The meeting was due to (was supposed to) finish at six o'clock.	Kaigi wa rokuji ni owaru hazu deshita.
The meeting is supposed to have finished at six o'clock.	Kaigi wa rokuji ni owatta hazu desu.

The negative form is **hazu ga (wa) nai/arimasen**:

They're not due to finish yet.	Mada owaru hazu ga nai desu.

Exercise 15
Put into Japanese:

1 I suppose they've finished now?
2 We were planning to leave Japan tomorrow.
3 They may come tomorrow.
4 A book like that shouldn't be expensive, you know.
5 I meant to tell you but I forgot.

CONVERSATION 9a: Talking to Mrs Inoue

Brown (B) arrives for the first time at his friend Kunio's house, but as Kunio isn't back from his sports club yet, he is invited in by Mrs Inoue (I), who chats to him:

B: Konnichi wa, Inoue-san no o-taku [1] desu ka.

I: Hai, sō desu ga, Buraun-san de irasshaimasu ka.

B: Hai, sō desu ga.

I: O-machi shite orimashita [2]. Kunio wa mō sugu kaette kuru hazu desu no de dōzo o-agari kudasai.

B: O-jama shimasu. Kunio-san wa kurabu katsudō ka nanika [3] de osoku natta n'desu ka.

I: Sō nan' [4] desu. Mōshi-wake arimasen ne ... Buraun-san, kochira e dōzo. Tsumetai o-nomimono de mo o-mochi shimashō [5] ka.

B: O-negai shimasu.

Several moments later she returns:

I: Hai, mugicha dake desu ga dōzo.

B: A, arigatō gozaimasu. Tsumetakute oishii desu ne.

I: Buraun-san wa ato dore gurai Nihon ni irassharu yotei desu ka.

B: Sō desu ne, yoku wakarimasen ga, moshi ka suru to ato ichinen gurai iru ka mo shiremasen. O-kane shidai [6] desu.

I: Nanika go-kenkyū nasatte iru [7] n'desu ka.

B: Hai, anō [8] kindaishi desu ga.

I: A sō desu ka. Buraun-san wa dōshite Nihon no koto ni kyōmi o mochihajimeta [9] n'desu ka.

B: Sō desu ne, sore wa chotto fukuzatsu nan desu ga chichi [10] no eikyō ga atta kara desu ne.

CONVERSATION 9b: 'My family'

Kunio (K) comes home, and together they talk of their families:

K: Tadaima.

I: O-kaeri nasai. O-kyaku-sama ga irasshatte iru no yo [11].

K: Buraun-san, osoku natte gomen nasai. Mō chotto matte kudasai. Ima kigaete kimasu kara ... o-kā-san! o-tō-san wa?

I: O-tō-san wa mada kaette inai no yo. Hayaku kigaete 'rasshai [12] ... Buraun-san wa go-kyōdai wa nannin desu ka.

B: Kyōdai wa sannin [13] de watashi wa jinan [14] desu.

I: Otoko bakari [15] desu ka.

B: Hai, sō desu. Ani hitori to otōto hitori desu.

I: A, sō desu ka. O-nīsan wa nani o shite irassharu n'desu ka.

B: Ani mo otōto mo kōkūgaisha ni tsutomete imasu. Futaritomo rainen Nihon ni kuru ka mo shirenai n'desu.

I: Sō desu ka. Sore wa tanoshimi desu[16] ne. Goryōshin mo itsuka Nihon ni irassharu[17] n'deshō.

B: Dō deshō ka. Chichi wa kuru ka mo shiremasen ga haha wa chotto muri desu ne. Hikōki ga kowakute ...

K: O-matase. Nan no hanashi desu ka.

I: Buraun-san no go-kyōdai no hanashi o shite ita no yo.

Notes:

1. **o-taku:** 'house'; **o-taku** is a polite word for **ie**. As an adjective **o-taku no ...** can mean 'your ...'

2. **O-machi shite orimashita:** 'I was waiting for (expecting) you'; the stem of the verb preceded by **o-** and followed by **suru/shimasu** is one way to make the verb humble. See Lesson 20. Note throughout this conversation and the next that Mrs Inoue, typically of women, uses very polite language to her guest.

3. **ka nanika:** 'or something or other'.

4. **sō nan'desu:** emphatic form of **sō desu,** 'that's right'; remember that **na** and not **da** comes before **n'desu**.

5. **O-mochi shimashō ka:** 'Shall I bring ...'; see above, note 2.

6. **O-kane shidai desu:** 'It depends on the money'... *cf.* **tenki shidai,** 'it depends on the weather' and **anata shidai,** 'it depends on you'.

7. **go-kenkyū nasatte iru n'desu ka:** 'are you researching (into) something?'; **nasaru/nasaimasu** is an honorific form of **suru/shimasu,** and **go-** is added to certain words to make them honorific (see Lesson 20). **Kenkyū suru/shimasu** is one of a vast number of compound verbs made up of a noun (here **kenkyū,** 'research') and **suru/shimasu,** 'do'. Note you can say either **... o kenkyū shimasu** or **... no kenkyū o shimasu.**

8. **anō:** 'umm'.

9. **mochihajimeta:** 'begin to have an interest in'; replace **masu** with **hajimeru/ hajimemasu** to mean 'begin to' (*cf.* **kenkyū shihajimeru,** 'begin to research').

10. **chichi:** 'my father'; in Japanese two different family terms have to be distinguished – (a) plain terms, (b) polite terms. The plain terms are used for <u>referring</u> to one's own family members; the polite terms are used for <u>referring</u> to others' family members. Those polite terms marked with an asterisk in the table below are also

used in <u>addressing</u> one's own family members:

	Plain	Polite
father	chichi	o-to-san*
mother	haha	o-kā-san*
parents	ryōshin	go-ryōshin
husband	shujin	go-shujin
wife	kanai	oku-san
brothers/sisters	kyōdai	go-kyōdai
older brother	ani	o-nī-san*
older sister	ane	o-nē-san*
younger brother	otōto	otōto-san
younger sister	imōto	imōto-san
son	musuko	musuko-san
daughter	musume	musume-san
grandfather	sofu	o-jī-san
grandmother	sobo	o-bā-san
uncle	oji	oji-san
aunt	oba	oba-san

Note that **oji-san** and **oba-san** are also, respectively, informal words for 'man' and 'woman'.

11. **irasshatte iru no yo: no yo** is characteristic of women's speech; **irasshatte iru** is honorific for **kite iru**, which is used out of deference for Mr Brown; the plain form ending is used because mother is speaking to son.

12. **'rasshai:** 'go and get changed'; an abbreviation of **irasshai**, the imperative of **irassharu/irasshaimasu**. The use of **rasshai** is characteristic of women's speech.

13. **kyōdai wa sannin:** 'I've got two brothers'; in Japan the speaker includes him/herself when counting numbers of brothers/sisters.

14. **jinan:** 'second son'; **chōnan** is 'eldest son', **chōjo** is 'eldest daughter', **jijo** is 'second daughter'.

15. **otoko bakari:** 'nothing but boys'.

16. **tanoshimi desu:** 'that's something to look forward to'; **tanoshimi** literally means 'enjoyment'.

17. **Nihon ni irassharu n'deshō:** 'they'll be coming to Japan, won't they?'. N.B. **irassharu/irasshaimasu** is the honorific form of both **iku/ikimasu** and **iru/imasu,** as well as **kuru/kimasu.** See Lesson 20.

Lesson 10

MAIN POINTS: Verbs of giving and receiving; doing things for people; having things done.

CONVERSATIONS: (a) 'What shall we buy for him?' (b) 'Happy Birthday!'

62 Verbs of giving and receiving

Verbs of giving and receiving can appear rather complex at first, since the verb you use will depend on your understanding of the relationship between yourself, the giver and the listener and the receiver. For example, if you are either doing the giving or at the time of speaking 'feel closer' to the giver than the receiver, for whatever reason (the giver may be your relative or friend), then one verb will be used. If, however, someone else is giving to you, or to someone with whom you identify more closely than with the giver, then another verb will be used. In practice, this is not as complex as it sounds! It is important, though, to take care with verbs of giving and receiving as impoliteness can result from misuse.

63 Verbs of giving (i)

Both **sashiageru/sashiagemasu** and **ageru/agemasu** mean 'give'. They often have 1st person (I/we) subjects and may also have 2nd person (you), and 3rd person (he/she/they) subjects but only if, at the time of speaking, you identify more closely with the giver than the receiver. For example, they will therefore be used if you were saying that you or your friend gave to someone else or that you or a member of your family gave to a member of another family, or that you or a member of your company gave to a member of another company.

The difference between **sashiageru/sashiagemasu** and **ageru/agemasu** is that the former is more respectful: **sashiageru/sashiagemasu** will therefore be used if you deem the receiver to be of higher status than the giver, or if, for whatever reason, you wish to show special respect to the receiver.

Ageru/agemasu is used when you deem the receiver to be either of lower status than or equal status to the giver. **Ageru/agemasu** may also be used when the receiver is of higher status than the giver provided that the receiver is not actually present, and provided that there is no one else present who may expect respect to be shown. As will be seen from the first example below, it's not normally thought necessary to use the more respectful forms when referring to (or addressing) members of one's own family.

Study very carefully the following examples, noting the speaker–giver–receiver relationships, and note too the difference between those sentences marked (a) and those marked (b): (b) rather than (a) should be used if you are speaking in the presence of the Professor himself or to his wife, or a colleague of his, all of whom would expect respect to be shown:

I'll give this to my mother.	**Haha ni kore o agemasu.**
I'll give it to you, Sir.	**Sensei, kore o sashiagemasu.**
(a) I'll give it to the Professor.	**Sensei ni agemasu.**
(b) I'll give it to the Professor.	**Sensei ni sashiagemasu.**
(a) Kunio gave it to the Professor.	**Kunio wa sensei ni agemashita.**
(b) Kunio gave it to the Professor.	**Kunio wa sensei ni sashiagemashita.**
Kunio gave Yumiko the paper.	**Kunio wa Yumiko ni shinbun o agemashita.**
Kunio, did you give Yumiko the paper?	**Kunio, Yumiko ni shinbun o agemashita ka.**

In these last two examples, both Kunio and Yumiko are acquaintances of yours, but the use of **ageru/agemasu** indicates that you identify more closely with Kunio than with Yumiko.

64 Verbs of giving (ii)

Both **kudasaru/kudasaimasu** and **kureru/kuremasu** mean 'give', but they can never be used with a 1st person (I/we) subject. They are often used with 1st person indirect objects (i.e. when someone gives to me/us) and may be used with 2nd and 3rd person indirect objects (to you, to him/her/them) but only if you identify more closely with the receiver than the giver. For example, you could use them if you were saying that someone else gave to you or a friend of yours or that a member of another family gave to you or a member of your family, or that a member of another company gave to you or a member of your company.

Kudasaru/kudasaimasu is more respectful than **kureru/kuremasu**, so you should use **kudasaru/kudasaimasu** if you deem the giver to be of superior status to the receiver or if, for whatever reason, you wish to show special respect to the giver.

Kureru/kuremasu is used when you deem the giver to be of similar status to or of lower status than the receiver. You may also use it when the giver is of superior status to the receiver if the giver is not present and if there is no one else present who may expect respect to be shown to the giver. Study this selection of examples:

My mother gave this to me.	**Haha ga kuremashita.**
Kunio, will you give this to me?	**Kunio, kore o kuremasu ka.**
Professor, will you give me this?	**Sensei, kore o kudasaimasu ka.**
Did Kunio give this to you?	**Kunio ga kureta n'desu ka.**
(a) The Professor gave it to me.	**Sensei ga kuremashita.**
(b) The Professor gave it to me.	**Sensei ga kudasaimashita.**

As in the preceding section, example (a) you might say to a friend or fellow student, but you should use (b) if the Professor himself or his wife or colleague was present at the time or if you were addressing yourself to his wife or a colleague of his.

In the final example below, both Kunio and Yumiko are acquaintances of yours, but the use of **kureru/kuremasu** (as opposed to **ageru/agemasu**) indicates that you feel much closer to Yumiko than you do to Kunio:

Kunio gave this to Yumiko.	**Kunio ga Yumiko ni kureta n'desu.**
Kunio, did you give this to Yumiko?	**Kunio, Yumiko ni kore o kureta n'desu ka.**

65 Verbs of receiving

Itadaku/itadakimasu and **morau/moraimasu** both mean 'receive'/'be given' and may have 1st, 2nd or 3rd person subjects. The difference between them is that **itadaku/itadakimasu** is more respectful. It is used when you deem the receiver to be of humbler status than the giver, or when you wish to show special respect to the giver.

Morau/moraimasu will be used when you deem the receiver to be of equal status to or superior status than the giver. You may also use it when the receiver is of inferior status than the giver, provided that the giver is not actually present and provided that there is no one else present who may expect respect to be shown. Study the following examples, and note that the person from whom something is received may be followed by either **ni** or **kara**:

I got a letter from Kunio.	**Kunio kara tegami o moraimashita.**
(a) I got a letter from the President.	**Shachō kara tegami o moraimashita.**
(b) I got a letter from the President.	**Shachō kara tegami o itadakimashita.**
Did you get a letter from Kunio?	**Kunio kara tegami o moraimashita ka.**
Kunio got a letter from Yumiko.	**Kunio wa Yumiko kara tegami o moraimashita.**
(a) He got a letter from the President.	**Shachō ni tegami o moraimashita.**
(b) He got a letter from the President.	**Shachō ni tegami o itadakimashita.**

Again, (a) in each case you may say to a friend or colleague, but (b) would be preferred if the company President himself were present or you were speaking to or in the presence of his wife or a colleague of his.

In practice, you may well find that Japanese tend to use **morau/moraimasu** and **itadaku/itadakimasu** more than **kureru/kuremasu** and **kudasaru/kudasaimasu**. That is, they may well prefer to say **kare ni moraimashita** ('I received it from him') rather than **kare ga kuremashita** ('he gave it to me').

Exercise 16
Put into Japanese:

1 My mother gave me this for my birthday.
2 Professor, I'll give you this.
3 The President got a book from his wife.
4 Tom (i.e. my colleague), I'll give you this.
5 Did Yumiko give Kunio a present?

66 Having things done/doing things for others

The verbs for receiving and giving are used with the **te** form of verbs to mean 'having things done' and 'doing things for others' respectively. Basically the same rules apply to the use of these constructions as to the use of the verbs of receiving and giving when used alone.

66a Having things done

The **te** form of a verb followed by **itadaku/itadakimasu** and **morau/moraimasu** means 'have something done' or 'get somebody to do something'. The person who is made to perform the action (the agent) is followed by **ni**. Note that both forms may either mean 'get somebody to do something', or 'someone was kind enough to do something for (me)'. Study the following examples:

I got my brother to help.	**Otōto ni tetsudatte moraimashita.**
I got the teacher to explain.	**Sensei ni setsumei shite moraimashita (or itadakimashita).**
Did you get Kunio to help?	**Kunio ni tetsudatte moraimashita ka.**
Did you get the teacher to explain?	**Sensei ni setsumei shite moraimashita ka (or itadakimashita ka).**
Kunio got Yumiko to help.	**Kunio wa Yumiko ni tetsudatte moraimashita.**
Kunio got the teacher to explain.	**Kunio wa sensei ni setsumei shite moraimashita (or itadakimashita).**

67 Doing things for others (i)

Te kudasaru/kudasaimasu and **te kureru/kuremasu** both mean '(be kind enough to) do something for somebody'. The recipient of the action is followed by **ni**. Consider the following examples:

Kunio, would you pass the salt?	**Kunio, shio o totte kuremasu ka.**
Teacher, will you explain this to me?	**Sensei, kore o setsumei shite kudasaimasu ka.**
Did Kunio help you?	**Kunio wa tetsudatte kuremashita ka.**
Did the teacher explain it to you?	**Sensei wa setsumei shite kuremashita ka (or kudasaimashita ka).**
Kunio helped Yumiko.	**Kunio ga Yumiko o tetsudatte kuremashita.**

68 Doing things for others (ii)

Te ageru/agemasu means 'do something for others'. You are advised to exercise caution over its usage, however. Unless you are speaking to a very close friend or a child, it's best to avoid using **te ageru/agemasu** as this can sound patronizing. (N.B. When you are speaking to a child or a very close friend you are likely to be using the plain form.) Study the following examples:

I'll help you, Kunio.	**Kunio, tetsudatte ageru yo.**
Did you help Yumiko?	**Yumiko o tetsudatte ageta ka.**
Kunio helped Yumiko.	**Kunio wa Yumiko o tetsudatte ageta.**

69 Doing things for others (iii)

There are two ways of saying such sentences as 'Professor, shall I help you?', and 'Kunio bought it for the Professor'. One is simply to use the **masu** form alone:

Professor, shall I help you?	**Sensei, tetsudaimashō ka.**
Kunio bought it for the Professor.	**Kunio wa sensei ni kaimashita.**
Shall I make some tea?	**O-cha o iremashō ka.**

The other (more respectful) way is to use a humble form of the verb. Certain verbs have humble alternatives. Learn the following:

	Normal	*Humble*
do	**suru/shimasu**	**itasu/itashimasu**
go	**iku/ikimasu**	**mairu/mairimasu**

| come | kuru/kimasu | mairu/mairimasu |
| say | iu/iimasu | mōsu/mōshimasu |

Most verbs which have no humble alternatives can be made humble as follows:

oshiemasu → oshie → o-oshie shimasu
miseru → mise → o-mise shimasu

Professor, shall I help? Sensei, o-tetsudai shimashō ka.
My brother will show you the photos. Otōtō ga shashin o o-mise shimasu.
Shall I ask (on your behalf)? O-kiki shimashō ka.

Exercise 17
Put into Japanese:

1 I'll buy it for you, Kunio.
2 Would you be kind enough to write your name here?
3 I'll get him to come at six o'clock.
4 Kunio got the Professor to pay.
5 The President bought it for my wife.

CONVERSATION 10a: 'What shall we buy for him?'

Two of Mr Brown's female students, Akiko (A) and Tomoko (T), who are good friends, discuss what to buy him for his birthday:

A: Asatte wa Buraun-sensei no tanjōbi deshō. Purezento demo agemashō ka.
T: Sō ne[1]. Nani ga ii kashira[2].
A: Nihonteki[3] na mono ga ii n'ja nai? Sensu to ka furoshiki to ka.
T: Sō ne. Kokojidai no tomodachi ga Mitsukoshi[4] de baito shite iru kara nanika ii mono[5] o sagashite moraimashō ka. Asoko wa nandemo takai kedo sukoshi yasuku shite kureru ka mo shirenai wa[2].

CONVERSATION 10b: 'Happy Birthday!'

Chieko, Yumiko, Kunio and the Inoues all (= mina, M) come to Mr Brown's party:

K: Buraun-san ni kanpai shimashō. ... Kanpai!
M: Kanpai! Kanpai!
K: Tanjōbi o-medetō gozaimasu[6].
M: O-medetō gozaimasu.

K: Chotto supīchi demo shite kudasai yo, Buraun-sensei!

B: Supīchi desu ka. Sore ja, mina-san kyō wa kite kudasatte [7] hontō ni arigatō gozaimasu. Konna suteki na tanjōbi pātei wa hajimete desu. Oishii go-chisō o tsukutte itadaite, hontō ni arigatō gozaimasu. Suteki na purezento mo dōmo arigatō.

K: Purezento wa nani o moratta n'desu ka.

B: Sensu to furoshiki to hon desu. Sensu wa Chieko-san kara, soshite furoshiki wa Kunio to Yumiko-san kara desu. Hon wa Inoue-san-tachi [8] ni itadakimashita.

K: Tokoro de Buraun-san wa kyō ikutsu ni natta n'desu ka.

B: Sore wa himitsu desu yo.

Notes:

1. **Sō ne:** familiar form of **sō desu ne**. Since Akiko and Tomoko are good friends, they use familiar Japanese, including some plain forms.

2. **kashira: kashira** here and **wa** below are characteristic of women's speech.

3. **Nihonteki:** 'Japanese': there is a large group of **na** adjectives formed by adding **teki** to nouns, e.g. **seiji** (politics), **seijiteki** (political); **keizai** (economics), **keizaiteki** (economic, economical).

4. **Mitsukoshi:** One of Japan's best-known department stores.

5. **nanika ii mono:** 'something nice'; **nanika** = 'something', see Lesson 14.

6. **tanjōbi o-medetō gozaimasu:** 'Happy Birthday'; **o-medetō gozaimasu** is used to congratulate on many different occasions, e.g. **akemashite o-medetō gozaimasu**, 'Happy New Year'.

7. **kite kudasatte arigatō gozaimasu:** 'Thank you for coming'; it is also possible to say **-te itadaite arigatō gozaimasu.**

8. **Inoue-san-tachi:** 'the Inoues'; **tachi** is a plural suffix.

Lesson 11

MAIN POINTS: Indirect speech: indirect statements; indirect questions and commands; miscellaneous expressions.
CONVERSATIONS: (a) A Japanese inn; (b) A beer garden.

70 Indirect statements

When quoting what someone says, thinks, replies etc., the 'quotative particle' **to** must be used. Consider the examples, noting that there are two possible positions for the subject:

'It's six o'clock,' their mother said.	**'Mō rokuji desu' to okāsan ga iimashita.**
I said 'Good night'.	**Watashi wa 'o-yasumi-nasai' to iimashita.**
'I'm going to bed,' she said.	**'Nemasu' to kanojo wa iimashita.**

Here, the exact words the speaker used have been translated. A more common type of sentence is perhaps that where we relate <u>indirectly</u> what someone says (reported speech) or thinks. There are a few rules to remember:

(1) The verb which precedes **to** is in the plain form.

I think he'll be home soon.	**Mō kaette kuru to omoimasu.**

(2) As a rule, the **te imasu** form of **iu/iimasu** and **omou/omoimasu** is used with 3rd person subjects.

He says (that) he doesn't know.	**Kare wa shiranai to itte imasu.**

(3) Note that Japanese uses different tenses to English.

I said I wouldn't go (J: I will not go, I said).	**Watashi wa ikanai to iimashita.**
He said it was interesting (J: It is interesting, he said).	**Omoshiroi to kare wa iimashita.**
I thought it had finished (J: It's finished, I thought).	**Mō owatta to omoimashita.**

71 Indirect questions

Indirect questions are sentences such as 'I asked *what* ...', 'Tell me *when* ...', 'Do you know *why ...*', 'Have you decided *where ...*'. Sentences such as 'Do you know *whether (if) ...*, are also of this sort. Note once again the tenses:

Shall I ask what time it gets here? (J: What time does it get here? shall I ask?)	Nanji ni tsuku ka o-kiki shimashō ka.
Tell me where he lives. (J: Where does he live? tell me.)	Doko ni sunde iru ka oshiete kudasai.
Do you know why he left the company? (J: Why did he leave the company? do you know?)	Naze kaisha o yameta ka shitte imasu ka.
He asked why there wasn't any more beer. (J: Why isn't there any more beer? he asked.)	Dōshite bīru ga mō nai ka kikimashita.

'... whether ... or not ...' requires **... ka dō ka ...**

I didn't know whether or not you eat sashimi.	Sashimi o taberu ka dō ka shirimasen deshita.
I don't yet know whether I'll go to Japan or not.	Nihon e iku ka dō ka mada wakarimasen.

Da/desu after nouns or **na** adjectives in the present tense is usually dropped:

I'll ask when it is.	Itsu ka kikimasu.
Do you know where it is?	Doko ka shitte imasu ka.

'I think probably ... (I'm pretty sure)' is translated by **n'ja nai ka to omoimasu,** or **nan ja nai ka to omimasu** with **na** adjectives and nouns:

I'm pretty sure we'll be on time.	Ma ni au n'ja nai ka to omoimasu.
I think it'll probably be O.K.	Daijōbu nan ja nai ka to omoimasu.

72 Indirect commands

Indirect commands such as 'I told him not to go' may be translated in a number of ways. The first is with **kudasai** or its plain form **kure** (**kure** is less polite and will be used when the speaker says what he himself or someone of lower status was told to do):

We asked them to come early. (J: Please come early, we asked.)	Hayaku kite kudasai to tanomimashita.
I told him not to go.	Ikanaide kure to iimashita.
He told me to help.	Tetsudatte kure to kare wa watashi ni iimashita.

The second involves **yō ni** (lit. 'in such a way that') **iu/iimasu** or **tanomu/tanomimasu**:

I told him not to go.	**Ikanai yō ni iimashita.**
We asked them to come early.	**Hayaku kuru yō ni tanomimashita.**

If the person told or asked to perform the action is of superior status, then **te kureru** or the even more polite **te kudasaru yō ni** may be used:

I asked the Professor to come at six o'clock.	**Sensei ni rokuji goro kite kureru yō ni tanomimashita.**
My wife asked the Professor to help.	**Kanai ga sensei ni tetsudatte kureru yō ni tanomimashita.**

Exercise 18
Put into Japanese:

1 Ask him whether he knows where they live.
2 Would you be kind enough to tell me where they live?
3 We asked him to be here by lunchtime, but he said he'd be here by four o'clock.
4 The teacher told the students to stand up.
5 Did he ask her why she's going to give up Japanese?

73 'Call A, B'

'Call A, B' is **A o** (or **wa**) **B to iimasu**.

A: *What do you call this yellow thing?*	**Kono kiiroi no wa nan to iimasu ka.**
B: *We call it 'takuwan'.*	**Takuwan to iimasu.**

Note the following:

How do you say 'I love you' in Japanese?	**'I love you' wa Nihongo de nan to iimasu ka.**

74 'An A called B', 'the fact that A means B'

'An A called B' is **B to iu A**. Consider the following:

A singer called Nakajima Miyuki ...	**Nakajima Miyuki to iu kashu ga ...**
The film called 'Ran' ...	**'Ran' to iu eiga wa ...**

The Japanese word 'ai' ...   **Ai to iu Nihongo no kotoba wa ...**

Nouns and adjectives may be followed by **to iu no wa** or **to iu koto wa** (the latter only for abstract things) sometimes in the sense of 'what I mean by ...', 'what is meant by ...', but often with no extra meaning at all:

Japanese (lit. as for what we call Japanese)   **Nihongo to iu no wa omoshiroi desu yo.**
is interesting, you know.
Kanji are difficult to remember, aren't they?   **Kanji to iu no wa oboenikui desu ne.**

When **to iu koto wa** follows a verb or adjective it often conveys '(the fact) that':

Did you know that he's left the company?   **Kaisha o yameta to iu koto o shitte**
                                                   imashita ka.
I heard that she's getting married.   **Kanojo ga kekkon suru to iu koto o**
                                                   kikimashita.

'The fact that ... means that ...' may be translated by **... to iu koto** (or **no**) **wa ... to iu koto** (or **imi**) **desu**:

The fact that the light's on means he's back   **Denki ga tsuite iru to iu koto wa kare**
home now.   **ga mō kaette kita to iu koto desu.**

'That' in sentences such as 'the news that', 'the view that', 'a request that', etc. is translated with **to iu**:

Did you hear the news that there had been a   **Sugoi jishin ga atta to iu nyūsu o**
terrible earthquake?   **kikimashita ka.**
There was a call (saying) that he'd arrived.   **Tōchaku shita to iu denwa ga arimashita.**

Note how to ask 'what does <u>A</u> mean?':

A: *What does the word 'shuto' mean?*   **Shuto (to iu kotoba) wa dō iu imi desu ka.**
B: *It means 'capital city'.*   **'Capital city' to iu imi desu yo.**

75 Another word on *to omoimasu*

'I'm thinking of ...', 'I think I shall ...', 'I thought I would ...' are expressions which require the plain forms of the **mashō** ending in combination with **to omoimasu**.

Verbs in Group 1 have this plain form made in the following way:

taberu → tabeyō
miru → miyō

Verbs in Group 2 have this form made by changing the final syllable (e.g. **-u**, **-ku**, **-gu**, **-su**, **-tsu**, **-nu** etc.) to **-ō**, **-kō**, **-gō**, **-sō**, **-tō**, **-nō** etc.:

kaku → kakō
matsu → matō
arau → araō

The irregular verbs are:

suru → shiyō
kuru → koyō
da → darō

Check you can form the plain forms of the following:

ikimashō	→	**ikō**
deshō		**darō**
sagashimashō		**sagasō**
haraimashō		**haraō**
demashō		**deyō**
kaerimashō		**kaerō**
kaemashō		**kaeyō**

Consider these examples, and note that **ka** adds the idea of 'perhaps', 'might':

He was thinking of giving up whisky.   **Uisukī o yameyō to omotte mashita.**
I think I'll buy a radio.   **Rajio o kaō to omoimasu.**
I'm thinking I might go via Korea.   **Kankoku keiyu de ikō ka to omotte imasu.**
I think I'll perhaps go to bed now.   **Mō neyō ka to omoimasu.**

Exercise 19

Put into Japanese:

1 'What does the word hakubutsukan mean?' 'It means museum.'
2 He was going out with her for a long time and then I heard they were getting married.
3 I'm thinking of perhaps coming back next year.
4 They said that they wouldn't come.
5 'What did you say?' 'I said "I'm tired and I'm going to bed."'
6 The fact that he hasn't phoned yet doesn't mean that he's had an accident, you know.

CONVERSATION 11a: A traditional Japanese inn

Shortly after arriving in Japan Mr Brown (B) makes his first visit with Mr Inoue (I) to a 'ryokan', where they are met by the owner's wife (R):

I: Gomen kudasai.
R: Hai! Irasshaimase.
I: Sumimasen, heya wa arimasu ka.
R: O-futari-sama de gozaimasu ne. Hai, gozaimasu. Go-ippaku de gozaimasu ka.
I: Hai, sō desu.
R: Dōzo o-agari kudasai. O-heya e go-annai itashimasu.

They are taken to their room and wait for tea to be brought. Mr Inoue points to a low table in the middle of the room:

I: Buraun-san, kore wa nan to iu ka shitte imasu ka.
B: Oboete imasen.
I: Kore wa kotatsu to itte, shita ni hīta ga tsuite iru n'desu. Attakakute totemo kimochi ga ii n'desu. Dōzo suwatte ashi o nobashite kudasai.

Mr Brown points to the sliding paper door:

B: Inoue-san, ano doa wa fusuma to iimasu ka shōji to iimasu ka. Dotchi ga dotchi ka[1] mata wasuremashita.
I: Are wa fusuma desu yo. Shikashi, Nihonma de ichiban omoshiroi no wa[2] Buraun-san no ushiro ni aru n'desu. Tokonoma to iu tokoro desu yo. Asoko ni kakejiku toka hana toka o oku n'desu.
B: Sō desu ka. Suteki desu ne. Kakejiku wa 'scroll' to iu imi deshita ne.
I: Sō desu. Shikashi kono kakejiku ni nan to kaite aru no ka watashi ni sappari wakarimasen[3]. Ji ga furukute totemo yominikui desu ne.
R: Shitsurei shimasu!

CONVERSATION 11b: A beer garden

Mr Murata (M) is waiting at a beer garden for Mr Brown (B) and others to appear:

B: Osoku natte mōshiwake nai desu. Basho (o) shitte iru ka to omotta n'desu ga kekkyoku wakaranakute keisatsukan ni oshiete moratta n'desu.
M: Warukatta desu[4] ne.
B: Tonde mo arimasen. Nakanaka ii tokoro desu ne. Inoue-san wa? kuru to itte ita deshō.
M: N, kuji ni natta kara mō chotto de[5] kuru to omoimasu ga.
B: Yamamoto-san wa?
M: Yamamoto-san wa nē okāsan ga kinō nyūin shita no de kyō wa chotto muri[6] nan

ja nai ka to omoimasu yo.

B: Taihen desu ne. Katayama-san wa?

M: Iya, Katayama-san wa kaisha no yōji de osoku naru darō to itte imashita. Hatashite kuru ka dō ka wakarimasen ga.

B: Sō desu ka. Kinō watashi wa Sumisu-san ni kyō kuru yō ni itta n'desu ga kyō wa muri da to itte imashita yo!

M: Zannen desu ne. Jā, sannin dake de nomimashō! *To the waiter:* Sumimasen! Bīru o kudasai!

Notes:

1. **Dotchi ga dotchi ka ...:** 'I've forgotten which is which'; **dotchi** is an abbreviation of **dochira**.

2. **de ichiban omoshiroi no wa:** 'the most interesting thing in a Japanese room is ...'. Superlatives are dealt with in Lesson 16.

3. **nan to kaite aru ka ...:** 'I've no idea what is written on it'; **te aru/arimasu** is dealt with in Lesson 19.

4. **Warukatta:** here, it means 'I'm sorry'.

5. **mō chotto de:** 'in a moment', 'before long'.

6. **muri:** here, 'impossible'.

Lesson 12

MAIN POINTS: *like/dislike; want to do; want someone to do;* more on *wa* and *ga;* more on *naru* and *narimasu;* more on *yō ni.*
CONVERSATIONS: (a) Likes and dislikes; (b) 'What sports are you good at?'

76 'Like/dislike'

The **na** adjectives **suki** ('liked') and **kirai** ('disliked') are normally used in place of a verb. '<u>A</u> likes <u>B</u>' and '<u>A</u> dislikes <u>B</u>' are <u>A</u> **wa** <u>B</u> **ga suki desu** and <u>A</u> **wa** <u>B</u> **ga kirai desu:**

My wife likes jazz. (J: As for my wife, jazz is liked.)	**Kanai wa jazu ga suki desu.**
I dislike manju.	**Watashi wa manjū ga kirai desu.**

The subject is omitted when the context makes clear who or what this is:

A: *Do you like Japanese food?*	**Washoku ga suki desu ka.**
B: *Yes, I do, very much.*	**Hai, totemo suki desu.**

'Really like' and 'really loathe' are **daisuki** and **daikirai** respectively. When referring to people one likes and dislikes **no koto ga** is often used:

You really like her, don't you?	**Kanojo no koto ga daisuki desu ne.**
I really loathe that song.	**Ano uta ga daikirai desu.**

In the negative, and when two things are being contrasted, and when replying to a question using **wa,** the object of the like or dislike may be followed by **wa** and not **ga:**

I don't like the rainy season in Japan.	**Nihon no tsuyu wa suki ja arimasen.**
I like Japanese magazines, but I don't like Japanese comics.	**Nihon no zasshi wa suki desu ga manga wa suki ja arimasen.**
A: *What about some beer?*	**Bīru wa ikaga desu ka.**
B: *I don't like beer.*	**Bīru wa suki ja nai n'desu.**

Both **suki** and **kirai** are **na** adjectives and can of course be placed before nouns:

... a drink which I (etc.) like (J: a liked drink) ...	**... suki na nomimono ...**
... a person I don't like ...	**... kirai na hito ...**

To clarify who is doing the liking in such expressions, add the pronoun plus **no:**

There is no food which I don't like.	**Watashi no kirai na tabemono wa nai desu.**
What is the food he likes?	**Kare no suki na tabemono wa nan desu ka.**

77 Some other *wa/ga* expressions

'<u>A</u> is good at <u>B</u>' and '<u>A</u> is bad at <u>B</u>' are <u>A</u> **wa** <u>B</u> **ga jōzu desu** and <u>A</u> **wa** <u>B</u> **ga heta desu:**

He was very good at the guitar.	**Kare wa gitā ga totemo jōzu deshita.**
Mrs Suzuki is not useless at singing.	**Suzuki-san wa uta ga heta ja arimasen.**

Jōzu and **heta** are both **na** adjectives and are to be found before nouns:

Sports he's good at are judo and baseball.	**Kare no jōzu na spotsu wa jūdō to yakyū desu.**
Languages she's not good at are French and German.	**Kanojo no heta na kotoba wa Furansugo to Doitsugo desu.**

Other very common **wa/ga** constructions include **wakaru/wakarimasu** 'understand':

She understands Japanese well.	**(Kanojo wa) Nihongo ga yoku wakarimasu.**
Do you understand the meaning of that joke?	**(Anata wa) sono jōdan no imi ga wakarimasu ka.**

and **dekiru/dekimasu** 'can (do)':

Mr Suzuki's son can do kendo.	**Suzuki-san no musuko wa kendō ga dekimasu.**
A: *Can you do (speak) English?*	**(Anata wa) Eigo ga dekimasu ka.**
B: *Just a little.*	**Sukoshi dake dekimasu.**

and, of course, **aru/arimasu:**

Have you got any money? (J: As for you, is there any money?)	**(Anata wa) o-kane ga arimasu ka.**
I haven't got a ticket.	**Watashi wa kippu ga arimasen.**

Note here that you can say either 'as for <u>A</u>, its <u>B</u> is ...', or '<u>A</u>'s <u>B</u> is ...'. Compare the following:

The cost of living in Tokyo is high.	(a) **Tōkyō wa bukka ga takai desu.**
	(b) **Tōkyō no bukka wa takai desu.**

Japan's population is great.   (a) **Nihon wa jinkō ga ōi desu.**
                                                      (b) **Nihon no jinkō wa ōi desu.**

In all of the above, **wa** will <u>generally</u> replace **ga** when the word before **ga** is being contrasted with something else, when the sentence is negative, and when a reply is being made to a question which uses **wa**:

He's good at judo but he's no good at kendo.   **Jūdō wa jōzu desu ga kendō wa heta desu.**
I can't speak Japanese, you know.   **Nihongo wa dekimasen yo.**
A: *What about the money?*   **O-kane wa?**
B: *I've got the money.*   **O-kane wa arimasu yo.**

78 'Want something'/'need something'

The adjective **hoshii** ('desired') is used for 'want something':

I want a cigarette. (J: As for me, a cigarette   **Watashi wa tabako ga hoshii desu.**
is desired.)
Do you want a bit more money?   **Mō sukoshi o-kane ga hoshii desu ka.**

If the subject is a third person (he/she/they), **hoshii** is usually followed by **to itte iru/imasu** (**iimashita** in the past), or a word for 'seems' – see Lesson 13:

A: *What does she want?*   **Kanojo wa nani ga hoshii to itte imasu ka.**
B: *She doesn't want anything.*   **Nanimo hoshiku nai to itte imasu.**

Alternatively, the verb **hoshigaru/hoshigarimasu** may be used:

He doesn't want any money.   **O-kane wa hoshigatte imasen.**

Hoshii can also be used before a noun:

Is there something you want (J: a desired   **Hoshii mono wa arimasu ka.**
thing)?

'Need something' is translated by **iru/irimasu** ('is necessary'):

I need some more time. (J: As for me, more   **Watashi wa mō chotto jikan ga irimasu.**
time is necessary.)
Don't you need that?   **Irimasen ka.**

Often the meaning of **iru/irimasu** is close to 'want':

A: *What about some tea?*   **Kōcha wa?**
B: *I don't want any now.*   **Ima wa irimasen.**

Exercise 20

Put into Japanese:

1 'Don't you like that song?' 'No, I really loathe it.'
2 'What sports is your brother good at?' 'He's good at baseball.'
3 She's got very pretty eyes.
4 I've got two children. What about you?
5 I can speak Japanese but I can't speak Korean yet.
6 I don't want that, so I'll give it to you.
7 She wants that expensive dress.
8 'Can you do it?' 'No, I can't. Would you (be kind enough to) ask him if he can?'

79 'Want to' (i)

'Want to' is made by adding **tai** to the stem of any verb. **Tai** works like an **i** adjective, and its negative is **taku nai**. Check you can make the **tai** and **taku nai** forms of the following:

suru/shimasu	→ **shitai**	→ **shitaku nai**
oriru/orimasu	**oritai**	**oritaku nai**
kuru/kimasu	**kitai**	**kitaku nai**
kau/kaimasu	**kaitai**	**kaitaku nai**
iku/ikimasu	**ikitai**	**ikitaku nai**
kaeru/kaerimasu	**kaeritai**	**kaeritaku nai**
kaeru/kaemasu	**kaetai**	**kaetaku nai**

Now check you can form the past positive and negative of the following:

shitai	→ **shitakatta**	→ **shitaku nakatta**
oritai	**oritakatta**	**oritaku nakatta**
owaritai	**owaritakatta**	**owaritaku nakatta**
kaitai	**kaitakatta**	**kaitaku nakatta**
kitai	**kitakatta**	**kitaku nakatta**
detai	**detakatta**	**detaku nakatta**
kaeritai	**kaeritakatta**	**kaeritaku nakatta**

The addition of **desu** or **n'desu** to these forms makes them polite:

We don't want to go home yet.	**Mada kaeritaku nai desu.**
I didn't want to go by plane.	**Hikōki de ikitaku nakatta desu.**
I should like to open a bank account.	**Kōza o hirakitai n'desu ga.**

Often the direct object of the **tai** form is followed not by **o**, but by **ga**:

Why do you want to read yesterday's newspaper?	**Dōshite kinō no shinbun ga yomitai n'desu ka.**
I wanted to buy that shirt.	**Ano shatsu ga kaitakatta desu.**

An alternative to the polite **desu** ending is **to omoimasu** ('think that'). Its meaning is often close to 'would like to':

I would like to go to bed now.	**Mō netai to omoimasu yo.**
Wouldn't you like to go out somewhere?	**Dokoka e asobi ni ikitai to omoimasen ka.**

80 'Want to' (ii)

A 3rd person subject generally requires either **to itte iru/imasu** or **deshō** (or a word for 'seems', see Lesson 13):

They want to go with us.	**Karera wa issho ni ikitai to itte imasu.**
The children want something to drink.	**Kodomo wa nanika nomitai deshō.**

A common alternative is to add **-garu** to the **tai** ending. Note the formation: **ikitai → ikitagaru**. This is generally found as **-gatte iru/imasu**:

She wanted to do it but she couldn't.	**Kanojo wa yaritagatte ita n'desu ga dekinakatta desu.**

81 'Want someone to ...'

The **te** form of the verb plus **hoshii** is used for 'want someone to do something'. The agent (the person required to perform the action) is followed by **ni**. The speaker will use it only when addressing those he deems to be of inferior status or when speaking to intimates. The form is frequently used interrogatively in polite speech to mean 'Do you want me/us to ...?':

Tanaka, I want you to come early tomorrow.	**Tanaka-kun ashita hayaku kite hoshii.**
Do you want me to phone?	**Denwa shite hoshii n'desu ka.**

82 More on *naru/narimasu*

Naru/narimasu is used with the **tai** form of verbs:

Yesterday I didn't want to, but today I do. (J: I have become want to)	**Kinō wa shitaku nakatta desu ga kyō wa shitaku narimashita.**

Do you (now) want to meet her? **Kanojo ni aitaku natta n'desu ka.**

Naru/narimasu is also used very often both with **nai** itself and the plain negative of verbs:

A: *Has the snow all gone?* **Yuki wa minna naku narimashita ka.**
B: *No, it hasn't (yet).* **(Mada) naku natte imasen.**
He's disappeared. **Kare wa inaku narimashita yo.**
I can't speak Japanese any more. **Nihongo wa dekinaku narimashita.**

Naku narimashita used of people means 'die':

My teacher died the day before yesterday. **Sensei wa ototoi naku narimashita.**

'Come to ...' is often expressed by **yō ni naru/narimasu:**

You will (come to) understand one day. **Itsuka wakaru yō ni naru deshō.**
I couldn't do it a week ago, but now I can. **Isshūkan mae wa dekimasen deshita ga ima wa dekiru yō ni narimashita.**

83 More on *yō ni*

Yō ni has the literal meaning of 'so as to', 'in such a way that' (see Lesson 11). The same **yō ni** can be used with **suru/shimasu** to mean 'be sure to' ('do in such a way as to'):

Be sure to be back by seven. **Shichiji made ni kaette kuru yō ni shite kudasai.**

Be sure to ring, won't you. **Denwa suru yō ni shite kudasai ne.**

Yō ni is used with a large number of other verbs too. Below is a selection:

Open the window (J: so as) to let some air in. **Kaze ga haitte kuru yō ni mado o akete kudasai.**

Let's pray (J: in such a way) that they arrive safely. **Buji ni tōchaku suru yō ni inorimashō.**

I got up early so as to be in time for the plane. **Hikōki ni ma ni au yō ni hayaku okimashita.**

Let's take care (J: in such a way that we do) not to smoke too much. **Tabako o suisuginai yō ni chūi shimashō*.**

(*This is the health warning found on the side of Japanese cigarette packs.)

Exercise 21

Put into Japanese:

1 I don't want to go, neither does she.
2 You don't need that, do you?
3 Does your brother want to go too?
4 Be sure to lock the door, won't you.
5 My money's all gone.
6 Take care not to break it.

CONVERSATION 12a: Likes and dislikes

Mr Amai (A) asks Mr Brown about his preferences:

A: Buraun-san wa sukikirai wa arimasu ka.
B: Sō desu ne. Kirai na mono wa amari nai desu ne. Nattō to manjū gurai[1] desu ne. Ato wa[2] kirai na mono wa betsu ni nai to omoimasu.
A: Sashimi to sushi wa daijōbu desu ka.
B: Sashimi mo sushi mo daikōbutsu desu yo. Saisho wa chotto dake teikō ga atta n'desu ga ima wa totemo suki desu.
A: Nihonshu wa dō desu ka. Gaikokujin wa minna Nihonshu ga suki da to kikimashita ga.
B: Dō deshō. Watashi wa reigai ka mo shiremasen ga Nihonshu wa chotto dame desu!

CONVERSATION 12b: 'What sports are you good at?'

They go on to discuss sports:

A: Buraun-san wa supōtsu ga jōzu deshō?
B: Sō desu ne. Ragubī wa wari to jōzu desu kedo ato wa[2] amari dekinai n'desu yo. Amai-san wa nanika supōtsu ga dekimasu ka.
A: Yakyū to sofutobōru gurai[3] desu ne.
B: Yakyū wa Nihon de sugoi ninki ga arimasu ne. Sonna ni[4] ninki ga aru nante[5] shirimasen deshita. Yakyū no heta na Nihonjin wa inai n'ja nai desu ka[6].
A: Sō ka mo shiremasen ne. Kodomo no toki kara minna yatte imasu kara ne. Buraun-san, yakyū no shiai o mi ni ikimasen ka[7].
B: Zehi ikitai desu ne.
A: Doko no fuan[8] desu ka.
B: Watashi wa Kyojin[9] ga suki desu ne. Amai-san wa?
A: Yappari Hanshin Taigāsu[9] desu ne!

Notes:

1. **Nattō to manjū gurai:** 'Natto and manju are about the extent of my likes and dislikes'; **gurai** here means 'and not much else'. **Nattō** is fermented soya, mostly eaten at breakfast, and **manjū** are bean cakes.

2. **ato wa:** 'apart from that', 'as for the rest'.

3. **gurai:** see note 1 above.

4. **sonna ni:** 'that' as in 'I didn't know it was *that* popular'. See Lesson 16.

5. **nante:** informal alternative for **to iu koto wa.**

6. **n'ja nai desu ka:** 'Isn't it the case that …?'; this is a very common sentence ending.

7. **ikimasen ka:** distinguish between **ikimasen ka,** a suggestion meaning 'would you like to' and **ikitai desu ka** ('do you want to?').

8. **Doko no fuan:** 'Who do you support?'; **doko** refers to 'which team?'

9. **Kyojin, Hanshin Taigasu** ('Tigers') are both top professional baseball teams.

Lesson 13

MAIN POINTS: Appearance; feel; taste; sound.
CONVERSATIONS: (a) The weather; (b) The news.

84 'Appears to be', 'looks like' (i)

There are two types of expression involving **sō desu**:

(1) after the plain form of adjectives or verbs it means 'it appears from what I've heard that ...' or simply 'I hear that ...', 'it is said that ...':

I hear that she's given up Japanese.	**Nihongo o yameta sō desu.**
I hear it's quiet there.	**Asoko wa shizuka da sō desu.**

(2) **Sō desu** is also added to the stem of both types of adjective:

shizuka na → shizuka → shizukasō
oishii → oishi → oishisō

N.B.: **ii** ('good') has an irregular form **yosasō**; **nai** ('there isn't') has an irregular form **nasasō**.

Sō desu is also added to the stem of verbs of any group:

dekimasu → deki → dekisō

Here the meaning is 'it looks, from what I see, (or sounds from what I hear) that (it's going to be) ...'. Compare:

It looks (as if it's going to be) tasty.	**Oishisō desu.**
I hear it's tasty.	**Oishii sō desu.**
It looks quiet.	**Shizukasō desu.**
They say it's quiet.	**Shizuka da sō desu.**
She looks as if she wants to eat manju.	**Manjū ga tabetasō desu.**
I hear she wants to eat manju.	**Manjū ga tabetai sō desu.**
She looks as if she speaks Japanese.	**Nihongo ga dekisō desu.**
I hear she speaks Japanese.	**Nihongo ga dekiru sō desu.**

Sō, added to the stem of an adjective or verb, functions as a **na** adjective:

That's tasty-looking food.	**Sore wa oishisō na gohan desu ne.**
This is a quiet-looking town.	**Kore wa shizukasō na machi desu.**

85 'Appears to be', 'looks like' (ii)

Whereas **sō desu** (2) is used for evidence based largely on sight and refers to something that has not yet been realized, **yō desu** is used generally for a situation that exists at the time of speaking. Moreover, **yō desu**'s usage is broader and not confined to sight. Consider the following:

He seems to have a temperature.	**Netsu ga aru yō desu.**
He didn't appear to understand.	**Wakaranakatta yō desu.**
All the shops are shut, it seems.	**O-mise wa minna shimatte iru yō desu.**
It appears to be quite useless.	**Zenzen dame na yō desu.**

With nouns the particle **no** is needed:

That person looks like a businessman.	**Ano hito wa sararīman no yō desu ne.**

Yō is also used as a **na** adjective with a variety of meanings:

There are few beautiful places like Kamikochi.	**Kamikōchi no yō na utsukushii tokoro wa sukunai desu.**
There are many short people such as myself in Japan.	**Nihon ni wa watashi no yō na se ga hikui hito wa takusan imasu yo.**
It's a spring-like day.	**Haru no yō na hi desu.**

Yō may also be followed by **ni** in a variety of different ways:

She speaks Japanese like a Japanese.	**Nihonjin no yō ni Nihongo o hanashimasu.**
Do it quickly, as the teacher said.	**Sensei ga itta yō ni hayaku shite kudasai.**

(See also Lessons 11 and 12.)

'Just like' is to onaji yō ni:

The Japanese, just like the English, always talk about the weather.	**Nihonjin wa Igirisujin to onaji yō ni itsumo tenki ni tsuite hanasu n'desu.**
Pronounce it just like the teacher does.	**Sensei to onaji yō ni hatsuon shite kudasai.**

'Unlike' is to chigatte:

Unlike Chinese, Japanese is easy.	**Chūgokugo to chigatte Nihongo wa kantan desu yo.**

Finally, learn this set of useful words:

what sort of (in what way)?	**dono yō na (ni)**
this sort of (in this way)	**kono yō na (ni)**
that sort of (in that way)	**sono yō na (ni)**
that sort of (in that way)	**ano yō na (ni)**

Consider the following:

In what way is it different?	**Dono yō ni chigaimasu ka.**
What sort of problem is it?	**Dono yō na mondai desu ka.**

86 'Appears to be', 'looks like' (iii)

Mitai and **rashii** are two common words which at the end of a sentence mean 'appears', 'looks like' in all but the sense of **sō desu** (2). In conversation, **mitai** is the most common of all the 'appearance' words:

The water seems to have boiled.	**O-yu ga waita mitai desu yo.**
I hear he's coming home tomorrow.	**Ashita kaette kuru mitai desu ne.**
It seems to be very old.	**Totemo furui mitai desu ne.**
It appears to be useless.	**Dame mitai desu.**
He's a businessman, it seems.	**Ano hito wa sararīman mitai desu.**

In all the above **rashii** could be used as well.

Differences between **mitai** and **rashii: mitai** is a **na** adjective; **rashii** is an **i** adjective. When used before nouns or as adverbs their meanings differ. Consider first **mitai**:

I loathe days like today.	**Kyō mitai na hi wa daikirai desu.**
Do it like I did.	**Watashi ga yatta mitai ni yatte kudasai.**

B rashii A, however, means 'an A typical of B':

He's a manly person.	**Otoko rashii otoko desu.**
It's a typical spring day.	**Haru rashii hi desu.**

Exercise 22
Put into Japanese:

1 I understand that he married a Japanese girl last year.
2 That sashimi really does look tasty, you know.
3 The concert seems to have finished now, so shall we go for a drink?
4 'How do I use chopsticks?' 'Use them like I do.'
5 I loathe people like her. I hear she argues with everyone.

87 Feel, sense, taste, smell, sound, looks, shape

Learn the following idiomatic expressions:

Feel (like) ...   ki ga suru/shimasu
Taste (like) ...   aji ga suru/shimasu
Smell (like) ...   nioi ga suru/shimasu
Sound (like) ...   oto ga suru/shimasu
Feel (as if) ..., get the impression   kanji ga suru/shimasu
  (that) ...
Look ...   kao o shite iru/imasu
Have a ... shape   katachi o shite iru/imasu

Many of these expressions are preceded by **(no) yō na** or **to iu**. Study the following:

I don't feel like getting up today.	Kyō wa okiru ki ga shinai n'desu.
This fish has got a rather odd taste.	Kono sakana wa chotto hen na aji ga shimasu.
It smells like gas.	Gasu no yō na nioi ga shimasu yo.
It sounds as if it's raining, doesn't it?	Ame ga futte iru yō na oto ga shimasu ne.
I feel that it's expensive.	Chotto takai kanji ga shimasu.
I get the impression it's a bit difficult.	Chotto muzukashii to iu kanji ga shimasu yo.
He looks sad.	Kanashii kao o shite imasu.
She's good-looking.	Kanojo wa ii kao o shite imasu.
That temple is a funny shape, isn't it?	Ano o-tera wa hen na katachi o shite imasu ne.

Note finally the very common intransitive verbs **mieru/miemasu** (lit. be visible) and **kikoeru/kikoemasu** (lit. be audible);

Excuse me, I can't see.	Sumimasen. (Chotto) miemasen.
Can you see the sea?	Umi ga miemasu ka.
It looks very pretty.	Totemo kirei ni miemasu.
I can't hear. Would you turn the sound up, please?	Chotto kikoemasen. Oto o mō chotto okiku shite moraemasu ka.

Exercise 23
Put into Japanese:

1 One gets the feeling that it's spring already.
2 Don't you feel like going out tonight?
3 He looks as if he hasn't eaten for a long time.

4 That house is shaped like a temple.
5 Can't you smell something (J: isn't there a smell)?

CONVERSATION 13a: The weather

Mr Amai and Mr Brown discuss today's weather:

A: Kyō no tenki wa dō naru n'deshō ka.
B: Tenki yohō ni yoru to[1] hare da sō desu ga dōmo haresō na kanji ga shimasen ne.
A: Sō desu ne. Ame ga furisō desu kara pikunikku wa chūshi ni naru n'deshō. Mō ame ga furihajimeta mitai desu yo.
B: Un, potsupotsu futte iru yō desu ne. Komarimashita. Demo nishi no hō wa akarui desu kara ato kara hareru yō na ki mo shimasu[2] yo.

CONVERSATION 13b: The news

Mr Amai talks about an earthquake in Tokyo:

A: Kesa no nyūsu o mimashita ka.
B: Mada mite imasen. Dōshite desu ka.
A: Nyūsu ni yoru to[3] Tōkyō ni kanari ōkii jishin ga atta sō desu. Shindo 5[4] datta rashii desu yo. Ōkii deshō?
B: Shindo 5 wa ōkii desu ne. Fushōsha wa?
A: Fushōsha wa nannin deta ka oboete imasen ga nanninka[5] shinda mitai desu yo. Jishin wa kowai desu ne.
B: Kowai desu yo. Demo 1923nen no yō na ōkii jishin ja nakute yokatta desu[6] ne.
A: Sore wa sō desu ga nyūsu de mō sugu mō hitotsu jishin ga aru ka mo shirenai kara chūi suru yō ni itte imashita yo.

Notes:

1. **ni yoru to … sō desu:** 'according to …'; **yoru to …** followed by **sō da/desu** is a very common way of expressing 'according to …'.

2. **yō na ki mo shimasu:** 'I actually feel that …'

3. See note 1.

4. **Shindo 5:** 'magnitude 5'.

5. **nanninka:** 'quite a few people'; for other related expressions see Lesson 14.

6. **ja nakute yokatta desu:** 'it's lucky that it wasn't'.

Lesson 14

MAIN POINTS: Relative clauses, simple and complex; *anybody/somebody/nobody*.
CONVERSATIONS: (a) A radio interview; (b) A temple in Kyoto.

88 Relative clauses (i)

A relative clause in English is one which begins with 'who' (e.g. 'the child who ...')
or 'which' (e.g. 'the car which ...'). As you know, in Japanese there are no words for
'who', 'which', etc. in this sense. For example, 'a car which is fast' is simply **hayai
kuruma**; refer back to sections 37 and 40. Just as adjectives can come before nouns,
so too can verbs in the formation of 'relative clauses'. Study these examples:

The child who is crying (J: the 'is crying' child) is my son.	**Naite iru kodomo wa musuko desu.**
The man who is singing in the bar (J: the 'in the bar is singing man') is the President.	**Bā de utatte iru hito wa shachō desu.**
The car which crashed is a Toyota.	**Shōtotsu shita kuruma wa Toyota desu.**

89 Relative clauses (ii)

Consider how the Japanese say more complex relative clauses, noting in the examples
below that **no** may replace **ga**:

the man whose eyes are blue (J: the 'eyes are blue' man)	**me ga (no) aoi hito wa**
a student with no money (J: a 'there is no money' student)	**o-kane ga (no) nai gakusei ga**
a country with lots of mountains (J: a 'mountains are many' country)	**yama ga (no) ōi kuni ga**

Now consider how to say 'whom', 'to whom', 'in which', 'whose', 'on which', etc., and
note that the subject of the relative clause may be expressed either by **ga** or by **no**:

The man whom I saw (J: the 'I saw man') is a famous singer.	**Watashi no mita hito wa yūmei na kashu desu.**
The girl to whom I sent a card (J: the 'I sent a card' girl) will be twenty-one tomorrow.	**Watashi ga kādo o okutta onna no ko wa ashita nijū ichi desu.**
The bar in which we had arranged to meet (J: the 'we had arranged to meet' bar) is a haunt for foreigners.	**Watashitachi ga machiawase shita bā wa gaijin no tamariba desu.**

109

The man whose father had that accident (J: the 'father had an accident' man) lives near me.	**Otōsan ga jiko ni atta hito wa watashi no ie no chikaku ni sunde imasu.**
The road on which we came (J: the 'we came road') is different.	**Kita michi wa chigaimasu.**

The following are a type of relative clause: 'things to do', **suru koto;** 'places to see', **miru tokoro;** 'something to write with' or 'something to write on', **kaku mono;** 'something to eat', **taberu mono.**

N.B.: An abstract thing is **koto**, a concrete thing is **mono**.

Exercise 24
Put into Japanese:

1 I like that car with the red roof.
2 Who's that girl drinking coffee?
3 Japan is a country with a very large population.
4 Who was that man you were speaking to just now? Is he someone you've known for a long time?
5 This is the book Mr Tanaka bought for his wife.
6 This is the shop in which I bought it.

90 'Someone', 'something'

'Someone', 'something', etc. are made by adding **ka** to the question words 'who', 'what', etc.:

Positive statement	Negative or positive question	
someone, somebody	someone, somebody	**dareka**
	anyone, anybody	**donataka**
something	something, anything	**nanika**
sometime	sometime	**itsuka**
somewhere	somewhere, anywhere	**dokoka**
one or the other	one or the other	**dochiraka**
one (some) of them	one (some) of them	**doreka**
some, a fair number of	some, a fair number of, any	**ikutsuka**
some, a fair amount of	some, a fair amount of, any	**ikuraka**

With these words **ga** and **o** are often omitted. **Wa** is never used. Other particles such as **ni, e, kara, to,** etc. must, however, be used when the verb demands it:

Someone stole my purse.	**Dareka (ga) watashi no saifu o nusumimashita.**
Did you tell someone (anyone)?	**Dareka ni iimashita ka.**
Will you have something to drink?	**Nanika (o) nomimasu ka.**
Shall we go and see a No (play) sometime?	**Itsuka Nō o mi ni ikimashō ka.**
I saw that advertisement somewhere.	**Dokoka de sono kōkoku o mimashita.**
They live somewhere in Nagoya.	**Nagoya no dokoka ni sunde imasu.**
Have you chosen one of (the two of) them?	**Dochiraka (o) erabimashita ka.**
Have you chosen (any) one of these?	**Doreka (o) erabimashita ka.**
There are a fair number of possibilities, you know.	**Ikutsuka no kanōsei ga arimasu yo.**

Often these words are used just 'sitting' before an adjective plus noun or a relative clause, contributing no extra meaning. Study the examples below:

Shall we go and have something good to eat?	**Nanika oishii mono o tabe ni ikimashō ka.**
I'd like to go somewhere where there aren't any people.	**Dokoka hito ga inai tokoro ni ikitai desu ne.**

'Some people ... other people ...', 'some places ... other places ...' etc. require a different construction with **aru** ('certain') and **wa**:

Some people like manju, others don't.	**Aru hito wa manjū ga suki desu ga aru hito wa kirai desu.**
Some places I went to, others I didn't.	**Aru tokoro wa ikimashita ga aru tokoro wa ikimasen deshita.**

Ka is added to the appropriate question word to mean 'a fair number of', 'quite a few':

It took quite a few hours.	**Nanjikanka kakarimashita yo.**
A fair number of people were there.	**Nanninka kite imashita.**
He's been living in Japan for a fair number of years now.	**Nihon ni mō nannenka sunde imasu.**

91 'Nobody', 'nothing'

'Nobody', 'nothing', etc. in negative statements, and 'anybody', 'anything', etc. in negative questions are translated by the appropriate question word and **mo**:

Negative statement	*Negative question*	
no one, nobody	anyone, anybody	**daremo, donatamo**

nothing	anything	**nanimo**
nowhere	anywhere	**dokomo**
neither	either of two	**dochiramo**
none	any of three and more	**doremo**
not much at all	not much at all	**ikuramo**
not many at all	not many at all	**ikutsumo**

The particles **ga** and **o** need not be used with these words. **Wa** is never used. All other particles are used. Note that the particle is inserted between the question word and **mo** (e.g. **dare ni mo; doko e mo**, etc.):

I haven't told anyone yet.	**Mada dare ni mo itte imasen.**
There's nothing in the fridge.	**Reizōko ni nanimo haitte inai n'desu.**
The teacher isn't anywhere.	**Sensei wa doko ni mo irasshaimasen.**
I don't like either of them.	**Dochiramo suki ja nai desu.**
Don't you like any of them?	**Doremo suki ja nai desu ka.**

N.B.: 'Never' in the present and future tenses is translated by **kesshite** ('definitely') or **zettai ni** ('absolutely') – for 'have never' see Lesson 15:

I'll never marry her.	**Kanojo to zettai ni kekkon shimasen.**
They're never going to win, are they?	**Zettai ni katanai desu ne.**

Study these next examples, in which the question word followed by **mo** is an adjective:

They don't sell them in any shop.	**Dono mise de mo utte imasen.**
My son doesn't go to any school yet.	**Musuko wa mada doko no gakkō ni mo itte imasen.**

Often certain of these words are used just sitting before an adjective and noun or a relative clause, with no extra meaning. Study the following:

There was no one I know there.	**Asoko ni daremo shitte iru hito wa imasen deshita.**
There's no interesting programme on, is there?	**Nanimo omoshiroi bangumi wa yatte imasen ne.**
There's nowhere I want to go.	**Dokomo ikitai tokoro wa arimasen.**

Several of these words appear in positive sentences as well:

I can do both.	**Dochiramo dekimasu.**
They're all tasty.	**Doremo oishii desu.**

Mo is added to the appropriate question word to mean 'a great number of ...', 'any number of ...':

A great number of people were there.	Nanninmo kite imashita.
They've been married for a great number of years (years and years).	Mō nannenmo kekkon shite imasu.
We drank bottles and bottles of beer.	Bīru wa nanbonmo nomimashita.
I asked time and time again.	Nankaimo kikimashita.

92 'Anybody', 'anything'

'Anybody', 'anything' in positive sentences (e.g. 'Anybody can speak Japanese!') is translated by the appropriate question word followed by **demo**. The particles **wa, ga** and **o** are not used. All other particles are. Study the selection of examples below:

Anybody can speak Japanese.	Daredemo Nihongo ga dekimasu.
I'll eat anything tasty.	Nandemo oishii mono o tabemasu.
Please take whichever of the two you like.	Dochirademo suki na no o totte kudasai.
Please use any of them.	Doredemo tsukatte kudasai.
Come round any time.	Itsudemo asobi ni kite kudasai.
There's any amount of beer.	Bīru wa ikurademo arimasu yo.
They sell them in any country.	Dono kuni de demo utte imasu.

Exercise 25

Put into Japanese:

1 Is there anywhere quiet near here?
2 What sports can he do?
3 He bought loads and loads of (J: any number of) books.
4 There was nobody there who could speak English.
5 There isn't anything interesting on the TV. tonight.

CONVERSATION 14a: A radio interview

The interviewer (A) asks Mr Brown about his motives for visiting Japan:

A: Mina-san, o-hayō gozaimasu. Kyō no o-kyaku-san wa Igirisu kara oide ni natta [1] Jon Buraun-san desu. Buraun-san, Nihon ni kita dōki [2] wa nan desu ka. Yahari Nihongo no benkyō desu ka.

B: Sō desu ne. Watashi ga Nihon ni kitai to omotta dōki wa ikutsuka arimasu ga yappari hanasu chikara to kiku chikara [3] o tsuketakatta kara desu ne.

A: Naruhodo. Sore kara Buraun-san, Nihon de ichiban shitai koto wa – Nihongo o benkyō suru hoka ni [4] – nan desu ka.

B: Shitai koto wa takusan arimasu ga yappari Nihon no shakai ni tokekonde tomodachi o takusan tsukuritai desu ne.

A: Sore kara saigo ni Buraun-san, ichiban ikitai tokoro wa doko desu ka.

B: Sō desu ne. Gaikokujin ga amari ikanai tokoro ni ikitai desu ne. Tatoeba Gotō retto mitai na rekishi no omoshiroi tokoro[5] o tazunetai desu ne.

A: Sō desu ka. Arigatō gozaimashita.

CONVERSATION 14b: A temple in Kyoto

Mr Brown goes to visit a Zen temple in Kyoto with Mr Inoue (I):

B: Kyōto no doko ni ikimashō ka.

I: Sō desu ne. Teien no aru o-tera ga ii desu ka soretomo tatemono no omoshiroi tokoro[6] ga ii desu ka. Kyōto ni wa nandemo arimasu yo.

B: Zen no eikyō o uketa teien o mite mitai[7] desu ne.

I: Soshitara, mazu Ryōanji to iu o-tera ni ikimashō. Ryōanji wa totemo omoshiroi desu yo. Hito wa itsumo chotto ōi desu ga zettai ni miru kachi[8] wa aru to omoimasu yo. Ryōanji wa Zen no shisō o arawasu tenkeiteki na teien[9] de Nihon dokutoku no tokoro desu. Hakusa to ishi dake shika nai teien[10] desu yo.

B: Omoshirosō desu ne. Seiyō de iu teien[11] to zenzen chigau mitai desu ne.

Notes:

1. **oide ni natta Buraun-san:** 'Mr Brown, who has come from England'; **oide ni naru/narimasu** is an honorific form of **kuru/kimasu.**

2. **Nihon ni kita dōki:** 'your motives for coming to Japan'.

3. **hanasu chikara to kiku chikara:** 'my ability to speak and hear'.

4. **benkyō suru hoka ni:** 'in addition to (apart from) studying'.

5. **omoshiroi tokoro:** 'a place like the Goto Islands with an interesting history'.

6. **tatemono no omoshiroi tokoro:** 'a place whose buildings are interesting'.

7. **mite mitai:** 'have a look and see'.

8. **miru kachi wa aru:** 'worth seeing'.

9. **... arawasu tenkeiteki na teien de:** 'a typical garden which shows ...'.

10. **... dake shika nai teien:** gardens with only white raked sand and stones, such as Ryoanji, are typical of Zen-influenced gardens.

11. **Seiyō de iu teien:** 'what one calls a garden in the West'.

Lesson 15

MAIN POINTS: *Must/must not, may/may not, can/cannot;* some uses of *koto* and *no* with verbs.
CONVERSATION: (a) Culture shock? (b) 'Have you ever been to Kamikochi?'

93 'Must', 'have to', 'must not', 'may not'

You need to know two ways to express 'must', 'have to'. The first involves the negative plain form of the verb plus **to** ('if') plus **dame desu** ('it's no good'):

You must read it (J: if you don't read it, it's no good).	**Sore o yomanai to dame desu.**
You must have your registration card with you.	**Gaijin tōrokushō o motte inai to dame desu.**

The second is known as the **nakereba narimasen** form. First make the negative plain form: **suru/shimasu → shinai**, then substitute **nakereba** for **nai** and add **narimasen**: shinai → shinakereba → shinakereba narimasen. (**nakereba** means 'if (you do) not ...'; **narimasen** means 'it's no good'):

You must eat it all (J: if you don't eat it all, it's no good).	**Zenbu tabenakereba narimasen.**
I have to catch the 9.30 train.	**Kuji sanjuppun no densha ni noranakereba narimasen.**

'Had to' is formed by the past of **narimasen**:

We had to tell him.	**Kare ni iwanakereba narimasen deshita.**

'Must not', 'may not' is expressed by the **te wa ikemasen** form. Add **wa** to the **te** form of the verb: **suu/suimasu** ('smoke') → **sutte wa,** and then add **ikemasen**: **sutte wa ikemasen.** (**te wa** means 'if (you) ...' **ikemasen** means 'it will not do'). A very common abbreviated form involves substituting **tcha** for **te wa:**

You mustn't smoke in here (J: if you smoke here, it won't do).	**Koko de sutte wa ikemasen.**
We mustn't laugh, must we?	**Waratcha ikemasen ne.**

94 'May', 'don't have to', 'don't need to'

'May' (and 'can', in the sense of 'it's all right to') requires the **te** form plus **mo** ('even if') plus **ii desu** ('it's good, it's all right'):

You may stay (the night).	**Tomatte mo ii desu yo.**
May I sit here?	**Koko ni suwatte mo ii desu ka.**
A: *Do you mind if I smoke?*	**Tabako o sutte mo ii desu ka.**
B: *No, I don't.*	**Hai, ii desu yo.**

Kamaimasen ('(I) don't mind') may be used instead of **ii desu**:

A: *Do you mind if I open the window?*	**Mado o akete mo kamaimasen ka.**
B: *No, I don't mind.*	**Hai, kamaimasen.**

'Don't have to' and 'don't need to' are expressed by the negative **te** form plus **mo** plus **ii desu** (or **kamaimasen**):

A: *We don't have to pay now, do we?*	**Ima sugu harawanakute mo ii desu ne.**
B: *No, you don't.*	**Hai, ii desu.**
You don't have to eat the manju.	**Manjū wa tabenakute mo ii desu.**

Note the use of the **te** form of **desu** in the following (**mo** is often dropped):

Is this O.K.? (Will this do?)	**Kore de (mo) ii desu ka.**
One will do.	**Hitotsu de (mo) ii desu.**

The construction is found with adjectives too:

I don't mind if it's expensive.	**Takakute mo ii desu yo.**
It's O.K. if it's not cheap.	**Yasuku nakute mo kamaimasen.**

95 'Wherever', 'whoever', etc.

Question words used with the **te mo** form translate the idea of 'wherever', 'whoever':

wherever you go	**doko e itte mo**
wherever you eat	**doko de tabete mo**
whatever I say to her	**kanojo ni nani o itte mo**
whoever we ask	**dare ni kiite mo**
whenever (at whatever time) you leave	**itsu shuppatsu shite mo**
whatever school they go to	**doko no gakkō e itte mo**

All these forms may be followed by **ii desu** or **kamaimasen** to give 'I don't mind', 'it doesn't matter ...'

I don't mind where you go.	**Doko e itte mo kamaimasen.**
It doesn't matter what you say.	**Nani o itte mo ii desu.**

96 'Can', 'be able'

There are two ways of expressing 'can', 'be able': the first involves the so-called potential form of the verb, when the verb ending is changed as follows:

Group 1 verbs:
taberu → tabe → taberareru

There is an abbreviated form of this also in common use:

taberu → tabe → tabereru

Group 2 verbs:
oyogu → oyogeru
arau → araeru

Irregular verbs:
suru → dekiru
kuru → korareru (or koreru)

All these 'can' forms function as Group 1 verbs in their own right. Check you can make 'can' forms of the following:

deru/demasu	→	**derareru/deraremasu (dereru/deremasu)**
iku/ikimasu		**ikeru/ikemasu**
harau/haraimasu		**haraeru/haraemasu**
toru/torimasu		**toreru/toremasu**

o, **ga** or **wa** may follow the object of the potential:

Can you speak English?	**Eigo ga hanasemasu (dekimasu) ka.**
I can't eat all this.	**Kore wa zenbu taberaremasen (taberemasen) yo.**

The second way is to use the plain form of the verb plus **koto ga** (or **wa** or **mo**) **dekiru/dekimasu**:

He can write Japanese.	**Kare wa Nihongo o kaku koto ga dekimasu.**

You can't buy anything with 500 yen.	**Gohyakuen de wa nanimo kau koto wa dekimasen.**
I can walk but I can't run.	**Aruku koto wa dekimasu ga hashiru koto wa dekimasen.**
Can you both read and write Japanese?	**Nihongo o kaku koto mo yomu koto mo dekimasu ka.**

Note here that expressions such as 'it is too (hot) ... for me to (eat) ...' may be translated by the **te** form of an adjective plus one of the 'can' forms:

It was too hot for me to eat (J: it was hot and so I could not ...).	**Atsukute taberenakatta desu.**
He spoke too quickly for me to be able to keep up.	**Hanashi ga hayasugite oitsukemasen deshita.**

Exercise 26
Put into Japanese:

1 'Is it all right if I go with you?' 'No, I have to go on my own.'
2 Can you be back home by six o'clock?
3 You don't have to write it in Japanese. You can write it in romaji.
4 You mustn't talk like that.
5 '10,000 yen will do, won't it?' 'Yes, that will be fine.'
6 I had to phone the police.

97 Some uses of *koto* (i)

'Do/does ... ever ...?' is expressed with the plain form plus **... koto wa** (or **ga**) **arimasu ka,** often with an adverb like **tokidoki** ('sometimes'):

A: *Do you ever browse in bookshops?*	**Honya-san de tachiyomi suru koto wa arimasu ka.**
B: *Yes, I do sometimes.*	**Hai, tokidoki arimasu.**
A: *Do you sometimes eat out?*	**Tokidoki gaishoku suru koto wa arimasu ka.**
B: *No, hardly ever.*	**Ie, hotondo nai desu ne.**

'Has/have ... ever ...?' requires the **ta** form plus **... koto wa** (or **ga**) **aru/arimasu:**

A: *Have you ever been to Nagasaki?*	**Nagasaki e itta koto wa arimasu ka.**
B: *No, I haven't.*	**Nai desu.**

A: *I've never been skiing, have you?*	**Watashi wa sukī e itta koto wa arimasen ga anata wa.**
B: *I have (actually).*	**Watashi wa arimasu yo.**
Sometimes I go out for a drink but not often for a meal.	**Tokidoki nomi ni iku koto wa arimasu ga shokuji ni iku koto wa amari nai desu.**

Mo may also be used:

I have also been to Taiwan.	**Taiwan e itta koto mo arimasu yo.**
I haven't even been to Kyushu.	**Kyūshū e itta koto mo arimasen.**

98 Some uses of *koto* (ii)

'Decide to ...' is translated by **... koto ni suru/shimasu,** and 'be decided (come about) that ...' by **koto ni naru/narimasu:**

We decided to call an ambulance.	**Kyūkyūsha o yobu koto ni shimashita.**
I've decided not to give up Japanese.	**Nihongo o yamenai koto ni shimashita.**
It's been decided that I'm going back to America next week.	**Raishū Amerika e kaeru koto ni natte imasu.**

99 Some uses of *koto* and *no*

By adding **koto** or **no** to the plain form of a verb you are in effect turning that verb into a noun: **hon o yomu** – read books; **hon o yomu koto (no)** – (the) reading (of) books. In many cases **no** and **koto** are interchangeable, but **no** is probably more frequent in conversation. Study the following:

I like reading books.	**Hon o yomu no ga suki desu.**
Speaking Japanese is easy but writing it is difficult.	**Nihongo o hanasu no wa kantan desu ga kaku no wa muzukashii desu.**
I'm tired of studying.	**Benkyō suru koto ni akita n'desu.**

In the following expressions **no** is more common. Consider them carefully:

I saw him talking to her.	**Kanojo to hanashite iru no o mimashita.**
Let's not go (J: let's stop going).	**Iku no o yamemashō.**
I'm waiting for him to come back.	**Kaette kuru no o matte imasu.**
Don't forget to phone!	**Denwa suru no o wasurenaide kudasai.**
Would you help me make it?	**Tsukuru no o tetsudatte kuremasu ka.**

100 Some uses of *no* (i)

No is frequently used in emphatic questions such as 'When is it that you're off?', 'Why is it that you're studying Japanese?' Study the examples below:

When is it that you're off? (J: As for your going, when is it?)	**Iku no wa itsu desu ka.**
Why is it that you're studying Japanese?	**Nihongo o benkyō shite iru no wa naze desu ka.**
Where is it that you met?	**Shiriatta no wa doko desu ka.**
Who is it that she married?	**Kanojo ga kekkon shita no wa dare desu ka.**

101 Some uses of *no* (ii)

No ni after a plain form is used to mean either 'for the purpose of (in order to)' or 'although'. In the first sense either **no ni wa** or **ni wa** may be used instead:

What do you use to make sukiyaki?	**Sukiyaki o tsukuru no ni nani o tsukaimasu ka.**
It takes about sixteen hours to fly to Japan, I hear.	**Nihon e iku no ni wa jūrokujikan gurai kakaru sō desu.**
How long did it take to get used to Japanese food?	**Nihon no tabemono ni nareru no ni dore gurai kakatta n'desu ka.**
I came to Nara (in order) to see a friend.	**Tomodachi ni au tame ni Nara e kimashita.**

You already know **ga, shikashi** and **keredomo** in the sense of 'but', 'although'. **No ni** differs in three respects: (1) it is never used to begin a sentence; (2) even in polite speech it is preceded by a plain form; (3) it is generally more emphatic than the other words. Note also that **no ni** cannot be preceded by **da. Na** must be used instead:

Although she slept for hours she's still tired.	**Nanjikanmo neta no ni mada tsukarete imasu.**
Although I said he mustn't go, he went.	**Itte wa ikenai to itta no ni itta n'desu.**
He said he'd go although he's ill.	**Byōki na no ni iku to itte imashita.**

The context will make clear which of the two meanings of **no ni** is intended.

Exercise 27
Put into Japanese:

1 'Do you like going to see temples?' 'Yes, I do. What about you?'
2 'Have you ever eaten manju?' 'No, I haven't. Why?'

3 We've decided to go by car and not by train.
4 'Do you ever speak Japanese at home?' 'Yes, sometimes we do.'
5 Why is it that he's always late?

CONVERSATION 15a: Culture shock?

Mr Inoue (I) asks Mr Brown if he's experienced a culture shock:

I: Nihon de karuchā shokku o keiken shimashita ka.
B: Sō desu ne, karuchā shokku to iu hodo ja nai [1] desu ga yappari iroiro nareru no ni jikan ga kakarimashita ne.
I: Kotoba toka tabemono toka desu ka.
B: Sō desu ne. Sore kara doko o mite mo kōkoku to ka hyōshiki toka wa mina kanji desu kara saisho wa mekura no yō na ki ga shimashita.
I: Sō deshō. Sore kara nichijō seikatsu de shite mo ii koto to shite wa ikenai koto mo sukoshi wa atta deshō.
B: Sukoshi dake desu. Tatoeba ie no naka de kutsu o haite [2] wa ikenai deshō. Sore kara suwarikata mo chigaimasu ne. Nihon de wa nanjikan mo agura o kaite suwaru [3] koto mo aru deshō. Nareru no ni sore wa jikan ga kakarimashita yo.
I: O-furo no hairikata mo zuibun chigau deshō. O-furo no naka de sekken o tsukatte wa ikenai deshō. Sore kara sen o nuite wa ikenai deshō, ato de minna hairimasu kara ne.

CONVERSATION 15b: 'Have you ever been to Kamikochi?'

Mr Brown tells Mr Inoue about his holiday plans:

B: Inoue-san, Kamikōchi e itta koto wa arimasu ka.
I: Mada nai desu yo. Nagano made shigoto de iku koto wa tokidoki arimasu ga Kamikōchi made wa itte kita koto wa nai desu ne. Dōshite desu ka.
B: Raishū tomodachi to issho ni iku koto ni natte iru n'desu.
I: Kamikōchi o miru no ni chōdo ii jiki deshō ne. Hachigatsu demo suzushikute kimochi ga ii mitai desu ne.
B: Inoue-san, issho ni itte mo ii desu yo.
I: Chotto muri desu. Kaisha no shigoto ga isogashikute kotoshi wa yasumi ga torenai n'desu yo.

Notes:

1. **to iu hodo ja nai desu ga:** 'it's not quite what I'd call a culture shock'.

2. **kutsu o haite:** Japanese uses different words for wear depending on where the article is worn:

wear a hat = **bōshi o kaburu/kaburimasu.**

wear glasses = **megane o kakeru/kakemasu.**

wear a coat, shirt, jacket = **kōto, shatsu, uwagi o kiru/kimasu.**

wear a dress = **doresu o kiru/kimasu.**

wear a skirt, trousers, socks, shoes = **sukāto, zubon, kutsushita, kutsu o haku/ hakimasu.**

wear a watch, tie, scarf, gloves = **tokei, nekutai, mafura, tebukuro o suru/ shimasu.**

3. **agura o kaite:** 'sit cross-legged'. 'Sit on one's knees' is **seiza o suru/shimasu.**

Lesson 16

MAIN POINTS: Comparing things: _A is ... er than B; A is the biggest; A is (not) as ... as B._

CONVERSATIONS: (a) Comparing England and Japan; (b) The doctor's.

102 Comparing things (i)

Consider first the following:

A: _Which is better?_   **Dochira ga ii desu ka.**
B: _The cheap(er) one is better._   **Yasui no ga ii desu.**
A: _Which car do you prefer?_   **Dochira no kuruma ga suki desu ka.**
B: _I prefer the red one._   **Akai no ga suki desu.**

It will be seen that Japanese adjectives have no comparative forms of their own. **Dochira**, 'which (of two)', itself implies a comparative. 'Which is ... er, A or B?' is translated like this:

A: _Which do you prefer, sumo or baseball?_   **Sumō to yakyū to dochira ga suki desu ka.**
B: _I prefer baseball._   **Yakyū ga suki desu ne.**

103 Comparing things (ii)

You need to know two ways of translating 'A is ... er than B'. The first is **A wa B yori ... desu**:

My word processor was cheaper than yours.   **Watashi no wā-puro wa anata no yori yasukatta desu.**

Today's weather is better than yesterday's.   **Kyō no tenki wa kinō yori ii desu ne.**

The second is **B yori A no hō ga ... desu**:

Japanese is easier than Chinese, you know.   **Chūgokugo yori Nihongo no hō ga kantan desu.**

I prefer the Kansai area to the Kanto.   **Kantō yori Kansai no hō ga suki desu.**

The difference between them reflects the difference between **wa** and **ga**. **A wa B yori** is a general statement about **A**. It may be thought of as answering 'Tell me something about **A**'. **B yori A no hō ga** is more emphatic. It emphasizes **A**, and

123

may be thought of as answering 'Which is ... er?'. **Yori** may be omitted:

Summer is better.	**Natsu no hō ga ii desu ne.**
Chieko is prettier.	**Chieko no hō ga kirei desu.**

Both constructions are also used with adverbs:

He speaks faster than I do.	**Kare wa watashi yori hayaku hanashimasu.**
She can sing better than you.	**Anata yori kanojo no hō ga jōzu ni utaemasu.**

Study carefully the following, in which verbs are used:

Playing golf is more fun than staying at home.	**Gorufu o suru no wa uchi ni iru yori tanoshii desu ne.**
Going by train is quicker than walking.	**Aruku yori densha de iku hō ga hayai desu ne.**

When in English 'would' is used, in Japanese the verb placed before **hō** is in the **ta** form, but <u>only</u> in the positive:

It would be easier to walk than to take the bus.	**Basu de iku yori aruite itta hō ga kantan desu.**
It would be cheaper to stay at home.	**Uchi ni ita hō ga yasui desu.**
It would be more sensible not to do that.	**Sō shinai hō ga gōriteki desu yo.**

'Should (not)' and 'should (not) have' are translated by **-ta (-nai) hō ga ii desu** and **-ta (-nai) hō ga yokatta desu** respectively:

You should apologize immediately.	**Sugu ayamatta hō ga ii desu.**
You shouldn't interrupt.	**Kuchi o dasanai hō ga ii desu.**
Perhaps I shouldn't have said that.	**Sō iwanai hō ga yokatta ka mo shiremasen.**
You should have brought your alien registration card.	**Gaijin tōrokushō o motte kita hō ga yokatta desu.**

Exercise 28
Put into Japanese:

1 Do the Japanese work harder than the British?
2 We shouldn't have taken the taxi.
3 In winter Japan is colder than Britain, you know.
4 Which is faster, the bullet train or the new French train?
5 Drinking at a bar is more fun than drinking at home.

104 Comparing things (iii)

'Much ... er', 'far ... er' may be translated by either **motto** or **zutto**:

A: *That car is much faster than this.* — Ano kuruma wa kore yori motto hayai desu yo.

B: *It's much more expensive.* — Zutto takai n'desu.
You speak far more fluently than I do. — Watashi yori zutto ryūchō ni hanashimasu.

'A little ... er' is **(mō) chotto ...** or **(mō) sukoshi ...** :

It's a little colder than yesterday. — Kinō yori sukoshi samui desu.
Prices in Tokyo are a little higher than in London. — Tōkyō no bukka wa Rondon yori chotto takai desu.

105 Superlatives

There is no special superlative form of the adjective. Superlatives are made by adding **mottomo** or **ichiban** ('number 1'):

Learning kanji is one of the most enjoyable things. — Kanji o oboeru no wa mottomo tanoshii koto no hitotsu desu.
She's the best at table tennis. — Takkyū ga ichiban jōzu na no wa kanojo desu.

'Which is the ... est, A, B, or C?' requires **naka** or **uchi**:

A: *Which is the prettiest, Nagasaki, Yokohama or Hakodate?* — Nagasaki to Yokohama to Hakodate no naka de doko ga ichiban kirei desu ka.

B: *Isn't Nagasaki the prettiest of them?* — Sono* naka de Nagasaki wa ichiban kirei ja nai desu ka.

*Sono, as here, means 'of it/he/she/them' as well as 'that'.

Note the use of the particle **de** to mean 'in':

She's the cleverest pupil in the class. — Kanojo wa kurasu de mottomo atama ga ii seito desu.

106 'How much ... ?' 'How ... is it?' 'It's this ...'

'How (much) ... ?' is **dore hodo, dore gurai** or **dore dake**:

How much do you need?	**Dore gurai irimasu ka.**
How much can you eat?	**Dore dake (takusan) taberemasu ka.**
How tired are you?	**Dore hodo tsukarete imasu ka.**

Study the following expressions with adjectives and adverbs:

How late is it?	**Dore gurai osoi desu ka.**
How fast does it go?	**Dore hodo hayaku hashirimasu ka.**
How big is it?	**Dore dake ōkii desu ka.**

'This big', 'that much', etc. are translated by **kore** (or **sore, are**), **hodo, gurai** or **dake** plus an adjective or adverb. **Hodo** is used more in negative sentences:

Was it about this big?	**Kore gurai ōkikatta n'desu ka.**
It wasn't that good, you know.	**Sore hodo yoku nakatta n'desu yo.**

Learn also the following: **Donna ni** asks 'how?' (meaning 'to what extent?'), and is answered by **konna ni** ('this, to this extent'), **sonna ni** or **anna ni** ('that, to that extent').

A: *How big is it?*	**Donna ni ōkii n'desu ka.**
B: *It's not that big.*	**Sonna ni ōkiku nai n'desu yo.**

107 'As ... as ...'

Gurai and **hodo** both appear in 'as ... as ...' sentences. **A wa B hodo ...** is used most in negative sentences. Study the following:

I'm not as clever as him.	**Watashi wa kare hodo atama ga yoku nai desu.**
Today isn't as hot as yesterday.	**Kyō wa kinō hodo atsuku nai desu ne.**

In positive sentences, <u>A</u> **wa** <u>B</u> **to onaji gurai ...** is perhaps the most common:

Is Japan (about) as big as Britain?	**Nihon wa Igirisu to onaji gurai ōkii desu ka.**
He's as bad at Japanese as I am.	**Kare wa watashi to onaji gurai Nihongo ga heta desu.**

'As ... as possible' is **dekiru dake** plus an adverb or adjective:

Please come as quickly as possible.	**Dekiru dake hayaku kite kudasai.**
Go and get as cheap a one as possible.	**Dekiru dake yasui no o katte kite kudasai.**

Exercise 29

Put into Japanese:

1 He drinks about as much as I do.
2 You shouldn't have said that.
3 'Which do you like the best?' 'My favourite one is that blue one.'
4 'How big was the fish? Was it this big?' 'No, it wasn't that big, it was a bit smaller than that.'
5 I'm not as tall as my big brother, but I'm (about) as strong as he is.

CONVERSATION 16a: Comparisons

Mr Inoue and Mr Brown compare Britain and Japan:

B: Inoue-san, Nihon to Eikoku to menseki wa dotchi[1] ga hiroi ka shitte imasu ka. Eikoku no hō ga sukoshi hiroi desu ka.
I: Chigaimasu yo. Eikoku wa Nihon hodo hiroku nai desu yo.
B: Ā, sō desu ka. Shikashi jinkō wa Nihon no hō ga zutto ōi deshō?
I: Sore wa sō desu. Eikoku no nibai[2] ijō[3] ōi n'ja nai desu ka. Sore kara, Nihon no hotondo ga yama na no de sumeru[4] tokoro wa sonna ni nai n'desu yo.
B: Sō desu ne, jinkō mitsudo wa totemo takai n'desu ne.
I: Eikoku ni wa yama to iu hodo no mono[5] wa nai mitai desu ne.
B: Sō demo nai desu yo[6]. Fuji-san hodo takai no wa nai ka mo shiremasen ga Uēruzu toka Sukottorando toka ni wa yama wa ikutsumo arimasu yo.
I: Hontō desu ka[7]. Sore kara kikō wa zuibun chigaimasu ne. Nihon wa shiki ga hakkiri shite ite[8] Eikoku wa natsu demo fuyu mitai na hi ga takusan aru sō desu ne.
B: Sono tōri desu. Shikashi Eikoku ni tsuyu toka taifū toka wa nai desu.
I: Urayamashii desu ne. Eikoku no hō ga anzen na yō desu ne.
B: Kazan mo nai shi jishin mo arimasen kara ne!

CONVERSATION 16b: The doctor's

Mr Brown goes to the doctor's (I):

I: Dō shimashita ka.
B: I ga itakute tamaranai[9] n'desu.
I: Sore wa ikemasen ne. Itsu goro kara desu ka.
B: Mikka hodo mae kara desu.
I: Sore ja, shatsu o nuide soko de yoko ni natte kudasai ... Rentogen o totta hō ga ii desu ne.

Several minutes later:

I: Tada no ichōen dake desu. Shinpai wa irimasen. Shibaraku no aida o-sake mo tabako mo hikaeta hō ga ii desu ne.

B: Gohan wa futsū ni tabete mo ii desu ka.

I: Takusan tabesuginai hō ga ii desu yo. Sore kara karai mono mo hikaeta hō ga ii desu ne. Kusuri o agemasu kara shokuzen ni nonde kudasai.

B: Arigatō gozaimasu.

I: O-daiji ni.

Notes:

1. **dotchi:** abbreviation of **dochira**.

2. **no nibai ... ōi:** 'twice as large'; **bai** is the counter for 'times'.

3. **ijō:** 'more than'.

4. **sumeru tokoro:** 'places where people can live'.

5. **to iu hodo no mono:** 'there is nothing worthy of the name mountain'; lit. 'of the extent that you'd call it a mountain'.

6. **sō demo nai desu yo:** 'that's not quite true, you know'.

7. **hontō desu ka:** 'Really?'

8. **hakkiri shite ite: hakkiri suru/shimasu** is 'be clear'; **hakkiri saseru/ sasemasu** is 'make clear'. See Lesson 19.

9. **itakute tamaranai:** 'unbearably painful' (*lit.* 'painful and I can't bear it').

Lesson 17

MAIN POINTS: Some time expressions: *before/after/while/when*, etc.
CONVERSATIONS: (a) Climbing Mount Fuji; (b) A Japanese lesson.

108 'While' — *-nagara*

If the subject of both verbs in a 'while' sentence is the same, then **-nagara** is used attached to the stem of the verb:

tabemasu → tabe → tabenagara
shimasu → shi → shinagara

He always studies while he watches the TV.	**Itsumo terebi o minagara benkyō shimasu.**
She was looking at the magazine while having a meal.	**Gohan o tabenagara zasshi o mite imashita.**

109 'While' — *aida*

When the subjects of the two parts of the 'while' sentence are different, **aida (ni)** is used. The tense of the verb which precedes **aida** is generally the same as in English:

We played cards while the children were asleep.	**Kodomo ga nete ita aida toranpu o yarimashita.**
There's something I want to ask you while you're here.	**Koko ni irassharu aida o-kiki shitai koto ga arimasu ga.**
While I was at university, my elder brother was in Korea.	**Watashi ga daigaku ni itte ita aida ani ga Kankoku ni imashita.**

Study these miscellaneous expressions involving **aida**:

Where were you during the war?	**Sensō no aida doko ni irasshatta n'desu ka.**
I haven't seen her for a long time.	**Nagai aida atte imasen.**
He should be here between six and seven o'clock.	**Rokuji kara shichiji no aida ni kuru hazu desu.**
Nagoya is between Osaka and Tokyo.	**Nagoya wa Ōsaka to Tōkyō to no aida ni arimasu.**

110 'After' — *ato*

In addition to the **te** form plus **kara, ato (de)** is often used (always with the plain past):

After you've finished your meal, do come round, won't you?	**Gohan ga owatta ato (de) asobi ni kite kudasai ne.**
After I had gone to bed, my brother phoned.	**Watashi ga neta ato o-nī-san kara denwa ga arimashita.**

Study these additional 'after' phrases:

The concert began after six o'clock.	**Konsāto wa rokuji sugi ni hajimarimashita.**
After ten minutes we set off.	**Juppun tatte kara dekakemashita.**

Study these miscellaneous phrases with **ato**:

I'll do it afterwards.	**Ato de shimasu.**
What happened after that?	**Sono ato wa dō narimashita ka.**
After the lesson, we walked home.	**Jugyō no ato aruite kaerimashita.**
There are only two minutes left.	**Ato nifun shika arimasen.**

111 'Before' — *mae*

Irrespective of the English tense, <u>only</u> the present tense of the Japanese verb can be used with **mae (ni)**:

Before I leave Japan, I definitely want to climb Mt. Fuji.	**Nihon o tatsu mae ni zehi Fuji-san ni noboritai desu ne.**
They went out for many years before they got married.	**Kekkon suru mae ni nannenkan mo tsukiatte imashita.**

Study these miscellaneous expressions using **mae**:

Where did you live before (that)?	**(Sono) mae ni doko ni sunde irasshaimashita ka.**
Before the war, the cost of living was much cheaper.	**Sensō no mae bukka wa motto yasukatta desu.**
I gave it to a friend the other day.	**Kono mae tomodachi ni agemashita.**
It's a photo of my last girlfriend.	**Watashi no mae no kanojo no shashin desu.**

112 'When' — *toki*

Any tense of the verb or adjective may be used with **toki (ni)**:

He was already there when I got to the airport.	**Watashi ga kūkō ni tsuita toki kare wa mō kite imashita.**
When I was going out with her, we always went to that bar.	**Kanojo to tsukiatte ita toki itsumo ano bā ni ikimashita.**
I get very tired when it's humid like today.	**Kyō mitai ni mushiatsui toki ni taihen tsukaremasu.**

Study these miscellaneous expressions involving **toki**:

Which company were you working for then?	**Sono toki doko no kaisha ni tsutomete ita n'desu ka.**
When I was a student, I played rugby.	**Gakusei no toki ragubī o yarimashita.**
There are times when I think I'd like to give up Japanese.	**Nihongo o yametai to omou toki mo arimasu yo.**

Exercise 30
Put into Japanese:

1 Before you got married, did you go out with lots of girls?
2 Was that before you went to Japan or after you'd got there?
3 While they were talking, I listened to the news.
4 While you're out, I think I'll probably watch the TV.
5 We went there once before. Don't you remember?

113 'When', 'once', 'if' — *to*

To is slightly different from **toki** since it is used to translate 'whenever ..., ...'; 'when/once/if ..., (then inevitably) ...'. With **to**, the verb may be in either the plain or **masu** form.

To is only used with the present. Also **to** will often be followed by some adverb such as **itsumo** ('always') or **kanarazu** ('inevitably'). Study carefully these examples:

Whenever I phone her she's out.	**Kanojo ni denwa suru to itsumo rusu desu.**
Whenever I went to that coffee shop I bumped into him.	**Ano kissaten ni iku to kanarazu kare ni deaimashita.**
When (once) you start to learn Japanese you can't stop.	**Nihongo o narai-hajimeru to yamerarenaku narimasu.**

Once I've got into the swing of things, I'm O.K.	Chōshi ga deru to daijōbu desu yo.
If you turn left here you can't miss it.	Koko o hidari e magarimasu to, sugu wakarimasu.

'As soon as' may be expressed by ... **to sugu** ... (or **te kara sugu**):

Let's check in as soon as we get to the airport.	Kūkō ni tsuku to sugu chekku-in shimashō.
As soon as I got home, I made a meal and went to bed.	Uchi e kaette kara sugu gohan o tsukutte nemashita.

114 'Just about to'; 'has/have just'

The noun **tokoro** is used to say 'just about to ...', 'has just ...'. It may be used with the adverbs **ima** ('just now') and/or **chōdo** ('just'). Study the following, noting the tenses:

We're about to go home now.	Mō kaeru tokoro desu.
I was just about to phone.	Chōdo denwa o kakeru tokoro deshita.
I've just got back.	Ima chōdo kaette kita tokoro desu.
I had just started to learn Japanese then.	Sono toki wa Nihongo o narai-hajimeta tokoro deshita.

In order to say, for example, 'just as I was about to go out, the phone rang', the plain form of **mashō** (see Lesson 11) plus **to suru** is generally used with **tokoro, to,** or **toki**. Study the following:

I was just about to go out when the phone rang.	Chōdo dekakeyō to suru tokoro (e) denwa ga narimashita.
Just as I was about to go to bed the bomb went off.	Chōdo neyō to suru to bakudan ga bakuhatsu shita n'desu.
I was just about to phone the police, when she came back.	Chōdo keisatsu ni denwa shiyō to shita toki ni kanojo ga kaette kita n'desu.

Note here these other miscellaneous expressions involving **tokoro**:

I saw the cars collide.	Kuruma ga shōtotsu suru tokoro o mimashita.
Recently I've been really busy.	Kono tokoro sugoku isogashii n'desu.

115 Some other common time expressions

'Until' – **made**:

I shan't go to bed until I've learnt it off by heart.	**Kore o anki suru made nemasen.**
Wait until you're a bit bigger.	**Mō chotto ōkiku naru made matte kudasai.**

'In the middle of' – **saichū**:

I'm in the middle of writing a letter.	**Tegami o kaite iru saichū desu.**
I was in the middle of reading the comic.	**Manga o yonde iru saichū deshita.**

'Whenever' – **tabi**:

This is synonymous with ... **to itsumo ...**:

Whenever I go by train I leave something behind.	**Densha ni noru tabi ni nanika wasuremono o shimasu yo.**

'Before' – **uchi**:

'Before' will be translated by **uchi** plus a negative (rather than **mae**) when the idea is that 'something is going to happen soon, but before it does ...':

Let's tidy up before Mum gets home.	**Okāsan ga kaette konai uchi ni sōji shimashō ne.**
Eat it before it gets cold.	**Samenai uchi ni tabete kudasai.**

'As far as ...', 'as long as ...' – **kagiri**:

As far as I (can) remember, he's not married.	**Watashi ga oboete iru kagiri kare wa mada kekkon shite imasen yo.**
As long as you tell no one, I don't mind.	**Dare ni mo iwanai kagiri kamaimasen.**

Exercise 31
Put into Japanese:

1 What are you going to be doing while you're over here?
2 When I saw the girl he was going out with, I knew why he loved her.
3 Once you get to Japan, you won't want to come back home again.
4 I haven't eaten sushi for a long time.
5 Whenever I drink whisky and wine I get a hangover.

CONVERSATION 17a: Climbing Mt. Fuji

Mr Brown has been invited to the Inoues' for dinner and is telling them what he'd like to do before leaving Japan:

Mrs I: Jon-san, shokuji no yōi ga dekimashita. Samenai uchi ni dōzo o-meshiagari kudasai[1].

B: Itadakimasu.

Mrs I: Hai, dōzo.

Mr I: Jon-san, kikoku suru made ato wazuka[2] desu ne. Nihon o tatsu mae ni hoka ni shitai koto toka ikitai tokoro wa nai desu ka.

B: Arimasu. Kono mae shinkansen ni notte Fuji-san no mae o tōtta toki ni zehi ichido nobotte mitai[3] to omoimashita ga.

Mr I: Sō desu ka. Sore wa ii kangae desu ne.

B: Inoue-san wa nobotta koto wa arimasu ka.

Mr I: Wakai toki ni ichido dake arimasu yo.

B: Dō deshita ka. Yokatta desu ka.

Mr I: Nobotta ato no kimochi wa totemo yokatta desu ga nobotte iru aida wa tsura katta desu ne.

B: Sō desu ka. Igirisu ni kaeru mae ni zehi ichido nobotte mitai desu ne ... Gochisō-sama deshita.

Mrs I: O-somatsu-sama deshita.

CONVERSATION 17b: A Japanese lesson

The teacher (S) asks Tom (T), John (J) and Mary (M) some questions:

S: Kyō wa 'mae', 'ato', 'toki', 'to' nado no renshū o shimashō ne. Mazu 'mae' o tsukatte bunshō o tsukutte mimashō. Hai, Tomu-san, nandemo ii desu kara dōzo.

T: Etto, 'Nihon ni kuru mae wa Nihongo wa dekinakatta n'desu ga ima wa sukoshi dekiru yō ni narimashita.'

S: Ii desu ne. Kondo wa 'ato' o tsukatte bunshō o tsukutte mite kudasai.

J: 'Jugyō ga owatta ato de tomodachi to bā ni ikimasu. Sono ato ni mō hitotsu no bā e ikimasu.'

S: Kekkō desu[4]. Tsugi wa 'toki' desu ne.

M: 'Kono mae bā e itta toki ni o-sake o nondari uta o utattari shimashita.'[5]

S: Ii desu yo.

T: Mō hitotsu tsukutte ii desu ka.

S: Hai, dōzo.

T: 'Chōdo ie o deyō to shita toki ni Merī kara denwa ga arimashita.'

S: Totemo ii bunshō desu ne. Saigo ni 'to' no renshū desu ne. Hai, Jon-san.

J: 'Jugyō ga owaru to itsumo tomodachi to nomi ni ikimasu. Soshite, nomi ni iku to itsumo yopparatte kaette kimasu.'
S: Ii desu ne.

Notes:

1. **o-meshiagari kudasai:** 'please eat'; **meshiagaru/meshiagarimasu** is an honorific form of both **taberu/tabemasu** and **nomu/nomimasu** and is therefore used only of others to whom one wishes to show special respect; the form **o-meshiagari kudasai** is an honorific imperative. See Lesson 20.

2. **ato wazuka:** 'there's only a little time left'.

3. **nobotte mitai:** the **te** form plus **miru/mimasu** means 'do something and see' or 'try doing'.

4. **Kekkō desu:** here it means 'that'll do nicely'.

5. **o-sake o nondari, uta o utattari shimashita:** 'I drank alcohol and sang songs'; when describing a series of actions which are not consecutive the so-called **tari** form is used. This is formed by adding **ri** to the **ta** form. Usually the last of a series of **tari** forms is followed by **suru/shimasu: terebi o mitari toranpu o shitari shimashita,** 'I watched the TV. and played cards.'

Lesson 18

MAIN POINTS: *If* clauses; some related expressions.
CONVERSATIONS: (a) 'What should I do?' (b) 'We should have taken a taxi!'

116 'If' — the *ba* form

Before considering the applications of the various 'if' forms, we must consider their formation:

(1) The **ba** form of verbs

All verbs (except **da/desu**) have their **ba** form made in the same way: the final syllable, **-u, -ku, -gu, -su, -tsu, -nu, -bu, -mu, -ru** (see column 3 of the table on page 9), is changed to the corresponding syllable in column 4:

arau → **arae**
kaku → **kake**
oyogu → **oyoge**
taberu → **tabere**

To this **ba** is added. Check you can make the **ba** forms of the following:

yomu	→	**yomeba**
kuru		**kureba**
suru		**sureba**
deru		**dereba**
matsu		**mateba**
iu		**ieba**

Da/desu does not have a **ba** form. Instead, **nara** is used, both with nouns and **na** adjectives: 'if I were you' (lit. 'if it were me') is **watashi nara;** 'if I'm free' is **hima nara.**

(2) The **ba** form of **i** adjectives, of the **tai** form, and of negatives

In all these cases, the final **i** syllable is changed to **-kereba**. Check you can make the **ba** form of the following:

atatakai	→	**atatakakereba**
suzushii		**suzushikereba**
ikitai		**ikitakereba**

136

konai	**konakereba**
shitaku nai	**shitaku nakereba**
ja nai	**ja nakereba**
oishii	**oishikereba**
oishiku nai	**oishiku nakereba**

117 'If' — the *tara* form

The **tara** form of ALL verbs, without exception, is made by adding **-ra** to the **ta** form. Check you know the **tara** forms of the following:

iku	→	**ittara**
iru ('be')		**itara**
suru		**shitara**
da		**dattara**
kuru		**kitara**

While this **tara** form *is* found in polite speech, an extra degree of politeness is given by adding **-ra** to the **mashita** form of any verb:

arimashita	→	**arimashitara**
irasshaimashita		**irasshaimashitara**
deshita		**deshitara**

The **tara** form of **i** adjectives, of the **-tai** form and of the negative is made by adding **-ra** to their past tense. Check you know the **tara** form of the following:

atsui	→	**atsukattara**
kaeritai		**kaeritakattara**
ōkii		**ōkikattara**
dekinai		**dekinakattara**
nai		**nakattara**
oishiku nai		**oishiku nakattara**

118 'If' — application

Study the following examples, paying particular attention to the tenses:

If the plane crashes, we will all die, won't we? **Hikōki ga tsuiraku sureba (shitara) minna shinimasu ne.**

If the bomb blew up on the plane, **Hikōki no naka de bakudan ga**

(the plane) <u>would</u> crash.	**bakuhatsu sureba (shitara) tsuiraku suru deshō.**
If the wing <u>were</u> to come off, the plane couldn't fly.	**Tsubasa ga torereba (toretara) hikōki ga tobenaku naru deshō.**
If they <u>hadn't</u> shot the terrorist, she <u>would have</u> escaped.	**Terorisuto o uchikorosanakattara nigeta deshō.**

Moshi very frequently introduces 'if' clauses of all types:

If it's no good what shall we do?	**Moshi dame dattara dō shimashō.**
If I hadn't run I wouldn't have fallen over.	**Moshi hashiranakattara korobanakatta deshō.**

Another common type of 'if' clause has **n'dattara** or, more politely, **n'deshitara** attached to a present or past plain form. The meaning is 'if, in fact, ...', or 'if it's the case that ...':

If you are, in fact, coming to London do let me know.	**Moshi Rondon ni irassharu n'deshitara oshiete kudasai.**
If it's the case that he's decided to give up Japanese, what shall we do?	**Moshi Nihongo o yameru koto ni shita n'dattara dō shimashō ka.**

In many of the examples given above **deshō** has followed the final verb, but there are various other possibilities, such as **ka mo shiremasen**, or **darō to omoimasu**.

Exercise 32
Put into Japanese:

1 If I were you, I think I'd refuse.
2 If it rains tomorrow, let's not go.
3 If you had come ten minutes earlier, you might have caught the train.
4 If it's clean and new I'll buy it.
5 If you were to phone him now, he'll probably be in.

119 Miscellaneous expressions with *tara* and *ba*

Suggestions can be made with the **tara** form plus **dō** or, where extra politeness is demanded, **ikaga**:

Why don't you come along too, Kunio?	**Issho ni kitara dō desu ka, Kunio.**
Why don't you go too, Professor?	**Issho ni irasshaimashitara ikaga desu ka Sensei?**

Asking what one should do, where one should go, etc. may be done with either the **tara** form or the **ba** form followed by **ii desu ka** (lit. 'it'll be good if we do what/go where?'). Note also how to say, for example, 'I don't know what to say':

What should I say to him?	Nani o ittara (ieba) ii desu ka.
I don't know what to say.	Nani o ittara ii ka wakarimasen.
A: *How should I explain it?*	Dō setsumei shitara (sureba) ii desu ka.
B: *I'm not sure how you should explain it.*	Dō setsumei shitara ii ka chotto wakarimasen.

Note that 'I wish ...', 'I hope ...' is **ii n'desu (ga) (ne)** added to one of the 'if' forms:

I wish it would finish quickly.	Hayaku owattara ii n'desu ga ne.
I wish it were cheaper.	Mō chotto yasukereba ii n'desu ga.
I hope I don't have to go.	Ikanakute mo ii n'dattara ii n'desu ga.
I wish he hadn't come.	Ano hito ga konakattara yokatta n'desu ga ne.
I wish he hadn't said that.	Sore o iwanakereba yokatta n'desu ne.
I hope they're on time.	Ma ni aeba ii n'desu ga.

Expressions of the type 'the more ... the more...' are made with the form **sureba suru hodo ...** (lit. 'if one does something, to the extent one does it, it is ...'). Study carefully the following:

The more you speak in Japanese, the more fluent you'll become.	Nihongo de hanaseba hanasu hodo perapera ni narimasu yo.
The more nuclear weapons there are, the more dangerous the world becomes.	Kakuheiki ga ōku nareba naru hodo kono yo no naka ga abunaku narimasu ne.
The less you eat the thinner you'll get.	Tabenakereba tabenai hodo hosoku narimasu.

It should also be noted that the **tara** form is frequently used (1) to mean 'when', and (2) in negative 'must' clauses. Pay attention to the tenses:

When you've finished please tell me.	Owattara oshiete kudasai.
When I woke up this morning I had a bad headache.	Kesa okitara atama ga sugoku itakatta n'desu.
He said you mustn't talk.	Hanashitara dame da to itte imashita.
You mustn't smoke here.	Koko de tabako o suttara dame desu yo.

Exercise 33

Put into Japanese:

1 Why don't you learn how to write Japanese as well?
2 I didn't know what to do or where to go.
3 I hope the weather'll get better tomorrow.
4 I wish I hadn't bought that car.
5 The longer you stay in Japan, the more you'll get to like it.

CONVERSATION 18a: 'What should I do?'

Mr Brown asks Mr Inoue how he can improve his Japanese fluency:

B: Inoue-san, Nihon ni kite kara mō sankagetsu tatte iru[1] no ni Nihongo ga zenzen jōtatsu shite inai yō na ki ga shimasu ga.
I: Jōtatsu shite inai wake ja nai desu yo[2]. De mo, mō ni, san-kagetsu shitara[3] kitto motto umaku naru to omoimasu.
B: Demo motto hayaku jōzu ni naru ni wa dō shitara ii to omoimasu ka.
I: Sō desu ne. Tango no mondai nara mainichi nyūsu o kiite, shiranai kotoba o minna kakitottara dō desu ka. Sō sureba tango no kazu ga fueru deshō.
B: De mo, dō shitara motto ryūchō ni shabereru yō ni naru no deshō.
I: Sore wa jikan no mondai desu ne.
B: Nihon ni kuru mae ni motto benkyō shite okeba[4] yokatta n'desu ne.

CONVERSATION 18b: 'We should have taken a taxi!'

Mr Inoue and Mr Brown are looking for an address:

B: Moshi takushī de itta n'dattara mō tsuite ita ka mo shiremasen ne.
I: Iya, mō sugu tsukimasu.
B: Demo chizu o kaite moraeba yokatta n'ja nai desu ka.
I: Iya, chizu nanka[5] irimasen ... Koko wa Aoyamadōri deshō. Soshitara koko o massugu itte, mittsume no shingō o hidari ni magaru to 2 ban da to omoimasu yo.
B: Sō desu ka. Demo dareka ni kiite mitara dō desu ka.
I: Ii desu. Ii desu[6]. Sugu chikaku desu kara ...

After a short while, they're lost:

B: Yappari futatsume no shingō o magareba yokatta n'ja nai desu ka.
I: Sō ka mo shiremasen ne. Ato gofun gurai shite mitsukaranakattara takushī o hiroimashō ne.
B: *(to himself)* Attara ne.

Five minutes later, to a taxi driver:

I: Aoyama 1 chōme 2 ban 6 gō[7] made o-negai shimasu.

Notes:

1. **kara sankagetsu tatte iru:** 'three months have passed since ...', 'I've been here for three months'. **Tatsu/tachimasu** means 'pass' (of time).

2. **wake ja nai desu:** 'it's not the case that'.

3. **ni, san-kagetsu shitara:** 'in another two or three months', lit. 'if/when another two or three months have passed'; **suru/shimasu** here is used like **tatsu/ tachimasu.**

4. **benkyō shite okeba yokatta:** 'I should have studied'; when an action is performed for some future event **te oku/okimasu** is often used. Among very common phrases involving **te oku/okimasu** are **kangaete okimashō** ('Let's think about it') and **(asoko ni) oite oite kudasai** ('Leave it there').

5. **chizu nan ka:** 'a map or anything', informal.

6. **Ii desu, ii desu:** 'it's fine as it is', 'we don't need to (ask anyone)'.

7. **Aoyama 1 chōme 2 ban 6 gō:** the full address would be **Tōkyō-to, Minato-ku, Aoyama 1 chōme 2 ban 6 gō**; very few streets have street names in Japan, and the best way to reach your destination is by asking a policeman! The address-system in Japan works in sections rather than streets and begins with the largest unit, here **Tōkyō** city; **Minato-ku** (Minato 'ward') is a section of Tokyo; **Aoyama** is a section of Minato, **1 chōme (itchōme)** is a section of **Aoyama, 2 ban** is a subsection of **1 chōme,** and **6 gō** is the 6th plot in **2 ban.**

Lesson 19

MAIN POINTS: The passive, the causative and the passive causative.
CONVERSATIONS: (a) A hangover; (b) An arranged marriage.

120 The passive (i)

The passive is formed in the case of all verbs (except **suru/shimasu**) from the negative plain form. Study the following:

Group 1 verbs require **rareru**:
tabenai → tabe → taberareru
minai → mi → mirareru

Group 2 verbs require **reru**:
kakanai → kaka → kakareru
shiranai → shira → shirareru
kawanai → kawa → kawareru

Irregular verbs:
konai → ko → korareru
suru/shimasu → sareru

The passives of all verbs now function as Group 1 verbs.

121 The passive (ii)

As in English, the Japanese passive is used with <u>transitive</u> verbs. The human agent of the action, when expressed, is generally followed by **ni**. Consider the following:

I hear that the reporter was kidnapped by terrorists.	**Ano kisha wa terorisuto ni yūkai sareta sō desu.**
The politician was arrested by the police.	**Ano seijika wa keisatsu ni taiho saremashita.**
I was told off by the boss.	**Bosu ni shikararemashita.**

The passive is used frequently with verbs of asking and saying, where English may not always use a passive:

They asked me (J: I was asked) to interpret.	**Tsūyaku suru yō ni tanomaremashita.**
We were told to be there by twelve, you know.	**Jūniji made ni kuru yō ni iwareta n'desu yo.**

142

Who told you?	**Dare ni iwareta n'desu ka.**

The agent of the passive verb can also be followed by **ni yotte** (lit. 'by means of') or **kara** ('from'), particularly when the use of **ni** may lead to ambiguities:

I was invited to the party by my friend.	**Tomodachi kara pātei* ni shōtai sareta n'desu.**
It's a book written by Mishima.	**Mishima ni yotte kakareta hon desu.**

*Pronounce as in English 'party'.

122 The passive (iii)

There are two other important uses of the passive. The first is sometimes called the 'passive of inconvenience' because it is often, but not always, used in the sense of 'having something done to one against one's will'. Study carefully the following pairs of sentences:

(He) asked me lots of things.	**Takusan no koto o kikimashita.**
I was asked lots of things (by him).	**Kare ni takusan no koto o kikare-mashita.**
(They) checked my baggage.	**Nimotsu o shirabemashita.**
I had my baggage checked.	**Nimotsu o shiraberaremashita.**
Somebody stole my passport.	**Dareka ga watashi no pasupōto o nusumimashita.**
I had my passport stolen.	**Pasupōto o nusumaremashita.**
He corrected my Japanese.	**Nihongo o naoshimashita** (or **naoshite kuremashita**).
I had my Japanese corrected.	**Nihongo o naosaremashita.**

The second special use of the passive is with <u>intransitive</u> verbs. This passive also often expresses 'inconvenience'. Study carefully the following pairs of sentences, of which the first is neutral:

His father died.	**Otōsan ga shinimashita.**
He suffered the death of his father.	**Otōsan ni shinaremashita.**
A visitor came.	**O-kyaku-san ga kimashita.**
A visitor came (it was inconvenient) (J: I was 'come' by a visitor).	**O-kyaku-san ni koraremashita.**
The baby kept crying.	**Akachan ga zutto naite imashita.**
The baby kept crying (it was inconvenient) (J: I was 'kept cried' by the baby).	**Akachan ni zutto nakarete imashita.**

Exercise 34

Put into Japanese:

1 Our house was broken into (J: entered) by a burglar.
2 I had my fingerprints taken when I went to get my Alien Registration Card.
3 We were all told off for being late.
4 I was asked why I gave up Japanese.
5 He was told he would probably soon die.

123 The passive (iv)

'Has been done' ('is in a state of having been done') is translated not by a passive but by **te aru/arimasu:**

Has the beer been bought?	**Bīru wa katte aru n'desu ka.**
Everybody's been told.	**Minna ni itte arimasu yo.**
The letter has been sent.	**Tegami wa okutte arimasu.**

Note here the use of **kaite aru/arimasu:**

A: *What does it say on that signpost?*	**Ano hyōshiki ni wa nan to kaite aru n'desu ka.**
B: *It says 'No entry'.*	**Shinnyū kinshi to kaite aru n'desu.**
It says in the dictionary 'foreigner'.	**Jisho ni wa 'gaijin' to kaite arimasu.**

124 Transitive and intransitive verbs

It will be useful to mention here related pairs of transitive and intransitive verbs and some of their uses. First study the pairs in the following, by no means comprehensive, list:

open *vt.*	**akeru/akemasu**	(be) open	**aku/akimasu**
collect *vt.*	**atsumeru/atsumemasu**	collect, (be) collected	**atsumaru/ atsumarimasu**
put in *vt.*	**ireru/iremasu**	go in	**hairu/hairimasu**
close *vt.*	**shimeru/shimemasu**	(be) close(d)	**shimaru/ shimarimasu**
stop *vt.*	**tomeru/tomemasu**	stop, stay	**tomaru/ tomarimasu**
attach, turn on *vt.*	**tsukeru/tsukemasu**	(be) attached to, go on	**tsuku/tsukimasu**

build *vt.*	tateru/tatemasu	stand	tatsu/tachimasu
convey *vt.*	tsutaeru/tsutaemasu	(be) convey(ed)	tsutawaru/ tsutawarimasu
hand over *vt.*	watasu/watashimasu	cross over	wataru/ watarimasu

Care is needed in the use of these verbs. Study the examples with three of the most common of these pairs:

I'll open the door.	Doa o akemasu.
The door won't open.	Doa wa akimasen.
I'm opening the door.	Doa o akete imasu.
The door is open.	Doa wa aite imasu.
Has the door been opened?	Doa wa akete arimasu ka.

I'll put it in.	Iremasu.
It won't go in (fit).	Hairimasen.
I'm putting it in.	Irete imasu.
It is in.	Haitte imasu.
Has it been put in?	Irete arimasu ka.

I'll turn the radio on.	Rajio o tsukemasu.
The radio won't go on.	Rajio wa tsukimasen.
I'm putting the radio on.	Rajio o tsukete imasu.
The radio is on.	Rajio wa tsuite imasu.
Has the radio been put on?	Rajio wa tsukete arimasu ka.

The difference between **aite iru** and **akete aru,** between **haitte iru** and **irete aru,** and between **tsuite iru** and **tsukete aru** is that while both the former and the latter in each case describe a state, the latter implies more emphatically the existence of an agent.

125 The causative (i)

The causatives of all verbs (except **suru/shimasu**) are conveniently formed from the negative plain form:

Group 1 verbs require **saseru:**
tabenai → tabe → tabesaseru
tsukenai → tsuke → tsukesaseru

Group 2 verbs require **seru:**
ikanai → ika → ikaseru
yomanai → yoma → yomaseru
kawanai → kawa → kawaseru

Irregular verbs:
konai → ko → kosaseru
suru/shimasu → saseru

126 The causative (ii)

There are two uses of the causative. The first is 'let somebody do ...'. The second is 'make somebody do ...'. The object of the letting or making is always an inferior of the speaker.

When the verb is <u>intransitive</u> and the object of the letting or making is expressed, the difference is often brought out by the use of the particle **o** for 'make', and the particle **ni** for 'let'. Consider the following:

You must make your husband work more.	**Danna-san o motto hatarakasenakereba narimasen.**
Please don't make me laugh.	**Watashi o warawasenaide kudasai.**
You shouldn't cause people trouble.	**Hito o komarasete wa ikemasen.**
Let him go.	**Kare ni ikasete kudasai.**

When the verb is <u>transitive</u> even if the person is being <u>made</u> to do something, rather than <u>allowed</u> to do something, that person is followed by the particle **ni**. The context will make it clear to the listener what is intended. Consider the following:

I don't want to let my daughter read those comics.	**Musume ni sonna manga o yomasetaku nai desu yo.**
You should make your husband wash the dishes.	**Danna-san ni o-sara o arawaseta hō ga ii desu yo.**

127 The causative (iii)

The causative is used with **kudasaru/kudasaimasu** (and **kureru/kuremasu**) and **itadaku/itadakimasu** (and **morau/moraimasu**), in order to ask permission in a polite way, either from persons of superior status or from persons to whom one wishes, for whatever reason, to show respect:

Please let me do it (for you).	**Dōzo sō sasete kudasai.**
May I (J: Would you be kind enough to let me) use the phone?	**Denwa o tsukawasete kudasaimasu ka.**
I should like to (J: I'd like to get you to let me) say a word.	**Hitokoto iwasete itadakitai n'desu.**
May I (J: can I get you to let me) take tomorrow off?	**Ashita yasumasete itadakemasu ka.**

128 The passive causative

The passive causative (i.e. 'is made to', 'is allowed to') of all verbs is formed from the causative, but the most common form for Group 2 verbs is not quite the same as that for Group 1 verbs.

Group 1 verbs:
tabesaseru → tabesase → tabesaserareru
misaseru → misase → misaserareru

Group 2 verbs:
ikaseru → ika → ikasareru
kakaseru → kaka → kakasareru

Irregular verbs:
saseru → sase → saserareru
kosaseru → kosase → kosaserareru

I was made to speak in Japanese.	**Nihongo de hanasasareta n'desu yo.**
They were made to sit cross-legged for hours.	**Nanjikanmo agura o kakasaremashita.**
Did you want to marry her or were you made to?	**Kanojo to kekkon shitakatta n'desu ka soretomo kekkon saserareta n'desu ka.**

Exercise 35
Put into Japanese:

1 'Is the light on?' 'No, it won't go on.'
2 The window has been opened. Who opened it, I wonder?
3 We were made to pay for (the cost of) everybody's drinks.
4 It says that all the trains will be late.
5 I didn't want to go but I was made to.
6 Even if he doesn't want to do it, we'll have to make him.

CONVERSATION 19a: A hangover

Mr Brown tells Mr Inoue about his evening in a karaoke bar:

B: Ohayō gozaimasu.
I: Ohayō. Buraun-san dō shita n'desu ka. Mata futsuka-yoi mitai desu ne.
B: Sō desu. Sakuya tomodachi ni karaoke bā[1] e tsurete ikareta n'desu.
I: Omoshirokatta deshō, karaoke wa.
B: Sō desu ne. De mo utaitaku nai to itta no ni utawasareta n'desu. Ikura onchi da

to itte mo Igirisu no uta o kikasete kure to iwarete, kotowaru to okorareso na ki ga shite 'Gurīn Surībusu' o utaimashita.

I: Uketa deshō.

B: Uketa mitai desu ne. Demo hidokatta desu yo. Nomitaku nakutemo[2] nomasareru n'desu kara.

I: Mō chotto tsuyoku naranai to dame desu ne, Jon-san.

CONVERSATION 19b: An arranged marriage

Yumiko explains to Mr Brown why she's crying:

B: Dōshite naite iru n'desu ka.

Y: Chichi ga kaigai ryūgaku o sasete kurenai to itta n'desu.

B: Dōshite kyū ni dame da to iwareta n'desu ka.

Y: Chichi wa watashi ni gakkō o sotsugyō shitara hanayome shugyō o saseru tsumori nan desu.

B: Hanayome shugyō tte[3]?

Y: O-cha ya o-hana sore ni ryōri o narattari shite kekkon no junbi o suru koto desu.

B: Kekkon no junbi desu ka. Demo Yumiko wa aite ga iru n'desu ka.

Y: Īe, o-miai o saserareru n'desu.

B: O-miai desu ka. Sore ja, dō suru n'desu ka.

Y: Yappari iwareru tōri ni[4] shinai to dame mitai desu ne.

Notes:

1. **karaoke:** lit. 'empty **(kara)** orchestra **(oke)**'; many Japanese bars are equipped with **karaoke**, which are cassette players that play only the backing track of songs; a microphone is passed around and customers are 'invited' to sing.

2. **nomitaku nakutemo:** 'even though I didn't want to drink'; the **te** plus **mo** means 'even if', 'even though'.

3. **tte: 'what do you mean by …';** **tte** is an abbreviation of **to iu koto wa.** See Lesson 20.

4. **iwareru tōri ni:** 'as I am told'.

Lesson 20

MAIN POINTS: Informal and honorific language – a summary.
CONVERSATIONS: (a) Out shopping; (b) A telephone message.

129 Informal Japanese

A few of the characteristics of informal speech are dealt with here principally to enable you to understand it when it is spoken either to you or in your presence. Informal speech is used in informal situations when addressing family members, close friends and social inferiors. It is not used in more formal situations and never used when addressing strangers or people of superior status. The speaker has to judge for him- or herself when informal speech is permissible.

There are various features of informal speech. Omission, particularly of particles, is common and abbreviated forms are also very common. The most characteristic feature, though, is the use of the plain form of verbs and adjectives. In each case below only a small selection of the many possibilities has been given.

130 Plain forms

In informal speech note that (a) with nouns and **na** adjectives, **da** is frequently omitted; (b) in requests **ka** is often omitted, and **no** may replace it; (c) **no (ka)** is used as the plain form of **n'desu (ka).** Study the following pairs:

A: *Are you off now?* — **Mō kaeru?**
B: *Yeah, I'm off.* — **N, kaeru.**
A: *Is it tomorrow?* — **Ashita?**
B: *It's tomorrow, it seems.* — **Ashita mitai yo.**
A: *Is she pretty?* — **Kirei na no*?**
B: *Yep.* — **Kirei da* yo.**
A: *What's up?* — **Dō shita no?**
B: *I've hurt my leg.* — **Ashi ga itakute.**
A: *That's expensive, isn't it?* — **Are wa takai ne.**
B: *Yep, that is expensive.* — **N, takai (no)* yo.**
A: *Shall we go out for a drink?* — **Nomi ni ikō.**
B: *Yeah, let's.* — **N, ikō.**
A: *What's that?* — **Are wa nani?**
B: *I don't know.* — **Shiranai.**
A: *Who's that?* — **Ano hito wa dare?**
B: *I wonder.* — **Dare darō?**

A: *It's useless, isn't it?*	**Dame da* ne.**
B: *Yep, it's useless.*	**N, dame da* yo.**
A: *You've understood, haven't you?*	**Wakatta ne?**
B: *I've got it.*	**N, wakatta wa*.**

* **da** will be omitted in women's informal speech
no is particularly characteristic of women's informal speech
wa is characteristic of women's informal speech

131 Omission

In informal speech, particles **wa, ga, o, ni, e** may be omitted provided that the meaning remains clear; **kudasai** in imperatives may be omitted; entire clauses after conjunctions like **kara** and **ga** may be omitted; other omissions are also possible. Consider the following pairs with particles omitted:

A: *I'll do it.*	**Watashi yaru.**
B: *Really?*	**Sō?**
A: *What's that?*	**Are nani?**
B: *I don't know.*	**Wakaranai.**
A: *Can you write?* (e.g. Japanese)	**Kaku koto dekiru?**
B: *Yes.*	**Dekiru yo.**
A: *It feels good, doesn't it?*	**Kimochi ii ne.**
B: *It does, doesn't it?*	**Kimochi ii ne.**
A: *What're you doing?*	**Nani shite'ru?**
B: *I'm reading.*	**Hon yonde'ru.**
A: *Where are you going?*	**Doko iku?**
B: *Nowhere.*	**Doko mo ikanai yo.**

Imperatives without **kudasai**:

Don't (J: stop)!	**Yamete.**
Come here!	**Kotchi kite.**
Drink this!	**Kore nonde.**

Clauses omitted:

A: *Have you got any money?*	**O-kane arimasu ka.**
B: *Yes, I have; (e.g. why do you ask?).*	**Arimasu ga ...**
I want to be off early tomorrow (so e.g. I need an early night tonight).	**Ashita hayaku dekaketai kara ...**
I must be off now.	**Mō kaeranakucha ...** (e.g. **narimasen**)
Why don't you go to sleep straight away?	**Sugu netara ...** (e.g. **dō desu ka**)?
Don't forget.	**Wasurenai yō ni ...** (e.g. **chūi shite kudasai**).

132 Abbreviations

Here is a selection of common abbreviations, some of which have been covered above. The non-abbreviated form is given in brackets:

You mustn't eat that.	**Tabecha (te wa) dame yo.**
O.K. then, let's go.	**Sore ja (de wa) ikō ka.**
I don't want anything.	**Nanimo iran (iranai).**
What're you doing?	**Nani shite'ru (te iru)?**
I'm not doing anything.	**Nanimo shite'nai (te inai).**
I was waiting for hours.	**Nanjikan mo matte'ta (te ita) yo.**
I'll leave it there.	**Asoko ni oit'oku (te oku).**
I'll make it for you.	**Tsukutt'ageru (te ageru).**
Even I can't do it.	**Watashi datte (de mo) dekinai.**
Where did he say he was going?	**Doko iku'tte (to itta/itte ita)?**
What does o-miai mean?	**O-miai'tte (to iu no wa)?**

Finally note that in informal Japanese there are some alternatives for 'I' and 'you': 'I' (in men's speech only) may be **boku** or **ore**; 'you' may be **kimi** or **o-mae**.

CONVERSATION 20a: Out shopping

A boy (B) and his girlfriend (A) buy some clothes:

A: Kore haite mitara?
B: Kore?! Jōdan! Konna no iran!
A: Dō shite? Ii no ni[1].
B: Shumi ja nai yo. Kore dō?
A: Ii yo. Haite miru?
B: N, haite miyō.

Several minutes later:

B: Chotto nagai n' ja nai?
A: Sonna koto nai wa yo. Chōdo ii n'ja nai no?
B: Ja, kaō ka ... Sumimasen, kore (o) o-negai shimasu.
X: Hai, yonsen en de gozaimasu ... chōdo yonsen en o-azukari itashimasu.
B: Yokatta ne. Kōcha demo nomi ni ikō ka.

Notes:

1. **ii no ni:** 'they're nice'; **no ni** expresses regret.

133 Honorific Japanese

Here it will be possible to touch on only a few of the more common features of honorific speech. Honorific language will be used when you wish to show respect, appreciation or concern, especially to the person you are talking to but also to the person you are talking about. Two types of honorific language may be distinguished: 'deferential' and 'humble'. Deferential language involves 'elevating' the person spoken to (or about) by certain verbs or verb forms; humble language involves the speaker 'lowering' himself or others out of respect for the person spoken to (or about) by the use of certain verbs and verb forms. Many of these have already appeared in conversations above.

134 Deferential & humble verbs and verb forms

Consider first some common verbs which have deferential and humble alternatives:

Neutral	Deferential	Humble
iru/imasu	irassharu/irasshaimasu	oru/orimasu
iku/ikimasu }	irassharu/irasshaimasu	{ mairu/mairimashita
kuru/kimasu }	oide ni naru/narimasu	{ ukagau/ukagaimasu
suru/shimasu	nasaru/nasaimasu	itasu/itashimasu
iu/iimasu	ossharu/osshaimasu	mōsu/mōshimasu
taberu/tabemasu }	meshiagaru/meshiagarimasu	{ itadaku/itadakimasu
nomu/nomimasu }		{ itadaku/itadakimasu
miru/mimasu	goran ni naru/narimasu	haiken itasu/itashimasu
kiku/kikimasu	(o-kiki ni naru/narimasu)	ukagau/ukagaimasu
shiru/shirimasu	gozonji desu	zonjiru/zonjimasu

Those verbs which do not have special deferential or humble forms can be made deferential or humble in various ways, the most common being as follows. Note that the passive is frequently used as a deferential form:

Neutral	Deferential	Humble
kaku/kakimasu	o-kaki ni naru/narimasu	o-kaki suru/shimasu
kaku/kakimasu	kakareru/kakaremasu	
yomu/yomimasu	o-yomi ni naru/narimasu	o-yomi suru/shimasu
yomu/yomimasu	yomareru/yomaremasu	

Study the following:

This is the book the Professor wrote.   **Kore wa Sensei ga o-kaki ni natta hon desu.**

You know when it is, don't you?	**Itsu ka gozonji desu ne.**
What did he say?	**Nan to osshaimashita ka.**
I'm not doing anything.	**Nanimo shite orimasen.**
I've met you before.	**Mae ni o-me ni kakarimashita.**
Do start (your meal)!	**Dōzo meshiagatte kudasai.**
What do you think, Professor?	**Sensei, dō omowaremasu ka.**
When will he be going home?	**Itsu o-kaeri ni naru n'desu ka.**
I wonder if you could help me (J: I should like to inquire) ...	**O-tazune shimasu ga ...**

Remember the use of **itadaku/itadakimasu** in honorific language:

I should like to take you around Nara.	**Nara o (go-)annai sasete itadakitai n'desu ga.**
May I use the phone?	**Denwa o tsukawasete itadakemasu ka.**
Would you be kind enough to wait just a little longer?	**Mō sukoshi matte itadakemasen ka.**

Honorific imperatives you should be able to recognize:

Please wait a minute.	**Shōshō o-machi kudasai.**
Please start!	**O-mashiagari kudasai.**
Please take a seat.	**Dōzo o-kake kudasai.**

135 Honorific nouns and adjectives

Nouns and adjectives too have honorific forms. Some nouns and adjectives have honorific <u>alternatives</u>: **hito** becomes **kata**; **dare** becomes **donata** or **dochira-sama**; **doko** becomes **dochira**; **ii** becomes **yoroshii**. Some nouns are made honorific, as you know, by placing either **go** or **o** in front of them. Some adjectives are made honorific by placing **o** before them. A number of verbs are regularly preceded, in honorific speech, by **o** and followed by **desu: dekakeru → o-dekake desu.** Study the examples below:

Is this O.K.?	**Kore de yoroshii desu ka.**
Who are you (who's speaking)?	**Dochira-sama de irasshaimasu ka.**
What are you studying?	**Nani o go-benkyō nasatte iru n'desu ka.**
When did you get married?	**Itsu go-kekkon nasaimashita ka.**
A: *Will you eat here?*	**Kochira de o-meshiagari desu ka.**
B: *No, I'll take it away.*	**Ie, motte kaerimasu.**

Note too some examples of adjectives preceded by **o**:

I'm sure you are very busy, but ...	**O-isogashii deshō ga ...**

154

You are young, aren't you?   **O-wakai desu ne.**

Before finishing this lesson you are advised to refer back to the following Conversations which contain various examples of honorific speech: 2c, 3a, 4a, 5c, 7b, 9a,b, 10b, 14a, 17a.

CONVERSATION 20b: A telephone message

Mr Tanaka (A) talks to a secretary (B):

A: Yoshida-san wa irasshaimasu[1] deshō ka.
B: Dochira-sama de irasshaimasu ka.
A: Tanaka to mōshimasu ga.
B: Shōshō o-machi kudasai ... Tadaima seki o hazushite orimasu ga ...
A: Sō desu ka. O-kotozuke o o-negai dekimasu[1] deshō ka.
B: Hai dōzo.
A: Ashita 11ji goro o-ukagai shimasu[2] no de sō osshatte kudasai.
B: Kashikomarimashita. O-tsutae itashimasu.

Notes:

1. **masu deshō ka:** in honorific speech **masu** forms are commonly used where plain forms would otherwise be expected.

2. **o-ukagai shimasu:** here it means 'I shall visit'.

Key to the Exercises

Exercise 1

1. (Watashi wa) gakusei ja arimasen. Anata wa?
2. '(Sore wa) shinkansen desu ka.' 'Chigaimasu.'
3. '(Kanojo wa) Nihonjin desu ka. Chūgokujin desu ka.' 'Sō desu ne.'
4. '(Kore wa) kanai desu.' 'Hajimemashite.'
5. '(Kanojo wa) Kankokujin desu.' 'A, sō desu ka.'

Exercise 2

1. '(Sore wa) hontō no kōhī desu ne.' 'Īe chigaimasu. Insutanto desu.'
2. 'Ki-iro no kuruma wa anata no desu ka.' 'Chigaimasu. Watashi no kuruma wa midori-iro desu.'
3. 'Kōhī wa?' 'O-negai shimasu.'
4. Asoko no hito wa Nihonjin ja arimasen.
5. (Kore wa) kyō no shinbun ja arimasen yo.

Exercise 3

1. 'Asoko no hito wa dare desu ka.' 'Mado no mae no hito desu ka.'
2. (Kore wa) kyō no shinbun desu ka. Kinō no shinbun desu ka.
3. 'Sumimasen. Toire wa dochira desu ka.' 'Achira desu.'
4. 'Nan desu ka.' 'Watashi no kippu desu yo.'
5. 'Sashimi wa dō desu ka.' 'Māmā desu.

Exercise 4

1. Kōhī wa arimasu ka.
2. Basu de kūkō made (e) ikimasu ka.
3. Pasupōto wa asoko desu/ni arimasu.
4. (Watashi wa) Nihongo de hanashimasu.
5. Ikeda-san wa ashita irasshaimasen/orimasen/imasen.

Exercise 5

1. 'Saifu ni o-kane ga arimasu.'
2. 'O-kane wa hikidashi no naka ni arimasen.' 'Doko ni arimasu ka.'
3. 'Kare wa Nihongo mo Chūgokugo mo hanashimasu.' 'Sō desu ka.'
4. 'Dare ga tegami o dashimasu ka.' 'Watashi ga dashimasu.'
5. Kyō wa ikimasen. Ashita wa ikimasu.

Exercise 6

1. Yūbe nomi ni ikimasen deshita.

2. Sugu uchi e kaerimashita.
3. Sashimi wa tabemasen deshita.
4. Shōyu to sashimi wa asoko ni arimasu.
5. Mō sugu owarimasu.
6. Hanbāgā to kōhī (o) o-negai shimasu.
7. Kanojo to Nihongo de hanashimasen deshita ka.

Exercise 7

1. 'Nannin issho ni ikimashita ka.' 'Hitori de ikimashita.'
2. Rokujūen no kitte o jūmai kudasai.
3. 'Koko kara Nagasaki made ikura desu ka.' 'Niman'en desu.'
4. Kare ni jukkai denwa shimashita.
5. Watashi no denwa bangō wa 654 no 2908 desu.

Exercise 8

1. 'Pātei e nannin kimashita ka.' 'Sannin shika kimasen deshita.'
2. Bīru o mō ippai dake o-negai shimasu.
3. Itsu goro ikimasu ka.
4. Sore ni kami o nanmai tsukaimashita ka.
5. (Kore wa) roppaime no bīru desu.

Exercise 9

1. Kyō wa totemo atsukatta desu ne.
2. Shikki o kai ni ikimashita ga arimasen deshita.
3. Kono o-cha wa amari oishiku nakatta desu ne.
4. Se no takai hito wa chichi desu. Se no hikui hito wa chichi no tomodachi desu.
5. Totemo yasashii hito desu.

Exercise 10

1. 'Dō yatte gakkō e ikimasu ka.' 'Watashi wa basu de ikimasu.'
2. Totemo jōzu ni hanashimasu ne.
3. 'Ōkisa wa?' 'Ōkisa wa chōdo ii desu.'
4. Ano Toyota wa tomodachi no to onaji desu.
5. Yoku sukī ni ikimasu ka.

Exercise 11

1. Hagaki o nimai to (ni) kitte o rokumai katte kimasu.
2. Asoko ni suwatte matte kudasai.
3. Kyōto e itte Ryōanji o mite kaette kimashita.
4. 'Aruite nanpun gurai kakarimasu ka.' 'Chotto wakarimasen ga basu de (wa) nijuppun gurai kakarimasu.'
5. O-tō-san o yonde kite kudasai.

Exercise 12

1. 'Ano Nakajima Miyuki no uta wa oboete imasen ka.' 'Oboete imasen ne.'
2. 'Doko no daigaku e itte imasu ka.' 'Watashi wa daigaku e itte imasen. Hataraite imasu.'
3. 'Sumimasen. Yūbinkyoku wa nanji kara nanji made aite imasu ka.' 'Shirimasen.'
4. 'Sakana-ya no tonari no kissaten o shitte imasu ka.' 'Īe, shirimasen.'
5. 'Ryōshin no tokoro e kaette imasu.' 'Itsu kaerimashita ka.'

Exercise 13

1. 'Itsu kara shodō o renshū shite imasu ka.' 'Rokunen gurai mae kara desu.'
2. Maitoshi rokugatsu ni sanshūkan gurai ryokō shimasu.
3. Kono utsukushii kuni ni itsu kara imasu/irasshaimasu ka.
4. Isogashikute mada yonde imasen.
5. Yonjū gonenkan kekkon shite imasu.

Exercise 14

1. 'Dōshite atarashii sūtsukēsu o futatsu katta n'desu ka.' 'Raishū kaigai e iku n'desu.'
2. 'Osoku kaette kita n'desu.' 'Dōshite desu ka.'
3. Nihongo o yameta n'desu.
4. Naze konakatta n'desu ka.
5. Bōifurendo ga Amerika ni kaetta no de naite iru n'desu.

Exercise 15

1. Mō owatta deshō?
2. Ashita Nihon o tatsu yotei deshita.
3. Ashita kuru ka mo shiremasen.
4. Sonna hon wa takaku nai hazu desu.
5. Iu tsumori deshita ga wasuremashita.

Exercise 16

1. Haha ga tanjōbi ni kore o kureta n'desu.
2. Sensei, kore o sashiagemasu.
3. Shachō wa oku-san ni hon o moraimashita.
4. Tomu-san, kore o agemashō.
5. Yumiko wa Kunio ni purezento o agemashita/kuremashita ka.

Exercise 17

1. Kunio, katte ageru yo.
2. Koko ni o-namae o kaite kudasaimasu ka.
3. Rokuji ni kite moraimasu.
4. Kunio wa sensei ni haratte itadakimashita.
5. Shachō ga kanai ni katte kudasaimashita.

Exercise 18

1. Doko ni sunde iru ka shitte iru ka dō ka kiite kudasai.
2. Doko ni sunde iru ka oshiete itadakemasen ka.
3. Hiru made ni kuru yō ni (kite kureru yō ni) tanomimashita ga yoji made ni kuru to itte imashita.
4. Sensei wa seito ni tatte kure to (tatsu yō ni) iimashita.
5. Naze Nihongo o yameru ka kikimashita ka.

Exercise 19

1. 'Hakubutsukan (to iu kotoba) wa dō iu imi desu ka.' '"Museum" to iu imi desu.'
2. Kanojo to nagai aida tsukiatte imashita. Sore kara kekkon suru to iu koto o kikimashita.
3. Rainen mata koyō ka to omotte imasu.
4. Konai to itte imashita.
5. 'Nan to iimashita ka.' 'Tsukarete iru kara mō neru to iimashita.'
6. Mada denwa shite inai to iu koto wa jiko ni atta to iu imi ja nai desu yo.

Exercise 20

1. 'Ano uta wa suki ja nai desu ka.' 'Daikirai desu.'
2. 'O-nī-san no jōzu na supōtsu wa nan desu ka.' 'O-nī-san wa yakyū ga jōzu desu.'
3. Kanojo wa me ga totemo kirei desu.
4. Watashi wa kodomo ga futari imasu. Anata wa?
5. Nihongo wa dekimasu ga Kankokugo wa mada dekimasen.
6. Irimasen kara agemasu.
7. Kanojo wa ano takai doresu ga hoshii to itte imasu yo.
8. 'Dekimasu ka.' 'Dekimasen. Kare ni dekiru ka dō ka kiite kuremasu ka.'

Exercise 21

1. Watashi wa ikitaku nai desu. Kanojo mo ikitaku nai to itte imasu.
2. Iranai deshō?
3. O-nī-san mo ikitai to itte imashita ka.
4. Doa no kagi o shimeru yō ni shite kudasai ne.
5. O-kane wa minna naku natte imasu.
6. Kowasanai yō ni chūi shite kudasai.

Exercise 22

1. Kyonen Nihonjin no onna no ko to kekkon shita rashii/mitai/sō desu.
2. Ano sashimi wa hontō ni oishisō desu ne.
3. Konsāto ga mō owatta mitai/rashii/yō desu, kara nomi ni ikimashō ka.
4. 'Hashi o dō yatte tsukaimasu ka.' 'Watashi no yō ni tsukatte kudasai.'
5. Kanojo no yō na hito ga daikirai desu. Minna to kenka suru rashii/mitai/sō desu kara.

Exercise 23

1. Mō haru ni natta to iu ki ga/kanji ga shimasu.

2. Konban dekakeru ki ga shimasen ka.
3. Nagai aida tabete inai yō na kao o shite imasu.
4. Ano ie wa o-tera no yō na katachi o shite imasu.
5. Nanika nioi ga shimasen ka.

Exercise 24

1. Ano yane no akai kuruma wa suki desu.
2. Kōhī o nonde iru onna no ko wa dare desu ka.
3. Nihon wa jinkō ga/no totemo ōi kuni desu.
4. Ima anata ga hanashite ita otoko no hito wa dare desu ka. Mukashi kara shitte iru hito desu ka.
5. Kore wa Tanaka-san ga oku-san ni katte ageta hon desu.
6. Koko wa sore o katta o-mise desu.

Exercise 25

1. Kono chikaku ni dokoka shizuka na tokoro wa arimasu ka.
2. Ano hito wa donna supōtsu ga dekimasu ka.
3. Hon o nansatsumo kaimashita.
4. Asoko ni daremo Eigo ga dekiru hito wa inakatta n'desu.
5. Konban terebi de nanimo omoshiroi bangumi wa yatte imasen.

Exercise 26

1. 'Issho ni itte mo ii desu ka.' 'Īe, hitori de ikanakereba narimasen.'
2. Rokuji made ni kaette koraremasu (koremasu) ka.
3. Nihongo de kakanakute mo ii desu. Rōmaji de kaite mo ii desu.
4. Sono yō ni hanashite wa ikemasen.
5. 'Ichiman'en de ii deshō?' 'Ii desu yo.'
6. Keisatsu ni denwa o shinakereba narimasen deshita.

Exercise 27

1. 'O-tera o mi ni iku no/koto wa suki desu ka.' 'Suki desu yo, anata wa?'
2. 'Manjū o tabeta koto wa arimasu ka.' 'Nai desu. Dōshite desu ka.'
3. Densha ja nakute kuruma de iku koto ni shimashita.
4. 'Ie de Nihongo o hanasu koto wa arimasu ka.' 'Tokidoki arimasu.'
5. Itsumo okurete iru no wa dōshite desu ka.

Exercise 28

1. Nihonjin wa Eikokujin yori yoku hatarakimasu ka.
2. Takushī de ikanai hō ga yokatta desu.
3. Fuyu wa Eikoku yori Nihon no hō ga samui desu yo.
4. Dochira ga hayai desu ka. Shinkansen soretomo Furansu no atarashii densha?
5. Ie de nomu yori bā de nomu hō ga tanoshii desu.

Exercise 29

1. Kare wa watashi to onaji gurai (takusan) nomimasu.
2. Iwanai hō ga yokatta desu.
3. 'Dore ga ichiban suki desu ka.' 'Watashi no ichiban suki na no wa ano aoi no desu.'
4. 'Sakana wa dore gurai/dake/hodo ōkikatta desu ka. Kore gurai/dake/hodo ōkikatta desu ka.'
   'Chigaimasu. Sonna ni ōkiku nakatta desu. Mō chotto chīsakatta desu.'
5. Ani hodo se ga takaku nai desu ga kare to onaji gurai tsuyoi desu.

Exercise 30

1. Kekkon suru mae ni takusan no onna no ko to tsukiaimashita ka.
2. Nihon ni iku mae desu ka Soretomo Nihon ni tsuita ato desu ka.
3. Karera ga hanashite ita aida watashi wa nyūsu o kiite imashita.
4. Dekakete iru aida terebi o miyō ka to omoimasu.
5. Mae ni ikkai ikimashita ga oboete imasen ka.

Exercise 31

1. Koko ni iru aida nani o suru tsumori desu ka.
2. Kare ga tsukiatte iru onna no ko o mita toki dōshite kare ga kanojo o aishite iru ka sugu
   wakarimashita.
3. Nihon ni iku to kaette kitaku naku narimasu.
4. Nagai aida sushi o tabete imasen.
5. Uisukī to wain o nomu tabi ni/to itsumo futsukayoi ni narimasu.

Exercise 32

1. Watashi nara kotowaru to omoimasu yo.
2. Ashita ame nara/dattara/deshitara iku no o yamemashō.
3. Moshi juppun hayaku kita n'dattara densha ni ma ni atta ka mo shiremasen.
4. Kirei de atarashikattara kaimasu.
5. Ima sugu denwa shitara iru darō to omoimasu.

Exercise 33

1. Nihongo o kaku koto mo narattara dō desu ka.
2. Dō shitara ii ka doko e ittara ii ka wakarimasen deshita.
3. Ashita tenki ga yoku nattara ii desu ga ne.
4. Ano kuruma o kawanakattara yokatta n'desu ga ne.
5. Nihon ni nagai aida ireba iru hodo suki ni naru n'desu.

Exercise 34

1. Ie wa dorobō ni hairareta n'desu.
2. Gaikokujin tōrokushō o tori ni itta toki ni shimon o torareta n'desu.
3. Okureta kara minna shikararemashita.
4. Naze Nihongo o yameta ka kikaremashita.

5. Kare wa mō sugu shinu darō to iwaremashita.

Exercise 35

1. 'Denki wa tsuite imasu ka.' 'Īe tsukimasen.'
2. Mado wa akete arimasu. Dare ga aketa deshō ka.
3. Minna no nomimono-dai o harawasareta n'desu.
4. Densha wa minna okureru to kaite arimasu.
5. Ikitaku nakatta n'desu ga ikasareta n'desu.
6. Kare ga yaritaku nakutemo yarasenakereba narimasen.

Key to the Conversations

Conversation 2a

B: Chieko, this is Professor Emura from Tokyo University. Professor Emura, this is my wife Chieko.
C: Pleased to meet you.
B: My wife is an English teacher.
E: Oh, really? How do you do?
B: Professor, this is my son David. David's a primary school pupil.
E: Ah, is that so? Pleased to meet you.
D: Pleased to meet you.

Conversation 2b

A: Excuse me, are you an American?
B: No, I'm not. I'm English.
A: Oh, really? Are you a student?
B: Yes, I am. I'm a student in the Japanese department of London University.
A: I see. I'm a businessman, you know. Forgive me, but what's your name?
B: Mike.
A: Mike, is it? I'm Kunio, Sato Kunio. Pleased to meet you.
B: Pleased to meet you too.

Conversation 2c

B: Excuse me, but this is the Dai Ichi hotel, isn't it?
P: No, it's not, actually. The Dai Ichi is the hotel over there.
B: Ah, it's over there, is it? Thank you very much.
P: Not at all.

I: Excuse me, but are you Mr Brown of ICI?
B: Yes, that's right.

I: Pleased to meet you. My name is Ikeda, I'm from Mitsui. How do you do?
B: Pleased to meet you, too.
I: Here's my card.
B: Ah, thank you very much. And this is mine too.

Conversation 3a

B: Excuse me, my name is Brown. Is Mr Tanaka in?
C: Tanaka is not in at the moment.
B: Really? I'll call back later then.

Conversation 3b

A: Excuse me, where are we? Is this Shinjuku?
B: No, it's not. It isn't Shinjuku. Umm, it's Shibuya.
A: Is it? Does it go to Shinjuku?
B: Umm, just a sec. Yes, it stops in Shinjuku.
A: Is it the next one?
B: No, it isn't. It's the one after next.
A: Thank you.

Conversation 3c

B: Mr Katayama, hello!
K: Mr Brown? I haven't seen you for ages. Are you well?
B: Yes, thank you, I am. And you, Mr Katayama?
K: Yes, I'm well.
B: Mr Katayama, how about it, won't you have a cup of tea or something?
K: Yes, let's go and have a cup. Umm, how about the coffee shop by the station?
B: You mean Kadota, don't you? Yes, that'll be fine.
K: Shall we go by car or shall we walk?
B: Let's walk.

Conversation 4a

W: Welcome!
W: What will you have?
B: Umm, what's the breakfast today?
W: Egg and toast.
B: O.K. then, one breakfast, please.
W: A breakfast with coffee is that? Or with tea?
B: Coffee, please. No, no. I'll make it tea after all.
W: Will that be milk tea?
B: Yes.
W: Right, that's one breakfast with milk tea, isn't it. Please wait for a short while.

B: Excuse me. Have you got today's paper?
W: Yes, the papers are over there. We've got the Asahi and the Mainichi but we haven't got any English-language papers.

W: Your breakfast with milk tea. I'm sorry to have kept you waiting.
B: Thank you.

B: The bill, please.
W: Certainly, sir.

Conversation 4b

B: Excuse me, is there a taxi rank near here?
P: A taxi rank? Umm, just a second. There was one near the bus stop in front of that department store.
B: Thank you very much.

B: To Tarumi station, please.
D: Which part of the station do you want?
B: The front of the station, please.
D: O.K.

B: Driver, will we be there in a minute?
D: Yes, it's not far off now ... O.K., here we are at the front of the station.
B: Let me off somewhere around here please.

B: Keep the change.
D: Thank you.

Conversation 5a

A: When's your birthday, John?
J: It's next week, actually.
A: Is that so? My birthday's next week too, you know.
J: Eh? What day next week is it?
A: Tuesday, Tuesday the 17th.
J: Eh? Mine is on the 20th.
A: What year were you born in, John? I was born in (19)60.
J: Me too!

Conversation 5b

B: Two 70-yen stamps and four postcards, please. And this letter to France, please.
X: Airmail or seamail?
B: By air please. Oh, and one aerogramme, please.
X: Will that be all?
B: Yes, that's all.
X: That'll be 700 yen altogether. That's exactly 700 that you've given me. Thank you very much.

Conversation 5c

B: What time is the next train for Kyoto?

X: Ten past nine. You have fifteen minutes.

B: O.K. then, two adults to Kyoto, please.

X: Single or return?

B: Return. How much is it?

X: 9,000 yen. That's 10,000 yen you've given me. Here's your 1,000 yen change. Thank you very much.

B: What platform is it?

X: It's platform 5.

C: May I see your tickets, please? ... This isn't the train for Kyoto, you know, this is the Nagoya train.

B: Oh, what shall we do? We've got on the wrong train.

Conversation 6a

A: Your Japanese is good, isn't it?

B: No, it isn't really. I've got a long way to go.

A: No, really. Your accent is very nice. It's no different from a Japanese. You really speak well, you know.

B: Do I? Thank you.

A: Is it difficult, Japanese?

B: Yes, it's very difficult. I've suffered a lot! The accent is fairly easy, but the grammar is tricky. And writing and reading are a great problem. There's katakana and hiragana and kanji too. It's extremely difficult to remember.

A: Yes, you're right there. It's a question of memory. Good for you, anyway!

Conversation 6b

S: Makunouchi, mackerel sushi, eel and rice, tea, beer.

T: Two makunouchis please.

S: Two makunouchis, here you are. Anything to drink?

T: I'd like something cold. A beer please. What about you, Mr Brown?

B: I'll have a hot cup of tea, please.

S: Here you are, that'll be 1,200 yen. That's exactly 2,000 yen you've given me. Thank you.

T: Mr Brown, is this the first time you've had a packed lunch?

B: Yes, it is actually. But it looks delicious, doesn't it? What sort of things has it got in it?

T: First you've got rice. And this yellowish thing here is takuwan, a pickle(d radish).

B: There are all sorts of things, aren't there? What about this red one?

T: Umm, that's a shrimp. It's not really red, they've just dyed it red. Anyway, let's eat. Itadakimasu!

B: Itadakimasu! This long thin thing is deep-fried prawn isn't it? It's tasty. You put this sauce on top, do you?

T: That's right. It's a bit hot (spicy) ... Also, this blackish one is seaweed. It has an interesting taste.

B: I'm full up! I've eaten too much. But it was delicious.
T: Try this. It's sour plum. It's very sour, but it's excellent for indigestion!

Conversation 7a

A: Excuse me, would you be kind enough to tell me how to use the phone?
B: (You want to know) how to use it? Certainly. Have you got a lot of 10-yen coins?
A: Umm, I haven't got much change. I'm sorry, but would you mind changing this for me?
B: Certainly. O.K. then, so first you pick up the receiver, and put in about three 10-yen coins, and then you dial the number. Do you see?
A: Yes, thanks. So, umm, first you pick up the receiver, stick in about three 10-yen coins, dial the number – 06 678 9809 – and that's it, isn't it?
B: That's right.
A: Thank you very much indeed.
B: Not at all, the pleasure is mine.
A: Oh, as I thought, they're engaged. I'll wait a little and then try phoning again.

Conversation 7b

Mrs K: Hello?
B: I'm sorry to be ringing late at night, but is that the Katayamas' residence?
Mrs K: Yes it is.
B: Is Kunio there?
Mrs K: Yes, just a sec. I'll go and get him.
B: Thank you.

K: Hello, Kunio here.
B: Kunio? It's John here.
K: Ah, John. I've not seen you for a long time. How have you been?
B: Very well, thank you. And you, Kunio?
K: Yes, I've been well too.
B: Anyway, Kunio, are you free the day after tomorrow?
K: The day after tomorrow is Saturday, isn't it? Yes, I'm free.
B: Well, would you like to come to Kyoto with me?
K: I haven't been to Kyoto for ages. That's a good idea. Yes, let's go together.
B: That's good. Where shall we go in Kyoto?
K: Let's first decide on the time and place to meet.
B: You're right.
K: Let's meet at the main entrance to Osaka station at about 8 and take the 8.30.
B: Fair enough.
K: O.K. then, so I'll see you at 8 o'clock in the morning the day after tomorrow.
B: Yes, I'm looking forward to it.

Conversation 8a

B: Excuse me, I'm looking for a bank. Isn't there one near here?
P: I'm not familiar with this area, actually. Try asking that policeman over there.

B: Thank you. I wonder if you could help me, I'm looking for a bank.

K: There is a Dai Ichi Kangin Bank over there but it's closed now. Banks in Japan are open from 9 a.m. to 3 p.m., you know.

B: I see. What shall I do? That's a nuisance, isn't it?

K: Your Japanese is good. Where do you come from?

B: Canada.

K: How long have you been in Japan?

B: Umm, for about four months.

K: Let me have a look at your Alien Registration card.

B: Just a sec. It's in my bag. Ah, I've got it. There you are.

K: Oh, you're a student, aren't you?

B: I've been studying at Hitotsubashi University for a month.

K: I see. And you live in Kunitachi?

B: Yes. I'm living in a dormitory at the moment but I'm looking for an apartment.

K: I see. Yes, that's fine.

Conversation 8b

B: What's on T.V.?

I: I'll have a look and see. Documentaries and quizzes. Uninteresting programmes, the lot of them.

B: There's no film on, is there?

I: Umm, just a sec. No, there isn't. Oh, there is a period play on, though.

B: I'm not really interested.

I: Kurosawa's '7 Samurai' is on at the cinema, though. Do you know it?

B: I only know the name. Who's in it?

I: I don't remember. Mifune, isn't it?

B: Really? So then, what'll we do? Shall we go and see it?

I: Straight away, without eating?

B: Yes, let's go. And then after the film let's go and have something nice to eat somewhere!

Conversation 9a

B: Hello, is this the Inoues' house?

I: Yes, it is. Are you Mr Brown?

B: Yes, that's right.

I: We've been expecting you. Kunio should be back in a minute, so do come on in.

B: Thank you. I expect he's late with his sports club or something, isn't he?

I: Yes, that's right. I am sorry, Mr Brown ... Do come this way. Shall I bring you something cool to drink?

B: Yes, please.

I: It's only wheat-tea, but here you are.

B: Thank you. It's nice and cold.

I: How much longer are you planning to be in Japan?

B: I'm not quite sure. I may be here for another year, but it depends on the money.

I: Are you studying something?

B: Yes, modern history.

I: Really? Why did you begin to get interested in Japan?

B: Umm, the reason I became interested in Japan is a bit complex, but it was probably because of my father's influence.

Conversation 9b

K: Hello.

I: Hello. Your guest is here.

K: Mr Brown, I'm sorry I'm late. Wait just a bit longer, I'm going to go and get changed. Mum, where's Dad?

I: He's not back yet. Go and get dressed quickly! ... Mr Brown, how many brothers and sisters have you got?

B: Two, I'm the second son.

I: All boys, is it?

B: Yes, that's right. I've got one big brother and one younger brother.

I: Oh, really? What does your elder brother do?

B: Both of my brothers work for an airline company. Both may come to Japan next year.

I: Well! That's something to look forward to. Your parents'll be coming to Japan at some stage?

B: I wonder. My father might but my mother is unlikely to. She's afraid of flying.

K: I'm sorry to have kept you waiting. What have you been talking about?

I: We were talking about Mr Brown's family.

Conversation 10a

A: It's Mr Brown's birthday the day after tomorrow, isn't it? Shall we buy him a present?

T: Yes. I wonder what'd be good.

A: Something Japanese'd be good, don't you think? A fan or a furoshiki or something like that.

T: Yes. A school friend of mine is working at Mitsukoshi so I'll get her to look for something nice. That's an expensive place for everything, but maybe she'll give us a small discount!

Conversation 10b

K: Let's drink a toast to Mr Brown! Cheers!

M: Cheers! Cheers!

K: Happy birthday!

M: Happy birthday!

K: Mr Brown, a speech, if you please!

B: A speech? O.K. Thank you very much, everyone, for coming today. It's the first time I've had such a splendid party. Thank you so much for making this splendid meal for me. And thank you, too, for the presents.

K: What presents did you get?

B: I got a fan, a furoshiki and a book. I got the fan from Chieko, and the furoshiki from Yumiko and Kunio. The Inoues kindly gave me the book.

K: By the way, how old are you today?

B: That's a secret!

168

Conversation 11a

I: Excuse me (is anyone there?).
R: Hello.
I: Excuse me, do you have any rooms?
R: There are two of you, aren't there? Yes, we do. Just one night is it?
I: Yes.
R: Do come in, and I'll take you to your rooms.

I: Mr Brown, do you know what this is called?
B: I don't remember.
I: It's called a kotatsu. There's a heater underneath. It's lovely and warm. Do sit down and stretch your legs.
B: Mr Inoue, do you call this door a fusuma or a shoji? I've forgotten again which is which.
I: It's a fusuma actually. But the most interesting thing in a Japanese-style room is behind you. It's a place called the tokonoma (alcove). You place flowers and kakejiku there.
B: It's really splendid. Kakejiku means scroll, doesn't it?
I: That's right, but I've got no idea what's written on that scroll. The characters are so old it's very difficult for me to read!
R: Excuse me (I've brought the tea).

Conversation 11b

B: I'm sorry I'm late. I thought I knew the place but in fact I didn't, so I got a policeman to tell me (the way).
M: I'm sorry.
B: Not at all. It's a rather good place, this, isn't it? What about Mr Inoue? He said he'd be coming, didn't he?
M: Umm, I expect he'll be here in a minute as it's gone 9 o'clock.
B: What about Mr Yamamoto?
M: Mr Yamamoto's mother went into hospital yesterday so I think it's a little unlikely he'll come.
B: That's terrible. What about Mr Katayama?
M: He said he'd be late because of business at the office. I'm not sure if he'll finally turn up or not!.
B: Really? I told Mr Smith to come along today but he too said it was impossible!
M: What a pity! Let's drink together then, just the three of us! Excuse me! Some beer, please!

Conversation 12a

A: Mr Brown, do you have any likes and dislikes?
B: Umm ... There aren't many things I don't like, actually. Only natto and manju. Apart from that I don't think there is anything particular I dislike.
A: Sashimi and sushi are all right, are they?
B: Sashimi and sushi are favourites of mine. At first I wasn't too keen (*lit.* there was some resistance to them) but now I like them a lot.
A: What about Japanese (rice) wine? I heard that all foreigners like it.
B: I wonder, I may be the exception, but I'm not too fond of rice wine!

Conversation 12b

A: I expect you're good at sports aren't you, Mr Brown?

B: Umm, I'm quite good at rugby, but apart from that I can't do much. What about you, Mr Amai, is there a sport you're good at?

A: Baseball and softball. That's about it.

B: Baseball is very popular in Japan, isn't it? I didn't know it was so popular. There can't be many Japanese who are bad at baseball, can there?

A: Maybe you're right. Everybody plays it from when they're children, you see. Mr Brown, would you like to go and see a baseball match?

A: Yes, I'd really like to.

B: Who do you support?

A: Me, I like the Giants. What about you?

B: Me, I like the Hanshin Tigers!

Conversation 13a

A: I wonder how today's weather will turn out?

B: According to the weather forecast it's going to be clear, but somehow it doesn't look that way, does it?

A: Yes. It looks as though it's going to rain so I expect the picnic will be off, won't it? It looks as if it's started to rain already.

B: It's spitting, it seems. That's a nuisance. But it is clear over in the west, so I get the feeling it may clear up later.

Conversation 13b

A: Have you seen the news this morning?

B: Not yet. Why?

A: According to the news there was a big earthquake in Tokyo. It was magnitude 5, it seems. That's big, isn't it?

B: Magnitude 5 is big. What about injuries?

A: I don't remember how many injured there are, but quite a few people died. Earthquakes are frightening, aren't they?

B: They are. It's lucky it wasn't a big one like the one in 1923.

A: Of course, but on the news they said be careful as there may be another earthquake soon.

Conversation 14a

A: Good morning everybody! Today's guest is Mr John Brown from England. Mr Brown, what were your motives for coming to Japan? To study Japanese, I suppose?

B: Umm, yes. I had quite a few motives in wanting to come to Japan, but I suppose it was because I wanted to improve my speaking and listening ability.

A: I see. Next, apart from studying Japanese, what is it that you want to do most of all in Japan?

B: There are many things I want to do, but I want to fit into Japanese society and make lots of friends.

A: Next and last of all, what is the place you most want to visit?

B: Umm, I want to go somewhere where foreigners don't go much. I want to visit for example a place which has an interesting history, like the Goto Islands.

A: Really? Thank you very much.

Conversation 14b

B: Which parts of Kyoto shall we go to?

I: Umm, which'd be good, a temple with a garden or somewhere where the buildings are interesting? There's everything in Kyoto, you know!

B: I'd like to have a look and see a Zen-influenced garden.

I: O.K. then, let's go first to the temple called Ryoanji. Ryoanji is a very interesting place. There are always lots of people, but I think that it's definitely worth seeing. Ryoanji is a typical garden which expresses the influence of Zen thought. It's a peculiarly Japanese sort of place. The garden is one with only white pebbles and rocks.

B: That sounds interesting. It sounds quite different to what we'd call a garden in the West!

Conversation 15a

I: Have you experienced a culture shock in Japan?

B: Umm, it doesn't amount to a culture shock as such, but it took time to get used to all sorts of things.

I: Do you mean food, language, etc.?

B: Yes, and wherever you look it's all kanji, so at first I felt as though I was blind.

I: I bet you did. There were a few things you mustn't do and things you may do in everyday life, weren't there?

B: Yes, just a few. For example, you mustn't wear shoes inside the house. And the way of sitting is different too. It sometimes happens that you'll sit for hours cross-legged, doesn't it? That takes time to get used to!

I: Bathing is very different too, isn't it? You mustn't use soap in the bath, must you? And you mustn't pull the plug out either, must you? Because everyone else has to get in afterwards, haven't they?

Conversation 15b

B: Mr Inoue, have you ever been to Kamikochi?

I: Not yet, no. It sometimes happens that I go to Nagano on business, but I've never been as far as Kamikochi. Why?

B: I've arranged to go there next week with a friend of mine.

I: It's probably just the right time for seeing Kamikochi. They say it's lovely and cool even in August.

B: You can come with us, Mr Inoue.

I: No, I can't. I'm so busy at the office that I won't be able to take a holiday this year.

Conversation 16a

B: Do you know which has the bigger area, Great Britain or Japan? Is Britain a bit bigger?

I: No, Britain isn't as big as Japan.

B: Oh, really. But as for the population though, Japan has a much larger one, doesn't it?

I: Oh, yes. It's probably more than twice the size of Britain's, isn't it? And, almost all of Japan is mountain(ous) so there isn't that much space where people can live.

B: Yes, the population density is very high, isn't it?

I: In Britain, there aren't any real mountains, I've heard. Is that right?

B: Not really. There may not be any as high as Mt. Fuji, but in Wales and Scotland there are a good number of mountains.

I: Really? And then the climate is very different, isn't it? In Japan the four seasons are clear(ly defined) but in Britain I hear there are winter-like days even in summer.

B: You're right. But in Britain there isn't a rainy season, and there are no typhoons.

I: You're lucky (*lit.* I'm envious). Britain is safer, it seems!

B: Yes, there are no volcanoes and no earthquakes.

Conversation 16b

I: What's the matter?

B: My stomach is unbearably painful.

I: That's no good, is it? Since when?

B: Since about three days ago.

I: O.K. then, take off your shirt and lie down over there. Mmm, I'd better take an X-ray.

I: You've got gastroenteritis. There's no need to worry. For a while you ought to keep away from cigarettes and alcohol.

B: May I eat normally?

I: You shouldn't eat too much. And you should refrain from hot spicy things. I'll give you some medicine. Take it before meals.

B: Thank you.

I: Take care.

Conversation 17a

I: John, dinner is ready. Eat it before it gets cold.

B: Itadakimasu.

I: John, there's not long now before you go back home, is there? Before you leave Japan are there any other things you want to do or places you want to see?

B: There are. The other day when I passed Mt. Fuji on the bullet train, I thought I'd really like to try climbing it sometime.

I: Really? That's a good idea.

B: Have you ever climbed it?

I: When I was younger I climbed it just once.

B: What was it like?

I: The feeling on reaching the top is great, but it's hard work while you're climbing, you know.

B: I bet it is. Mmm, before I go back I'd love to try climbing it .. Thank you for the meal.

Mrs I: A pleasure.

Conversation 17b

S: Today let's practise *mae, ato, toki, to,* O.K.? First, let's try making sentences using *mae.* Yes, Tom, go ahead. Anything'll do.

T: Umm, 'Before I came to Japan, I couldn't speak Japanese, but now I can a little.'

S: Good. Next, try making a sentence using *ato.*

J: 'After lectures finish I'm going to a bar with friends and after that I'm going to another bar.'

S: That's fine. Next is *toki.*

M: 'The other day when I went to a bar, I drank alcohol and sang songs.'

S: Good.

T: Can I do another one?

S: Yes, go on.

T: 'Just as I was about to go out of the door, I got a call from Mary.'

S: That's a very good sentence. Lastly *to.* Yes, John!

J: 'I always go for a drink when lectures finish. And I always come back drunk when I go out for a drink.'

S: That's fine.

Conversation 18a

B: Mr Inoue, I've been in Japan for three months now but I get the feeling my Japanese hasn't progressed at all.

I: It's not true that it hasn't progressed. But in another two or three months, it'll get much better, I'm sure.

B: But what do you think I should do to get better much sooner?

I: Umm, if it's a question of vocabulary, why don't you listen to the news every day, and take down the words you don't know? If you do that, the number of words will grow, won't it?

B: But I wonder what I should do to be able to speak much more fluently.

I: That's a question of time.

B: I should have studied more before coming to Japan!

Conversation 18b

B: If we'd gone by taxi, we might have been there by now.

I: We'll soon get there.

B: Shouldn't we have got him to write us a map?

I: No, we don't need a map. This is Aoyamadori, O.K.? I think if we go straight down here and turn left at the third set of lights, it should be *2ban.*

B: Really? But why don't we try asking someone?

I: No need for that. It's close by here.

B: Shouldn't we have taken the <u>second</u> turning on the left?

I: Maybe. Let's take a taxi if we don't find it in another five minutes.

B: If there is one!

I: Take us to Aoyama 1 *chome,* 2 *ban,* 6 *go* please.

Conversation 19a

B: Good morning.

I: Morning. What's the matter, Mr Brown? It looks like another hangover, is it?

B: That's right. I was taken to a karaoke bar last night by some friends.

I: I bet that was fun, wasn't it? The karaoke, I mean?

B: Umm, I said I didn't want to sing, but I was made to. However much I said I was tone deaf, they said they wanted to hear an English song, and I thought I'd be told off if I didn't sing so I sang 'Greensleeves'.

I: I bet that went down well.

B: It seems to have done. But it was awful, being made to drink even though I didn't want to.

I: John, you've got to get a bit stronger!

Conversation 19b

B: Why are you crying?

Y: My father has said that he won't let me go and study abroad.

B: Why have you suddenly been told that it's no good?

Y: My father intends to make me do hanayome shugyo as soon as I've finished school.

B: What's hanayome shugyo?

Y: It's preparing for marriage, by learning the tea-ceremony, flower arranging, and cooking.

B: Preparation for marriage? But have you got a fiancé (*lit.* partner)?

Y: No, I'm going to be made to have an arranged marriage.

B: An arranged marriage? What are you going to do?

Y: I suppose I'll have to do as I'm told!

Conversation 20a

A: Why don't you try these on?

B: These?! You must be joking, I don't want these!

A: Why? they're nice.

B: They're not my cup of tea. What about these?

A: They're nice. Are you going to try them on?

B: Mmm, I will.

B: They're a bit long, aren't they?

A: Not really. They're just right, I think.

B: O.K. I'll have them. Excuse me, can I have these please?

X: Yes, that's 4,000 yen.

B: Great. Shall we go and have a cup of tea?

Conversation 20b

A: Is Mr Yoshida there?

B: Who is speaking?

A: My name's Tanaka.

B: Just a moment ... He's not at his desk at the moment.

A: I see. Can I leave a message?

174

B: Yes, do.
A: I shall call on him tomorrow at eleven. Would you tell him that, please?
B: Certainly, I'll pass that on to him.

Vocabulary List 1:   English–Japanese

Verbs are given in both plain and *masu* forms. Numbers refer to lesson, but where we give a lesson number immediately followed by n. and another number the latter identifies a particular note in that lesson's conversation piece.

ability chikara
able to dekiru/dekimasu; 15
about goro, gurai; 5, 8
about (regarding) ni tsuite
abroad kaigai (e)
accent hatsuon
accident (have an) jiko (ni au/aimasu)
according to ni yoru to ... sō desu; 13n.1
advertisement kōkoku
afraid kowai
after(wards) -te kara; 7, ato ni/de; 17
afternoon gogo
again mata
ages, I haven't seen you for (o-)hisashiburi desu
ago mae; 8
airmail kōkūbin
airport kūkō
alcohol arukōru
alcoholic drink o-sake
alien registration card gaikokujin tōrokushōmeishō
alive, be ikiru/ikimasu; 8
all zenbu
all (everyone) mi(n)na
all right ii
alone hitori de
along, go o iku/ikimasu; 4
already mō; 3
also mo
although no ni, ga; 4, 9
altogether zenbu de
always itsumo; 14
a.m. gozen
ambulance kyūkyūsha
amount ryō
amusing omoshiroi
and then, so sore kara, soshite; 4, 7, 9

anybody, 14
anyone, 14
anything, 14
anywhere, 14
apartment apāto
apologize ayamaru/ayamarimasu
appear, 13
April shigatsu
argue kenka suru/shimasu
arrest taiho suru/shimasu
arrive tōchaku suru/shimasu, tsuku/tsukimasu
article kiji
as ... as hodo gurai; 16
as soon/far/long as ..., 17
ask kiku/kikimasu; 11
ask (for) tanomu/tanomimasu; 11
asleep, be nete iru/imasu; 7
at ni, de; 3, 4
attach *vt.* tsukeru/tsukemasu
August hachigatsu
aunt oba(-san); 9
autumn aki
awful hidoi

back ushiro
back, come kaette kuru/kimasu
bad warui
bad at heta; 12
bag kaban
baggage nimotsu
bang *vt.* batan to shimeru/shimemasu; 6
bank ginkō
bank account kōza
bar bā
baseball yakyū
bath *n.* (o-)furo
bath *vt.* (o-)furo ni hairu/hairimasu

be da/desu, aru/arimasu, iru/imasu, irassharu/irasshaimasu, oru/orimasu; 2, 3, 20
be (on TV.) ni deru/demasu
beautiful utsukushii
because no de, kara; 9
become naru/narimasu; 6, 12
bed, go to neru/nemasu
beer bīru
before mae; 5, 17
begin (to) hajimeru/hajimemasu
behind ushiro
beside soba, tonari
best ichiban ii; 16
better, 16
between no aida (ni); 17
beyond mukō
big ōkii, ōki na; 6
bike ōtobai
birthday tanjōbi
bit sukoshi, chotto; 5
black kuroi
blow up *vi.* bakuhatsu suru/shimasu
blue aoi
board ni noru/norimasu
boil *vi.* waku/wakimasu
boil *vt.* wakasu/wakashimasu
bomb *n.* bakudan
book(shop) honya-(san)
boring tsumaranai
born, be umareru/umaremasu
borrow kariru/karimasu
boss bosu
both mo ... mo, ryōhō; 2, 14, 16
bottle bin
bottle *(counter)* hon; 5
bottom shita
box hako
boy otoko no ko
boyfriend bōifurendo
bread pan
break *vt.* kowasu/kowashimasu
break down koshō suru/shimasu
breakfast chōshoku, asagohan
bring motte kuru/kimasu, tsurete

kuru/kimasu; 7
brother otōto, ani, o-nī-san; 9
brothers (go-)kyōdai; 9
brown chairo (no); 3
browse tachiyomi suru/shimasu
building biru, tatemono
bullet train shinkansen
bump into ni deau/deaimasu
burglar dorobō
bus(stop) basu(tei)
business, on shigoto de
businessman kaishain, sararīman
busy isogashii
but ga, no ni, keredo(mo) shikashi; 4, 9
buy kau/kaimasu
by de, ni, ni yotte; 3, 4, 19
by (four o'clock) made ni

call (denwa o) kakeru/kakemasu, yobu/yobimasu
called, 11
calligraphy shodō
camera kamera
can koto ga dekiru/dekimasu; 15
can do dekiru/dekimasu; 12
capital shuto
car kuruma
card kādo
cards (playing) toranpu
care kamau/kamaimasu; 15
careful, be chūi suru/shimasu
cartoon manga
catch (a train) ni noru/norimasu
catch cold kaze o hiku/hikimasu
cause, 19
certainly mochiron
chair isu
change *n.* o-kaeshi, o-tsuri, komakai o-kane
change *vt.* kaeru/kaemasu
change *vi.* kawaru/kawarimasu
changed, get kigaeru/kigaemasu
character (Chinese) kanji
cheap yasui
cheaply yasuku
cheapo yasuppoi
check shiraberu/shirabemasu

child(ren) kodomo
China Chūgoku
Chinese *adj.* Chūgoku no
Chinese (language) Chūgokugo
Chinese (person) Chūgokujin
chips furaido poteto
choose erabu/erabimasu
chopstick hashi
church kyōkai
cigarette tabako
cinema eigakan
class(room) kyōshitsu
clean *adj.* kirei (na)
clean *vt.* sōji suru/shimasu
cleanly kirei ni
clean up katazukeru/katazukemasu
clearly hakkiri (to)
clever atama ga ii, kashikoi
climate kikō
climb noboru/noborimasu
close *vt.* shimeru/shimemasu
close *vi.* shimaru/shimarimasu
closed, be shimatte iru/imasu; 8
coat *n.* kōto
coffee kōhī
coffee shop kissaten
coin kōka, dama
coke kōra
cold *n.* kaze
cold (to the touch) tsumetai
cold (weather) samui
collect *vt.* atsumeru/atsumemasu
collect *vi.* atsumaru/atsumarimasu
collide shōtotsu suru/shimasu
come kuru/kimasu, mairu/mairimasu,
    irassharu/irasshaimasu; 20
come back kaette kuru/kimasu; 7
come in hairu/hairimasu, haitte
    kuru/kimasu, agaru/agarimasu
come off toreru/toremasu
come out deru/demasu; 8
come round asobi ni kuru/kimasu
comic manga
company kaisha
complete, be dekite iru/imasu

completely kanzen ni
concert konsāto
continue *vt.* tsuzukeru/tsuzukemasu
continue *vi.* tsuzuku/tsuzukimasu
convey tsutaeru/tsutaemasu
cooking ryōri
cool (weather) suzushii
cool tsumetai
corner kado
correct naosu/naoshimasu
cost *n.* nedan
cost (of living) bukka
cost *vi.* kakaru/kakarimasu
country (nation) kuni
country(side) inaka
crash (cars) shōtotsu suru/shimasu
crash (planes) tsuiraku suru/shimasu
crazy kichigai (na)
cross (over) (o) wataru/watarimasu; 4
cross, be okotte iru/imasu
cross-legged, sit agura o kaku/kakimasu
crowded, be konde iru/imasu; 8
cry naku/nakimasu
cup koppu
cup *(counter)* hai; 5
cut *vt.* kiru/kirimasu

danger kiken
dangerous abunai, kiken na
date hizuke; 5
date, what's the nannichi
daughter musume(-san); 9
day hi
day after tomorrow asatte
day before yesterday ototsui, ototoi
dead shinde iru/imasu
December jūnigatsu
decide koto ni suru/shimasu; 15
decide kimeru/kimemasu
definitely zettai ni
delicious oishii
density mitsudo
depart dekakeru/dekakemasu
department (academic) gakubu
department store depāto
desire(d) hoshii; 12

dialect ben
dictionary jisho
die shinu/shinimasu
difficult muzukashii
difficult to -nikui; 6n.5
disappear, 12
dishy suteki (na)
dislike(d) kirai; 12
do yaru, yarimasu, suru/shimasu, itasu/
   itashimasu, nasaru/nasaimasu, tsukuru/
   tsukurimasu; 10, 20
doctor (o-)isha(-san)
documentary dokyumentarī
door doa
down shita
drawer hikidashi
dress doresu
dressed, get kigaeru/kigaemasu
drink *vt.* nomu/nomimasu, itadaku/
   itadakimasu, meshigaru,
   meshiagarimasu; 20
drink *n.* nomimono
drunk, be yo(ppara)tte iru/imasu
due to hazu; 9
during ... no aida; 17

early *adj.* hayai
early *adv.* hayaku
earthquake jishin
easy yasashii, kantan (na)
easy to -yasui; 6n.5
eat taberu/tabemasu, meshiagaru/
   meshiagarimasu, itadaku/itadakimasu; 20
eat out gaishoku suru/shimasu
either mo ... mo, dochiraka; 2, 14
embarrassed, be hazukashii
empty, be suite iru/imasu; 8,19
end (of street) tsukiatari
England Igirisu, Eikoku
English (language) Eigo
English (person) Igirisujin, Eikokujin
enough jūbun
enter hairu/hairimasu; 8
entry, no shinnyūkinshi
escape nigeru/nigemasu
even if -te mo; 19n.2

evening yūgata, ban
ever, 15
every day mainichi
every month maitsuki
every week maishū
every year mainen, maitoshi
everyone, 14
everything, 14
everywhere, 14
example, for tatoeba
excuse (me) shitsurei suru/shimasu,
   sumimasen, gomen nasai
exit deguchi
expected to hazu; 9
expensive takai
experience *n.* keiken
experience *vt.* keiken suru/shimasu
explain setsumei suru/shimasu
explanation setsumei
extremely hijō ni
eye me

face kao
the fact is that n' (no) desu; 9
fact, in jitsu wa
fall down ochiru/ochimasu
fall over korobu/korobimasu,
   taoreru/taoremasu
family kazoku
famous yūmei (na)
far tōi
fast hayai
father chichi, o-tō-san; 9
favourite ichiban suki (na)
February nigatsu
feel (like) 13
few sukunai
film fuirumu
film (movie) eiga
fine kekkō (na)
fingerprint shimon
finish saigo
finish *vt., vi.* owaru/owarimasu
fish (shop) sakana (ya-san)
flood kōzui
floor yuka

floor (*counter*) kai; 5
flower hana
flower arranging ikebana
fluent ryūchō (na), perapera (na)
fluently ryūchō ni
fly tobu/tobimasu
fond of suki (na); 12
food tabemono
foot, on aruite; 7
foot ashi
for ni
for (time), 8
foreign gaikoku no
foreigner gai(koku)jin
forget wasureru/wasuremasu
free (no charge) tada
free (time) hima (na)
French (language) Furansugo
fresh shinsen (na)
Friday kinyōbi
fridge reizōko
friend tomodachi
from kara
front mae
full ippai (na)
fun *n.* tanoshimi
fun *adj.* tanoshii
funny omoshiroi, okashii

garden niwa, teien
German (language) Doitsugo
get (become) naru/narimasu; 6
get (call) yobu/yobimasu
get (receive) morau/moraimasu, itadaku/itadakimasu; 10
get someone to do, 10
get up okiru/okimasu
get used to nareru/naremasu
girl onna no ko
girlfriend gārufurendo
give, 10
give up akirameru/akiramemasu
given, be, 10
glass koppu
glass (*counter*) hai
go iku/ikimasu, irassharu/irasshaimasu,

mairu/mairimasu; 20
go home kaeru/kaerimasu
go in hairu/hairimasu; 8
go off (bomb) bakuhatsu suru/shimasu
go out deru/demasu, dekakeru/dekakemasu
go out for a drink nomi ni iku/ikimasu
go out with to tsukiau/tsukiaimasu
good ii, yoroshii; 4n.6
good at jōzu (na), umai; 12
good many, 14
grandfather, 9
grandmother, 9
great ōkii
green midori-iro (no)
guest (o-)kyaku(-sama)
guide *vt.* annai suru/shimasu
guitar gitā

hair kami no ke
half past han
hamburger hanbāgā
hand te
hand over watasu/watashimasu
hang *vt.* kakeru/kakemasu
hangover futsukayoi
hard *adv.* katai
hard to *adj.* -nikui
hard *adv.* yoku
hat bōshi
haunt tamariba
have (got) aru/arimasu, motte iru/imasu; 3, 8
have someone do, 10
have to, 15
he kare
head atama
headache zutsū
hear kiku/kikimasu
heart kokoro
heart, learn by anki suru/shimasu
heater hīta
hello konnichi wa
help (someone) (o) tasukeru/tasukemasu, (ni) tetsudau/tetsudaimasu
her kanojo (no)
here koko
high takai

high school kōkō
him kare
his kare no
hobby shumi
holiday yasumi
holiday, go on ryokō suru/shimasu
holiday, take a yasumi o toru/torimasu
home (o-)uchi
home, go kaeru/kaerimasu
hope, 18
hot atsui
hot (spicy) karai
hotel hoteru
hour ji, jikan; 5, 8
house ie, (o-)taku
housewife shufu
how dō yatte
how *(plus adj.)* dore dake/hodo/gurai; 16
how about, 3
how long, 8
how much, 5, 16
how old (o-)ikutsu, nansai
humid mushiatsui
hungry, be onaka ga suite iru/imasu; 8
hurry isogu/isogimasu; 7
hurry, be in a isoide iru/imasu
husband (go-)shujin, danna-san; 9

I watashi, ore, boku; 20
if moshi; 18
ill byōki (na)
immediately (ima) sugu
important jūyō (na), taisetsu (na), daiji (na)
impression, 13
in (no naka) ni; 2, 5
injure kizu o tsukeru/tsukemasu
injury kizu
in(side), be (no naka ni) haitte iru/imasu; 8
instant insutanto (no)
instead -naide, -nakute; 7
intend to tsumori; 9
interest kyōmi
interesting omoshiroi
interpret tsūyaku suru/shimasu
interrupt kuchi o dasu/dashimasu

invite yobu/yobimasu, shōtai suru/shimasu
it, 2
January ichigatsu
Japan Nihon, Nippon
Japanese (language) Nihongo
Japanese (person) Nihonjin
jazz jazu
joke jōdan
July shichigatsu
jumper sēta
June rokugatsu
just chōdo, dake
just like to onaji yō na/ni; 13
just right chōdo ii

kidnap yūkai suru/shimasu
kind yasashii, shinsetsu (na)
kind enough to, 7
know shitte iru/imasu; 8, go-zonji, zonjiru/
  zonjimasu; 20
know, get to shiru/shirimasu; 7
Korea Kankoku
Korean (language) Kankokugo
Korean (person) Kankokujin

lacquerware shikki
lady oba-san; 9
language kotoba
language, foreign gaikokugo
large ōkii, ōi
last *vi.* tsuzuku/tsuzukimasu
last *adj.* saigo (no)
last month sengetsu
last night yūbe
last week senshū
last year kyonen
late osoi
late, be okurete iru/imasu
laugh warau/waraimasu
learn narau/naraimasu
leave *vi.* tatsu/tachimasu,
  dekakeru/dekakemasu
leave *vt.* yameru/yamemasu
leave something behind wasuremono o
  suru/shimasu
lecture jugyō

left hidari (no)
leg ashi
leisurely yukkuri to
lesson jugyō
let, 19
let's -mashō
let ... off orosu/oroshimasu
letter tegami
lie down yoko ni naru/narimasu
light *adj.* karui
light *n.* denki
like(d) suki; 12
likes and dislikes sukikirai
listen (to) (o) kiku/kikimasu, ukagau/
 ukagaimasu; 20
little chīsa na, chīsai
live sumu/sumimasu; 8
loathe daikirai; 12
lonely samishii
long nagai
loo o-tearai
look at (o) miru/mimasu, go-ran ni naru/
 narimasu, haiken itasu/itashimasu
look for sagasu/sagashimasu
look, have a mite miru/mimasu
look forward to o tanoshimi ni
 suru/shimasu
loose yurui
lose nakusu/shimasu
a lot (of) takusan(no)
love *n.* ai
love *vt.* aisuru/shimasu; 8
low hikui
lucky un ga ii
lunch hirugohan
lunchtime hiru

mad kichigai (na)
magazine zasshi
magnitude shindo
main entrance chūōguchi
make tsukuru/tsukurimasu, suru/shimasu
man otoko (no hito), oji-san; 9
many takusan (no), ōi
March sangatsu

marriage kekkon
married, be kekkon shite iru/imasu
marry to kekkon suru/shimasu
match shiai
matter, it doesn't kamaimasen; 15
may(be) ka mo shiremasen, hyotto suru to;
 9, 15
May gogatsu
me watashi
meal shokuji, gohan
meaning *n.* imi
mean *vt.*, 11
mean to tsumori; 9
medicine kusuri
meet (ni) au/aimasu
meet, arrange to machiawase (o) suru/
 shimasu
meeting kaigi
memory kioku
message (o-)kotozuke
middle naka
middle of, in the saichū; 17
mind kamau/kamaimasu; 15
minute fun; 5
moment, at the ima no tokoro
Monday getsuyōbi
money o-kane
month, 7, 8
more motto; 16
more, the ... the more, 18
(bit) more mō (chotto)
morning asa
most ichiban, mottomo; 16
mother haha, o-kā-san; 9
motorbike ōtobai
mountain yama
move *vi.* ugoku/ugokimasu
move *vt.* ugokasu/ugokashimasu
much takusan
museum hakubutsukan
must, 15

name (o-)namae
name card meishi
near chikai

nearby chikaku ni
necessary hitsuyō (na)
need iru/irimasu; 12
neither mo ... mo; 2, 14
never, 14
new atarashii
news nyūsu
newspaper shinbun
next tsugi (no)
next month raigetsu
next week raishū
next year rainen
nice ii
nice and -te ii; 7
night yoru
no ie
no good dame (na)
none, 14
noon hiru
no one, 14
normal futsū (no)
normally futsū
not at all zenzen
not often amari
not very amari; 16
not yet mada
note nōto
note (money) satsu
nothing, 14
November jūichigatsu
now ima; 4
nowhere, 14
nuclear weapons kakuheiki
nuisance, that's a komaru/komarimasu
number kazu, bangō

o'clock ji; 5
October jūgatsu
odd okashii, okashi na
of, 2
off, be kaeru/kaerimasu, dekakeru/dekakemasu
office kaisha
often yoku; 6
O.K. (good) ii, daijōbu (na)
O.K. (not too good) mā mā

old (people) toshiyori
old (things) furui
on no ue ni
once ikkai, ichido, itsuka; 5, 14
only shika (*with negative*), dake; 5
open vt. akeru/akemasu, hiraku/hirakimasu
open vi. aku/akimasu
open, be aite iru/imasu; 8, 19
opinion iken
opposite n. hantai
opposite adj. hantai (no)
or ... ka ... ka, soretomo; 2
orange n. mikan
ordinary futsū (no)
other hoka (no)
ought, 9, 18
our watashitachi no
out, be dete iru/imasu, dekakete iru/imasu
outside soto
over, 4
over there (a)soko, sochira, achira
own, on my hitori de

packed lunch (o-)bentō
painful itai
paper kami
parcel kozutsumi
parent (go-)ryōshin; 9
party pātei
pass tōru/tōrimasu
passport pasupōto
pay (o-kane o) harau/haraimasu
pencil enpitsu
people hitobito
perhaps tabun, moshi ka suru to
period play jidai geki
person hito
phone (call) n. denwa
phone vt. (ni) denwa suru/shimasu, denwa o kakeru/kakemasu
photo shashin
piece mai; 5
place n. basho, tokoro
place vt. oku/okimasu
plan yotei; 9
plane hikōki

platform bansen
play asobu/asobimasu
play (e.g. rugby) yaru/yarimasu
please o-negai suru/shimasu, kudasai; 4
pleased to meet you dōzo yoroshiku
pleasure, my dō itashimashite
plug (bath) sen
plum (sour) umeboshi
p.m. gogo
pocket poketto
police box kōban
police(man) keisatsu(kan)
polite teinei (na)
politician seijika
popular ninki ga aru/arimasu
population jinkō
possibility kanōsei
possible dekiru/dekimasu; 15
possibly tabun, moshi ka suru to
post (a letter) tegami o dasu/dashimasu
postcard hagaki
post office yūbinkyoku
potato, fried furaido poteto
practice renshū
practise renshū suru/shimasu
pray inoru/inorimasu
prefer suki; 16
preparation junbi, yōi
prepare junbi suru/shimasu, yōi suru/
    shimasu
present n. purezento
present adj. ima (no)
president (company) shachō
presumably osoraku; 9
pretty kirei (na)
price nedan
prices bukka
primary school pupil shōgakusei
probably darō/deshō; 9
problem mondai
professor sensei
programme bangumi
pronounce vt. hatsuon suru/shimasu
pronunciation hatsuon
properly chan to

publish shuppan suru/shimasu
pull out nuku/nukimasu
pupil seito
purse saifu
put oku/okimasu
put (in) (ni) ireru/iremasu

question shitsumon
question (problem) mondai
quick hayai
quickly hayaku
quiet shizuka (na)
quite kanari
quiz kuizu

radio rajio
rain n. ame
rain vi. ame ga furu/furimasu
rainy season tsuyu
raw fish (o-)sashimi
reach todoku/todokimasu
reach (arrive at) tsuku/tsukimasu,
    tōchaku suru/shimasu
read yomu/yomimasu
ready (yōi ga) dekite iru/imasu
real hontō (no)
really hontō (ni), sugoku
receive, 10
recent saikin (no)
recently saikin
red akai
refuse kotowaru/kotowarimasu
remember oboeru/oboemasu; 8
reporter kisha
residence o-taku
rest vi. yasumu/yasumimasu
return vi. kaeru/kaerimasu
return vt. kaesu/kaeshimasu
rice go-han
right migi
right, just chōdo ii
ring (ni) denwa suru/shimasu, denwa o
    kakeru/kakemasu
road michi, tōri
roof yane, okujō
room heya

room (space) basho
roughly itsu goro
round *adv.* 4
rude shitsurei (na)
rugby ragubī
run hashiru/hashirimasu

sad kanashii
safe anzen (na), buji (na)
safely anzen ni, buji ni
sale bāgen sēru
same (as) (to) onaji; 6
Saturday doyōbi
sauce sōsu
say iu/iimasu, mōsu/mōshimasu,
　　ossharu/osshaimasu; 11, 20
school gakkō
sea(side) umi(be)
seasons, four shiki
seat, take a suwaru/suwarimasu,
　　kakeru/kakemasu
see *see* **look at**
seem, 13
sell *vt.* uru/urimasu
sell *vi.* ureru/uremasu
send okuru/okurimasu
sensible gōriteki (na)
sentence bunshō
September kugatsu
set off dekakeru/dekakemasu
shall we -mashō; 3
shape katachi; 13
she kanojo
shirt shatsu
shoe kutsu
shoot utsu/uchimasu,
　　uchikorosu/uchikoroshimasu
shop o-mise
short (people) se ga hikui
short (things) mijikai
should, 16, 18
show miseru/misemasu
shut *vt.* shimeru/shimemasu
shut *vi.* shimaru/shimarimasu
shut, be shimatte iru/imasu
sick byōki (na)

sick of, be ni akiru/akimasu
side soba
signpost hyōshiki
simple kantan (na)
since kara; 8
sing utau/utaimasu
singer kashu
single (unmarried) *adj.* dokushin (no)
Sir sensei
sister imōto, ane, o-nē-san; 9
sit suwaru/suwarimasu, kakeru/kakemasu
sit cross-legged agura o kaku/kakimasu
sixth glass roppaime
size ōkisa
ski sukī suru/shimasu
slam batan to shimeru/shimemasu
sleep neru/nemasu
slow osoi
slowly osoku, yukkuri to
small chīsai, chīsa na
smell *n.* nioi
smell *vi.* nioi ga suru/shimasu; 13
smoke tabako o suu/suimasu
snow *n.* yuki
so, 9
so as to, 12
society shakai
soft yawarakai
softball sofutobōru
sold out urikire
some, 14
some ... other, 14
somebody, 14
someone, 14
something, 14
sometime, 14
somewhere, 14
son musuko(-san); 9
song uta
soon mō sugu; 4
sorry sumimasen, shitsurei suru/shimasu,
　　gomen nasai
sorts of, all iroiro (na), ironna (na)
sound oto; 13
sound like, 13

soya sauce shōyu
speak hanasu/hanshimasu, hanashi o suru/shimasu
spend (time) kakeru/kakemasu
spend (money) tsukau/tsukaimasu
spicy karai
splendid kekkō (na), rippa (na)
spoon supūn
spoonful hai; 5
sport supōtsu
spring haru
stamp kitte
stand (up) vt. tateru/tatemasu
stand (up) vi. tatsu/tachimasu
start vt. hajimeru/hajimemasu
start vi. hajimaru/hajimarimasu
start to -hajimeru/-hajimemasu; 9n.9
station eki
stay (the night) tomaru/tomarimasu
stay behind nokoru/nokorimasu
steal nusumu/nusumimasu
still mada; 4
stop vt. yameru/yamemasu, tomeru/tomemasu
stop vi. yamu/yamimasu, tomaru/tomarimasu
story hanashi
straight massugu
straight away ima sugu
strange hen (na), okashii, okashii na
street michi, tōri
stretch vt. nobasu/nobashimasu
strong tsuyoi
student gakusei
study benkyō suru/shimasu
stupid baka (na)
sugar satō
suitcase sūtsukēsu
summer natsu
Sunday nichiyōbi
suppose, I darō/deshō; 9
supposed to hazu; 9
sure, I'm not quite chotto wakarimasen
sweet adj. amai
swim oyogu/oyogimasu

swing, get into the chōshi ga deru/demasu
table tēburu
take toru/torimasu
take care chūi suru/shimasu; 12
take (thing) motte iku/ikimasu
take off nugu/nugimasu
take (time) off yasumu/yasumimasu
take out dasu/dashimasu
take (person) tsurete iku/ikimasu
take (time) kakaru/kakarimasu
talk hanasu/hanashimasu
tall se ga takai
taste n. aji
taste vt. aji ga suru/shimasu; 13
tasty oishii
taxi takushī
tea (English-type) kōcha
tea (Japanese) o-cha
teach oshieru/oshiemasu
teacher sensei
telephone n. denwa
television terebi
tell iu/imasu, oshieru/oshiemasu; 11
tell off shikaru/shikarimasu
temperature (fever) netsu
temple (o-)tera, -ji
terrible hidoi, osoroshii, sugoi
terrorist terorisuto
thank you dōmo arigatō gozaimasu/gozaimashita
that n. sore, are; 2
that adj. sono, ano; 2
that sort of sonna, anna; 2
there (a)soko; 2
thin hosoi
thing (abstract) koto
thing (concrete) mono
think omou/omoimasu, kangaeru/kangaemasu; 11
thirsty, be nodo ga kawaite iru/imasu; 8, 19
this n. kore
this adj. kono
this year kotoshi
thought n. shisō

throw nageru/nagemasu
throw away suteru/sutemasu
Thursday mokuyōbi
ticket kippu
tidy (up) *vt.* sōji suru/shimasu, katazukeru/katazukemasu, kirei ni suru/shimasu
tidy *adj.* kirei (na)
tight kitsui
till made
time jikan
time, be on (for) (ni) ma ni au/aimasu
tire, become tired tsukareru/tsukaremasu
tired, be tsukarete iru/imasu; 8
to e, ni, made, to; 3, 4, 5
toast tōsuto
toast (drink a) kanpai suru/shimasu
today kyō
together (with) (to) issho ni; 4
toilet toire, o-tearai, benjo
tomorrow ashita
tonight konban, konya
too mo
too (much) sugiru/sugimasu; 6
top ue
town machi
toy o-mocha
traffic kōtsū
traffic lights shingō
train densha
translate yaku suru/shimasu
travel ryokō suru/shimasu
tree ki
tricky yayakoshii
trouble *n.* mondai
trouble *vt.* (ni) meiwaku o kakeru/kakemasu
true hontō (no)
try ...ing te miru/mimasu; 6n.17; 7n.4; 8n.1
try on (shoes, socks, trousers, skirt) haite miru/mimasu
Thursday mokuyōbi
Tuesday kayōbi
turn (corner) (o) magaru/magarimasu

turn down oto o chīsaku suru/shimasu; 6
turn off kesu/keshimasu
turn on tsukeru/tsukemasu
turn up oto o ōkiku suru/shimasu; 6
turning (magari)kado
typhoon taifū

umbrella kasa
umm sō desu ne, etto
unbearably te tamaranai; 16
uncle oji(-san); 9
under(neath) shita
understand wakaru/wakarimasu; 12
uninteresting omoshiroku nai
university daigaku
unlike to chigatte; 13
unpleasant iya (na)
until made; 17
us watashitachi
use tsukau/tsukaimasu
used to, be ni narete iru/imasu
used to, get ni nareru/naremasu
useless dame (na)
usual futsū (no)
usually futsū

various iroiro (na), iron(na)
very totemo, amari (*with negative*); 6
via keiyu
view keshiki
view (opinion) iken
visit tazuneru/tazunemasu
visitor o-kyaku-san
volcano kazan

wait (for) (o) matsu/machimasu
walk aruku/arukimasu
wallet saifu
want (to), 12
war sensō
ward ku; 18
warm atatakai, attakai
wash arau/araimasu
watch *n.* tokei
watch *see* **look at**
water mizu
water (drinking) o-mizu

way to/of -kata; 7n.1
we watashitachi
weak yowai
weapon buki, heiki
wear kiru/kimasu, haku/hakimasu,
  kaburu/kaburimasu; 15n.2
weather (forecast) tenki(yohō)
Wednesday suiyōbi
week shūkan; 5
well *adj.* (o-)genki (na)
well *adv.* yoku, jōzu ni
what *n.* nan(i); 3
what *adj.* dono; 3
whatever, 15
when itsu, toki; 3, 17
whenever, 15
where doko, dochira; 3
wherever, 15
whether ka dō ka; 11
which *n.* dore
which *adj.* dono
which one, 3
whichever, 15
while aida (ni), -nagara; 17
whisky uisukī
white shiroi
who dare, donata; 3
whoever, 15
whose dare, donata no
why naze, dōshite; 9, 18
wide hiroi
wife oku-san; 9
wife, my kanai; 9

win katsu/kachimasu
wind kaze
window mado
wine wain
wine, rice (o-)sake
wing tsubasa
winter fuyu
wish, 18
with de, to, (to) issho ni; 3, 4
without ...ing, 7
wonder, I deshō ka; 9
wood ki
word kotoba, tango
word processor wā puro
work *n.* shigoto, kaisha
work *vi.* hataraku/hatarakimasu; 8
world yo no naka
worry *n.* shinpai
worry *vi.* shinpai suru/shimasu
would, 16
write kaku/kakimasu
writer sakka
wrong, it's chigau/chigaimasu

year toshi, nen; 5, 8
yellow kiiroi, kiiro (no)
yen en
yes hai
yesterday kinō
yet mada, mo; 4
you anata(tachi)
young wakai
your anata(tachi) no

Vocabulary List 2:   Japanese–English

ā oh
ā that way; 6
abunai dangerous
achira over there
agaru/agarimasu go up, come in; 20
ageru/agemasu give; 10
agura o kaku/kakimasu sit cross-legged
ai love *n.*
aida while, during, between; 17
aisuru/shimasu love *vt.*; 8
aite another person, partner
aite iru/imasu be open; 8
aji taste
aji ga suru/shimasu taste; 13
aka-chan baby
akai red
akarui light *adj.*
akeru/akemasu open *vt.*
akiru/akimasu become sick of
akirameru/akiramemasu give up
aku/akimasu open *vi.*
amai sweet
amari too much, not very; 5, 6, 16
ame rain *n.*
ame ga furu/furimasu rain *vi.*
Amerika America
Amerikajin American (person)
ana hole
anata you
anatatachi you
ani big brother; 9
anki suru/shimasu learn off by heart
anna that sort of
anna ni that much
(go) annai suru/shimasu guide
ano that *adj.*; 3
anō umm
anzen (na) safe
aoi blue
apāto apartment, flat
arau/araimasu wash
arawasu/arawashimasu express

are that *n.*
arigatō/arigatō gozaimasu thank you; 4
aru/arimasu be, have; 3, 12
aru certain, some; 14
aruite on foot; 7
aruku/arukimasu walk *v.*
asa morning
asa-gohan breakfast
asatte the day after tomorrow
ashi leg, foot
ashita tomorrow
asobi ni kuru/kimasu come round
asobu/asobimasu play
asoko over there
atama ga ii clever
atama ga itai have a headache
atarashii new
atatakai warm
ato after(wards), remaining; 5n.9
atsui hot
atsumaru/atsumarimasu gather *vi.*
atsumeru/atsumemasu gather *vt.*
attakai warm
au/aimasu meet
ayamaru/ayamarimasu apologize
ā yatte, 6
(o-)azukari shimasu/itashimasu receive

-ba if; 15, 18
bā bar
bāgen sēru sale
baito part-time work
baka (na) stupid
bakari just, nothing but; 8n.10
bakudan bomb
bakuhatsu suru/shimasu blow up *vi.*
ban evening
bangō number
bangumi programme
basho place, space
basu bus
basu tei bus stop

batan to (shimeru/shimemasu) slam
ben dialect
benkyō suru/shimasu study
(o-)bentō packed lunch
betsu ni (not) particularly
biru beer
bōifurendo boyfriend
boku I; 20
bōshi o kaburu (kaburimasu) wear a
  hat
bosu boss
buji (na) safe
bukka prices, cost of living
bunpō grammar
bunshō sentence
byōki (na) sick, ill

cha/o-cha tea, tea ceremony
chairo (no) brown
chan to properly
chekkuin suru/shimasu check in
chichi father; 9
(to) chigatte unlike
chigau/chigaimasu be different; 2, 6
chikaku nearby
chikara strength, ability
chīsai/chīsa na small
chizu map
chōdo just; 17
chōshi ga deru/demasu get into the
  swing of things
chotto a bit, little
Chūgoku China
Chūgokugo Chinese (language)
Chūgokujin Chinese (person)
chūi suru/shimasu take care; 12
chūko second-hand
chūō(guchi) central (exit)
chūshi ni naru/narimasu be abandoned

da/desu be; 2
dai cost
daigaku university
daiji (na) important
daijōbu (na) O.K.
daikirai (na) loath(ed); 12

daikōbutsu favourite (thing)
daisuki really like(d); 12
dake only; 5
dake quantity; 16
(10en) dama (10-yen) coin
dame (na) useless, no good; 15
danna-san (your) husband
dare who; 3
dareka, 14
daremo, 14
darō/deshō (ka), 9
dasu/dashimasu get/take out
datte even; 20
de, 3, 7
(ni) deau/deaimasu bump (into)
de gozaru/gozaimasu be; 4n.3
deguchi exit
de irassharu/irasshaimasu be; 2
dekakeru/dekakemasu go out
dekiru/dekimasu able, be ready, be
  complete, can do; 12, 15
dekiru dake as much as possible; 16
demo even, but, or something; 3n.6, 14
denki light, electricity
densha train
denwa telephone *n.*
denwa o kakeru/kakemasu telephone *vt.*
depāto department store
deru/demasu go out, appear (on TV.)
deshō probably; 9
deshō ka I wonder; 9
dete iru/imasu be out, have gone out, be
  on (TV.)
dō how (about); 3, 6, 11, 18
doa door
dochira, 3, 16
dochiraka, 14
dochiramo, 14
dochira-sama who; 3, 20
dō itashimashite a pleasure
dōjo martial arts hall
dōki motive
doko where; 3
dokoka, 14
dokomo, 14

dokutoku (no) peculiarly, peculiar to, unique to
dokyumentarī documentary
dōmo (arigatō) (thank you), somehow
donata who; 3, 14
donatamo, 14
donna what sort of; 3
donna ni how; 6
dono what, which *adj.*; 3
dore which *n.*
dore dake, 16
dore gurai how much/long; 8, 16
dore hodo, 16
doreka, 14
doremo, 14
doresu dress
dorobō robber
dōshite why; 9
dō yatte, 6
** doyōbi** Saturday
dōzo go ahead, please do; 4

e to(wards); 3
earoguramu aerogramme
ebi prawn
ebifurai fried prawn
eiga film (movie)
eigakan cinema
Eigo English (language)
eiji shinbun English language newspaper
Eikoku Britain, England
eikyō influence
eki station
eki-mae in front of the station
en yen; 5
enpitsu pencil
erabu/erabimasu choose
erai good for you, great
etto umm

fuan fan
fueru/fuemasu increase *vi.*
fuirumu film (camera)
fuku fork
fukuzatsu (na) complex
fun minute; 5, 8

funabin seamail
furaido poteto fried potato
Furansu France
(o-)furo bath
furoshiki cloth for wrapping things in
(ame ga) furu/furimasu rain *v.*
furui old (things)
fushōsha injured (people)
fusuma paper (sliding) screen
futari two people
futsū (no) usual, normal; 2
futsū usually, normally
futsukayoi hangover
fuyu winter

ga but, and; 3, 4
gai(koku)jin foreigner, alien
gaishoku suru/shimasu eat out
gakkō school, university
gakubu (academic) department
gakusei(-san) student
gārufurendo girlfriend
gasu gas
gatsu month; 5
genki (na) well
getsu month; 8
getsuyōbi Monday
ginkō bank
gitā guitar
go-chisō meal
go-chisō sama deshita thank you for the meal
gogo afternoon, p.m.
gohan rice, (cooked) meal
gomen nasai/kudasai excuse me
go-ran ni naru/narimasu look; 20
gōriteki (na) sensible
goro about; 5
gorufu golf
gozaru/gozaimasu be; 2, 4n.9
gozen a.m.
go-zonji desu know; 20
gurai about, extent; 5, 12n.1, 16

hagaki postcard
haha mother; 9

hai yes
hai (*counter*), 5
haiken itasu/itashimasu see, look at; 5n.12, 20
hairu/hairimasu enter, go in
haitte iru/imasu be in(side)
hajimaru/hajimarimasu begin, start *vi.*
hajimemashite pleased to meet you
hajimeru/hajimemasu begin, start *vt.*
-hajimeru/-hajimemasu start to; 9n.9
hajimete for the first time
hakkiri clearly; 6
hakkiri shite iru/imasu be clear
hako box
haku/hakimasu wear
hakusa white sand
han half past; 5
hana flower
hanashi story, talk
hanashichū engaged (phone)
hanasu/hanashimasu talk, speak
hanayome shugyō bride's training
hanbāgā hamburger
harau/haraimasu pay
hare fine weather
hareru/haremasu clear up
haru spring
hashi chopsticks
hashiru/hashirimasu run
hataraku/hatarakimasu work
hatashite after all
hatsu departure
hatsuon accent
hayai fast, quick, early
hazu due to, supposed to; 9
hazukashii embarrassed
(seki o) hazushite iru/imasu be out of one's seat
hen area
hen (na) odd
heya room
hi day
hidari left
hidoi awful
higashi east

hijō ni extremely
hikaeru/hikaemasu refrain from
hikidashi drawer
hikōki plane
hikui low
hima (na) free
himitsu secret
hiraku/hirakimasu open *vt.*
hirau/hiraimasu pick up
hiroi wide, large (space)
hirou/hiroimasu pick up
hisashiburi not for a long time
hīta heater
hito person
hitokoto a word
hitori de alone
hitotachi people
hitsuyō (na) necessary
hō side; 16
hodo extent; 15n.1, 16n.5, 18
(no) hoka (ni) other, apart from, in addition to; 14n.4
hon(ya-san) book(shop)
hon (*counter*), 5
Hon Kon Hong Kong
hontō (no) real, true; 2
hoshigaru/hoshigarimasu want; 12
hoshii desire(d), want; 12
hosoi thin
hosonagai long and thin
hoteru hotel
hotondo almost (all)
hyōshiki signpost
hyotto suru to perhaps; 9
i stomach
ii good, nice, right
ichiban most, best; 16
ichido onetime, once
i-chōen gastroenteritis
ie house
īe no
Igirisu England
Igirisujin English (person)
ikaga how; 3, 18
iken opinion

ikite iru/imasu be alive; 8
iku/ikimasu go; 7, 20
ikura how much; 5
ikuraka, 14
ikura(de)mo, 14, 15
ikutsu how many, how old; 5
ikutsuka, 14
ijō more than; 16n.3
ima now; 4
ima (no) present
ima no tokoro at the moment
imi meaning; 11
imōto(-san) young sister; 9
inaka country(side)
inoru/inorimasu pray; 12
insutanto instant
ippai full
(go-)ippaku one night
irasshaimase welcome
irassharu/irasshaimasu be, come, go; 20
ireru/iremasu put in, make (tea)
iro colour
iroiro (na) various
ironna various
iru/imasu be; 3
iru/irimasu need, be necessary; 12
ishi stone
isogashii busy
isogu/isogimasu hurry
isoide in a hurry
(to) issho ni with; 4
isu chair
itadaku/itadakimasu have, eat, receive, get; 7, 10, 20
itai painful
itasu/itashimasu do; 4n.1, 10, 20
itsu when, what time; 3
itsuka, 14
itsukara since when; 8
itsumo, 14
itte kuru/kimasu go (for a short time)
iu/iimasu say, tell; 11
iya (na) unpleasant

ja arimasen, 2

jazu jazz
ji writing
ji(kan) time; 5, 8
jidaigeki period play
jiki time, season
jiko (ni au/aimasu) (have an) accident
jinan second son; 9
jinkō population
jishin earthquake
jisho dictionary
jitensha bicycle
jōdan joke
jōshaken ticket
jōtatsu suru/shimasu progress
jōzu (na) good at; 12
jugyō lectures
junbi preparation
juwaki receiver

ka, 2, 3
-ka, 14
ka … ka, 2
kaban bag
kaburu/kaburimasu, 15n.2
kachi worth; 14
kado corner
kādo card
kaeru/kaemasu change vt.
kaeru/kaerimasu go back/home
kaesu/kaeshimasu return vt.
kaette kuru/kimasu come home
kagiri as long as, extent; 17
kai floor, time (counter); 5
kaigai abroad
kaigi conference
kaisha company, work, the office
kaishain businessman
kakaru/kakarimasu take (time), cost (money)
kakejiku scroll
kakeru/kakemasu pour, phone, sit down
kakitoru/kakitorimasu write down
kaku/kakimasu write
kakuheiki nuclear weapons
kamau/kamaimasu care, mind; 15
kamera camera

kami paper
ka mo shiremasen maybe; 9
Kanada Canada
kanai my wife; 9
kanarazu necessarily, always
kanari quite
kanashii sad
(o-)kane money
kangae idea
kangaeru/kangaemasu think, consider
Kankoku Korea
Kankokugo Korean (language)
Kankokujin Korean (person)
kanji Chinese character
kanji feeling; 13
(o-)kanjō bill
kanpai cheers
kanpai suru/shimasu drink a toast
konojo she, her, girlfriend; 2
kanōsei possibility
Kansai Osaka/Kobe area
kantan (na) simple, easy
Kantō Tokyo area
kao face; 13
kara and so; 9
kara after, since, from; 3, 7, 8
karada body
karai spicy, hot
kare he, him; 2
karera they, them; 2
karimasu (kariru) borrow
karuchā shokku culture shock
karui light
kasa umbrella
kashikoi clever
kashikomarimashita I have understood
  (and will do as you say); 4n.7
kashu singer
kata shoulder
-kata way to; 7n.1
katachi shape; 13
katai hard
katamichi one way
katsu/kachimasu win
katsudō activity

kau/kaimasu buy
kawaii cute
(nodo ga) kawaite iru/imasu be thirsty; 8
(nodo ga) kawaku/kawakimasu get
  thirsty
(to) kawaru/kawarimasu differ from,
  change *vi.*
kayōbi Tuesday
kazan volcano
kaze wind
kaze o hiku/hikimasu catch a cold
kazu number
ke(re)domo but
keiken suru/shimasu experience
keisatsu(kan) police(man)
keiyu (de) via
keizai economy
keizaiteki economic(al)
kekkō (na) splendid, fine
kekkon shite iru/imasu be married
kekkon suru/shimasu marry
kekkyoku after all
kendō the art of the (bamboo) sword
kenkyū suru/shimasu research
keredomo but
kesa this morning
kesshite definitely
kichigai (na) mad, crazy
kigaeru/kigaemasu (get) change(d)
ki ga suru/shimasu feel; 13
kiiro(ppoi) yellow(ish)
kiji article
kikō weather, climate
kikoku suru/shimasu return to one's
  country
kiku/kikimasu ask, hear, listen to; 11
kimeru/kimemasu decide
kimochi feeling
kindaishi modern history
kinō yesterday
kinpen neighbourhood
kinshi forbidden
kinyōbi Friday
kioku memory
kippu ticket

kirai (na) dislike(d); 12
kirei (na) pretty
kiru/kimasu wear; 15n.2
kiru/kirimasu cut
kisha reporter
kissaten coffee shop
kita north
kitsui tight
kitte stamp
kō in this way; 6
kōban police box
kōcha (English-type) tea
kochira this one; 2, 16
kodomo child(ren)
kōhī coffee
koi thick, strong
koko here, this (place)
kōkō jidai high-school days
kōkoku advertisement
kōkūbin airmail
kōkū gaisha airline company
komakai o-kane small change
komaru/komarimasu be a nuisance, get stuck
komu/komimasu get crowded
konban this evening
konban wa good evening
konbu sea weed
konde iru/imasu be crowded; 8
kondo wa this time
konna this sort of; 3
konnichi wa hello
kono this *adj.*; 2
konsāto concert
koppu cup
kōra cola
kore this; 2
korobu/korobimasu fall over
koshō shite iru/imasu be broken down
koshō suru/shimasu break down
kotatsu table with heater attached
koto (abstract) thing; 15, 17
kōto coat
kotoba word, language

kotoshi this year
kotowaru/kotowarimasu refuse
(o-)kotozuke message
kowai afraid, frightening
kowasu/kowashimasu break
kōza o hiraku/hirakimasu open an account
kozutsumi parcel
ku ward (of a city)
kuchi o dasu/dashimasu interrupt
kudasai please; 4, 7
kudasaru/kudasaimasu give; 10
kuizu quizz
kūkō airport
kuni country (nation)
kurabu katsudō club activities
kurasu class
kureru/kuremasu give; 10
kurō suru/shimasu suffer
kuro(ppo)i black(ish)
kuru/kimasu come; 7, 20
kuruma car, taxi
kusuri medicine
kutsu shoes
kutsushita socks
kuzusu/kuzushimasu change (money)
(o-)kyaku-san/sama guest, customer
kyō today
(go-)kyōdai brothers; 9
kyōmi interest
(ni) kyōmi o motte iru/imasu have an interest in
kyonen last year
kyū ni suddenly
kyūkyūsha ambulance

mā well, anyway
machiawase arrangement to meet
machiawase suru/shimasu arrange to meet
machigaeru/machigaemasu get the wrong..., mistake *vt.*
mada not yet; 4, 8
made until; 17
mado window
mae before, in front of, to (time) ; 3, 5, 17

mafurā scarf
magaru/magarimasu turn
mai (*counter*), 5
mainen every year
mainichi every day
mairu/mairimasu go, come; 10, 20
maitsuki every month
maku-no-uchi lunch
mā mā all right (not too good)
manga comic, cartoon
ma ni au/aimasu be in time
manjū bean cake
-mashō (ka) let's, shall we; 3n.10
massugu straight (ahead)
mata again
matsu/machimasu wait for
mattaku completely
mawaru/mawarimasu go round
mawasu/mawashimasu dial, turn
  round *vt.*
mazu first (of all)
mazui poor tasting
me eye
-me, 5
(o-)medetō gozaimasu congratulations
megane o kakeru/kakemasu wear
  glasses
meishi name card
mekura blind
menseki area
meshiagaru/meshiagarimasu eat,
  drink; 17n.1, 20
(o-)miai arranged marriage
michi road, way
midori(iro)(no) green; 2
migi right
mijikai short
mikan (an) orange
mina/minna all, everybody
minami south
miru/mimasu see, look at, watch
(te) miru/mimasu try ... doing, do and
  see; 6n.17, 7n.7, 8n.4
miruku milk
miruku-tei milk tea

(o-)mise shop
miseru/misemasu show
mitai seem, look like; 13
mitsudo density
mitsukaru/mitsukarimasu be found
mitsukeru/mitsukemasu find
mo, 2, 4
-mo, 14, 15
mo ... mo also, too, even
mō already, now; 4
mō (hitotsu) (one) more; 5
mō sukoshi a little more; 5
mokuyōbi Thursday
mondai problem, question
mōningu (sābisu) light breakfast
mono (concrete) thing
morau/moraimasu have, get, receive; 10
moshi if; 18
moshi ka suru to perhaps; 9
moshi moshi hello
mōshi wake nai/arimasen/gozaimasen
  I'm sorry
mōsu/mōshimasu say; 3, 10, 20
motsu/mochimasu hold
motte iru/imasu have (got); 8
motte kuru/kimasu bring
mottomo most; 16
mugicha wheat tea
mukai opposite
mukashi a long time ago
mukō beyond; 3
muri (na) forced, impossible
mushiatsui humid, sticky
musuko(-san) son; 9
musume(-san) daughter; 9
muzukashii difficult

n umm
nado etcetera; 4
nagai long
-nagara while; 17
nai, 6
naifu knife
naka inside; 3
nakanaka rather, very
naku/nakimasu cry

naku naru/narimasu disappear, die; 12
namae name
nan(i) what; 3, 5
nanbai, 5
nanban what number
nanbansen what platform
nanbon, 5
nandemo, 15
n'an desu, 9n.4
nangatsu, 5
nanika, 14, 15
nanimo, 14
nanji(kan), 5, 8
nankagetsu, 8
nankai, 5
nanmai, 5
nannen(kan), 5, 8
nannichi, 5, 8
nannin, 5
nansai, 5
nansatsu, 5
nanshūkan, 5
nante, 12n.4, 20
nanyōbi, 5
naosu/naoshimasu repair, correct
nara if; 18
narau/naraimasu learn
nareru/naremasu get used to
narete iru/imasu be used to
naru/narimasu become; 6, 12, 15
naruhodo I see
nasaru/nasaimasu do; 9, 20
natsu summer
nattō fermented soya
naze why; 9
n'dattara if; 18
n'deshitara if; 18
n'desu the fact, reason is; 9
ne, 2
(o-)negai suru/shimasu please! request
nekutai tie n.
nen year; 5, 8
neru/nemasu sleep, go to bed
nete iru/imasu be asleep
netsu heat, temperature

ni in, to; 3, 4, 5, 19
nibai twice; 16
nichi day; 5
nichijō(seikatsu) daily life
nichiyōbi Sunday
nigeru/nigemasu escape
Nihon Japan
Nihongo Japanese (language)
Nihonjin Japanese (person)
Nihonma Japanese-style room
Nihonshu rice wine
Nihonteki (na) Japanese
nikui difficult to; 6n.5
nimotsu luggage
ninki ga aru/arimasu be popular
nioi smell; 13
nishi west
niwa garden
ni yotte by (means of); 19
n'ja nai desu ka isn't it the case that;
  12n.5
no 's, of; 2, 3
no the fact, thing, one; 15
nō 'No' play
nobasu/nobashimasu stretch vt.
noboru/noborimasu climb
nochihodo later
no de and so; 9
nodo throat
nokoru/nokorimasu remain, be left/stay
  behind
nomimono drink n.
nomu/nomimasu drink vt.
no ni although; 15, 20n.1
(ni) noru/norimasu get on, ride on, board
nugu/nugimasu take off
nuku/nukimasu pull out
nurui tepid
nusumu/nusumimasu steal
nyūin suru/shimasu enter hospital
nyūsu news

o, 4
o-azukari shimasu;/itashimasu I
  receive; 4, 5, 6, 20
o-basan aunt; 9

o-bāsan grandmother; 9

oboeru/oboemasu learn, remember

o-cha tea (ceremony), Japanese tea

o-daiji ni take care

ōfuku return

o-furo bath

o-genki well

o-hana flower arranging

o-hayō gozaimasu good morning

o-hisashiburi desu I haven't seen you for ages

ōi many

o-ide ni naru/narimasu be, come, go; 14n.1, 20

oishii tasty

oitsuku/oitsukimasu catch up

o-jama shimasu excuse me

ojisan uncle; 9

ojīsan grandfather; 9

o-jōzu good (at); 6, 12

o-kaeshi change

o-kage-sama de thanks to you

o-kane money

o-kanjō bill

okā-san mother; 9

okashii, okashi na funny, odd

ōkii, ōki (na) big, large

okiru/okimasu get up

okite iru/imasu be up

okoru/okorimasu get angry

okotte iru/imasu be angry

oku/okimasu put; 18n.4

okuru/okurimasu send

oku-san wife; 9

o-mae you; 20

o-medetō gozaimasu congratulations; 10n.5

o-me ni kakaru/kakarimasu meet; 20

o-miai arranged marriage

o-mise shop

o-mocha toy

omoshiroi interesting, funny

omou/omoimasu think; 11

(to) onaji same (as); 6

(to) onaji yō ni in same way (as)

o-naka stomach

onchi tone deaf

o-negai shimasu please; 4

o-nēsan big sister; 9

o-nīsan big brother; 9

onna woman

onna no hito woman

onna no ko girl

o-nomimono drink

ore I; 20

oriru/orimasu get off

orosu/oroshimasu let off

oru/orimasu be; 3, 20

Ōsaka-ben Osaka dialect

o-sake rice wine, alcoholic drink

o-saki ni after you

o-sara plate

oshieru/oshiemasu teach, tell

osoi late, slow

o-somatsu sama deshita I am sorry it was a poor meal

osoraku presumably; 9

ossharu/osshaimasu say; 20

o-sumai residence

o-taku residence

o-tearai toilet

o-tera temple

oto sound

ōtobai motorbike

otoko (no hito) man

otoko no ko boy

otona adult

otōto younger brother; 9

otōsan father; 9

ototoi day before yesterday

o-tsuri change

owaru/owarimasu finish, end (*vi.*, *vt.*)

o-yasumi nasai good night

oyogu/oyogimasu swim

o-yu hot/boiling water

pasupōto passport

pātei o hiraku/hirakimasu hold a party

perapera fluent

pikunikku picnic

poketto pocket

potsupotsu spit (rain)
purezento present
ragubī rugby
rainen next year
raishū next week
rajio radio
rashii, 13
rei example
reigai exception
reizōko fridge
rekishi history
renshū practice
renshū suru/shimasu practise
rentogen X-ray
repōto report, essay
riyū reason
rōmaji Romanized Japanese
ryō dormitory
ryōri cooking
(go)ryōshin parents; 9
ryūchō (ni) fluent(ly)
ryūgaku study abroad

sabazushi mackerel sushi
sagasu/sagashimasu look for
sai (*counter*), 5
saichū in the middle; 17
saifu wallet, purse
saigo last
saikin recently
saikin (no) recent
saikō excellent
saisho first
sakana fish
sakana-ya fish shop
sake rice wine
saki ahead; 2
sakka author, writer
sakkā soccer
sakuya last night
sameru/samemasu get cold
samishii lonely
samui cold (weather)
samurai warrior
sappari not at all

sararīman businessman
sashiageru/sashiagemasu give; 10
sashimi raw fish
satō sugar
satsu note (money), book counter; 5
sayonara goodbye
se ga hikui short
se ga takai tall
seiji politics
seijika politician
seijiteki (na) political
seikatsu life
seito pupil
seiyō the West
seki seat
seki o hazusu/hazushimasu be absent
  from one's seat
sekken soap
sen plug (bath)
sengetsu last month
senmenki basin
sensei teacher, professor, Sir
senshū last week
sensō war
sensu fan
setsumei explanation
setsumei suru/shimasu explain
shaberu/shaberimasu speak, talk
shachō company president
shakai society
shashin photo
shatsu shirt
shi and; 6n.4
shiai match
shibaraku for a while
shidai depending on; 9n.6
shigoto work
shika only; 5
shikaru/shikarimasu tell off
shikashi but
shiki four seasons
shikki lacquerware
shimaru/shimarimasu shut, close *vi.*
shimatte iru/imasu be shut, closed; 8
shimeru/shimemasu shut, close *vt.*

shimon fingerprint
shinbun newspaper
shindo magnitude
shingō traffic lights
shinkansen bullet train
shinnyūkinshi no entry
shinpai worry
shinsetsu (na) kind
shinu/shinimasu die
shiraberu/shirabemasu check
shiriau/shiriaimasu get to know
shiroi white
shiru/shirimasu (get to) know; 8
shisō thought(s)
shita under, below, bottom
shitsurei (na) impolite, rude
shitte iru/imasu know; 7
shiyakusho city office
shizuka (na) quiet
shodō calligraphy
shōgakusei primary school pupil
shōji paper window
shōka furyō indigestion
shokuji meal
shokuzen before meals
shōshō a little
shōtai invitation
shōtai suru/shimasu invite
shōtotsu collision
shōtotsu suru/shimasu collide
shōyu soya sauce
shufu housewife
(go-)shujin husband; 9
shujutsu operation
shūkan custom
shū(kan) week; 5, 8
shumi pastime, taste, 'cup of tea'
shuppan suru/shimasu publish
shuppatsu suru/shimasu depart
shuto capital city
sō, 2, 3, 6
sō appear; 13
sobo grandmother
sochira there
sofu grandfather

sofutobōru softball
sōji suru/shimasu clean
soko there
sonna that sort of
sonna ni, 16
sono that *adj.*
sore that *n.*
sore ja well then
sore kara and (then)
soretomo or
sorosoro soon, in a moment
soshitara so then
soshite and so
sōsu sauce
soto outside
sotsugyō suru/shimasu graduate from
sō yatte, 6
sugiru/sugimasu too ... ; 6n.16, 7, 12, 15
sugoi great, fantastic, terrible
sugosu/sugoshimasu spend, pass time
sugu immediately; 4, 17
(o-naka ga) suite iru/imasu be hungry; 8
suiyōbi Wednesday
sukāto skirt
sukī ski
suki (na) like(d); 12
sukikirai likes and dislikes
sukiyaki beef dish
sukoshi a little, bit; 5
(o-naka ga) suku/sukimasu get hungry
sukunai few
(o-)sumai residence
sumimasen I am sorry
sumu/sumimasu live
sunakku bar
sunde iru/imasu live
supīchi speech
supōtsu sport
suppai sour
suru/shimasu do, make, decide; 3n.11, 6,
    9n.7, 15, 18n.3
sushi rice and raw fish
suteki (na) dishy, attractive
suteru/sutemasu throw away
sūtsukēsu suit case

(tabako o) suu/suimasu smoke
suwaru/suwarimasu sit
suzushii cool

tabako cigarette
tabemono food
taberu/tabemasu eat
tabi whenever, every time; 17
tabun perhaps; 9
tachiyomi suru/shimasu browse
tada free
tadaima presently, I'm back
taifū typhoon
taihen (na) awful, very
taiho suru/shimasu arrest
takai tall, expensive
takkyū table tennis
takusan many, much; 5
takushī (noriba) taxi (rank)
takuwan pickled radish
tamago egg
tamariba haunt
tame ni for purpose of, in order to; 15
tango vocabulary
tanjōbi birthday
tanomu/tanomimasu request, ask (for);
    11
tanoshii enjoyable, fun
tanoshimi something to look forward to
tanoshimi ni suru/shimasu look
    forward to
taoru towel
tara if, when; 18
tari, 17n.5
tatemono building
tateru/tatemasu stand vt.
tatoeba for example
tatsu/tachimasu stand vi., leave, pass (of
    time); 18n.1
tazuneru/tazunemasu visit
tebukuro glove
tēburu table
tegami letter
teien garden
teikō resistance
teinei (na) polite

temae before; 3
te mo, 19n.2
tenkeiteki (na) typical
tenki weather
tenki(yohō) weather (forecast)
tera temple
terebi TV.
terorisuto terrorist
tetsudau/tetsudaimasu help
to that, with, and, if, when, once; 4, 11, 17,
    18
tōchaku suru/shimasu arrive
toire toilet
(to) issho ni together (with)
toka and, etcetera; 4
tokei watch
tokekomu/tokekomimasu fit into, melt
    into
toki when; 17
tokidoki sometimes; 9
tokonoma alcove
tokoro place; 17
tokoro de by the way
tomaru/tomarimasu stop vi., stay
tomeru/tomemasu stop vt.
tomodachi friend
tonari beside; 3
tonde mo arimasen ridiculous, not at all
toranpu cards (playing)
tōri as; 19n.4
toreru/toremasu come off
tōrokushō registration card
toru/torimasu take, pass vt.
tōru/tōrimasu pass vi.
tōsuto toast
totemo very (much)
totte iku/ikimasu take
totte kuru/kimasu go and get
tsubasa wing
tsugi next
tsuiraku suru/shimasu crash
(ni) tsuite regarding, about
tsuite iru/imasu be on (light, TV., etc.)
tsukareru/tsukaremasu become tired
tsukarete iru/imasu be tired

tsukau/tsukaimasu use
tsukemono pickle
tsukeru/tsukemasu put on (TV.), attach
tsukiatari end (of road)
tsukiau/tsukiaimasu go out (with)
tsuku/tsukimasu go on, arrive
tsukuru/tsukurimasu make
tsumaranai boring
tsumetai cool, cold (to the touch)
tsumori intention; 9
tsurai hard work, tiring
tsurete ikiu/ikimasu take (a person)
tsutaeru/tsutaemasu convey, pass on
(ni) tsutomeru/tsutomemasu work (for)
tsūyaku suru/shimasu interpret
tsuyoi strong
tsuyu rainy season
tsuzukeru/tsuzukemasu continue *vt.*
tsuzuku/tsuzukimasu continue *vi.*

uchi home, house
uchi before; 17
uchikorosu/uchikoroshimasu shoot dead
ue top, on, above; 3
uisukī whisky
ukagau/ukagaimasu visit, ask; 3n.3, 20
ukeru/ukemasu go down well, receive
umai good at, tasty
umareru/umaremasu be born
umeboshi sour plum
umi(be) sea(side)
un umm ...
unagi bentō eel lunch
untenshu(-san) driver
urayamashii envious
ureshii pleased
uriba sales department
uru/urimasu sell
ushiro behind
uta song
utau/utaimasu sing
utsu/uchimasu shoot
utsukushii beautiful
uwagi jacket

wa (*subject, object, topic particle*) 2, 3, 4, 12
wain wine
wakai young
wakaru/wakarimasu understand; 12
wake, 18n.2
waku/wakimasu boil *vi.*
wā puro word processor
warau/waraimasu laugh
wari to quite
warui bad
washoku Japanese food
wasureru/wasuremasu forget; 15
(o) wataru/watarimasu cross over; 4
watashi I, me
watashitachi we, us
watasu/watashimasu hand over
wazuka a little

ya and; 4
yabun osoku late at night
yakyū baseball
yama mountain
yameru/yamemasu stop *vt.*, give up; 12
yamu/yamimasu stop *vi.*
yane roof
yappari after all, as expected
yaru/yarimasu do, play
yasashii kind, easy
yasui cheap
-yasui easy to; 6n.5
yasumi holiday, rest
yasumu/yasumimasu rest
yawarakai soft
yayakoshii tricky
yo (no naka) the world
yo, 2
yō (ni) (na), 11, 12, 13
yobu/yobimasu call, invite, get (a person)
yōfuku clothing
yōi preparation
yōji business
yokatta *see* ii
yokatta desu that's good
yoko ni naru/narimasu lie down
yoku often, well
yomikaki reading and writing

yomu/yomimasu read
yopparatte iru/imasu be drunk
yopparau/yopparaimasu get drunk
yori than; 16
yoroshii good, all right, O.K.; 14n.6
(ni) yoru to according to; 13n.1
yotei plan; 9
yūbe last night
yūbinkyoku post office
yuka floor
yūkai suru/shimasu kidnap
yuki snow
yuki destination; 5n.7
yukkuri slow
yukkuri suru/shimasu take one's time

yūmei (na) famous
yurui loose

zannen (na) regrettable
zasshi magazine
zehi by all means
zenbu all, everything
zenbu de altogether
zenzen (not) at all
zettai (ni) definitely
zonjiru/zonjimasu think; 20
zubon trousers
zuibun a good deal
zutto much (more); 16

Appendix 1

The syllables represented in the table on page 9 are given here in *hiragana*:

a あ	i い	u う	e え	o お
ka か	ki き	ku く	ke け	ko こ
sa さ	shi し	su す	se せ	so そ
ta た	chi ち	tsu つ	te て	to と
na な	ni に	nu ぬ	ne ね	no の
ha は ¹	hi ひ	fu ふ	he へ ²	ho ほ
ma ま	mi み	mu む	me め	mo も
ya や		yu ゆ		yo よ
ra ら	ri り	ru る	re れ	ro ろ
wa わ				
o を ³				
n ん				

1 The *hiragana* symbol は (**ha**) is also used for writing the particle **wa**.

2 The *hiragana* symbol へ (**he**) is also used for **e** ('to', 'towards').

3 This *hiragana* symbol is used for the object particle **o** only.

The 'voiced sounds' **ga, gi, gu** etc., **za, ji, zu** etc., **da, ji, zu** etc., and **ba, bi, bu** etc. (rows 3, 5, 7 and 10 of the table on page 9) are made by adding a *nigori* mark (˝) to **ka, ki, ku** etc., **sa, shi, su** etc., **ta, chi, tsu** etc. and **ha, hi, fu** etc. respectively. (**Pa, pi, pu** etc. – row 11, page 9 – is made by adding a small circle to **ha, hi, fu** etc.)

2

Examples:

ながさき	**Nagasaki**
ぎんざ	**Ginza** (a main street in Tokyo)
だめ	**dame**
ぶぶん	**bubun**

Note that the long 'ō' syllable (ō, kō, sō etc.) is generally written 'ou', 'kou', 'sou', etc.

そう	**sō**
じょうず	**jōzu**
ほう	**hō**

But there are a small number of exceptions:

おおきい	**ōkii**
おおい	**ōi**

The 'double consonant' is written like this with a small **tsu**:

かった	**katta**
まった	**matta**
ちょっと	**chotto**

Other combined syllables are as explained in the Introduction. Study now the examples below:

げいしゃ	**geisha**
しゅじゅつ	**shujutsu**

しゅうかん	shūkan
おちゃ	o-cha
いちにちじゅう	ichinichijū
おばさん	obasan
おばあさん	obāsan
きょうと	Kyōto
きゅうしゅう	Kyūshū
あな	ana
あんな	anna
かた	kata
かった	katta

Appendix 2

The small selection of *kanji* (Chinese characters) given below represents some of the more common ones the visitor is likely to see on the streets of Japan. Some of these may appear in *hiragana* as well. The words marked with an asterisk are in *katakana*:

駅	**(eki)**	station
地下鉄	**(chikatetsu)**	subway station
切符売場	**(kippu uriba)**	ticket office
改札口	**(kaisatsu guchi)**	ticket gate
入口	**(iriguchi)**	entrance
出口	**(deguchi)**	exit
非常口	**(hijōguchi)**	emergency exit
押す	**(osu)**	push
引く	**(hiku)**	pull
中央口	**(chūōguchi)**	central exit
北口	**(kitaguchi)**	north exit
南口	**(minamiguchi)**	south exit
西口	**(nishiguchi)**	west exit
東口	**(higashiguchi)**	east exit
コインロッカー	**(koinrokka*)**	coin locker
待合室	**(machiaishitsu)**	waiting room
お手洗い	**(o-tearai)**	toilet

便所 **(benjō)** toilet

トイレ **(toire*)** toilet

化粧室 **(keshōshitsu)** powder room

男子用 **(danshiyō)** men

女子用 **(joshiyō)** women

使用中 **(shiyōchu)** engaged

故障中 **(koshōchū)** out of order

飲料水 **(inryōsui)** drinking water

タクシー 乗り場 **(takushī* noriba)** taxi rank

駐車場 **(chūshajō)** parking

駐車禁止 **(chūsha kinshi)** parking forbidden

土足厳禁 **(dosoku genkin)** shoes strictly forbidden

立入禁止 **(tachiiri kinshi)** no entry

禁煙 **(kin'en)** no smoking

銀行 **(ginkō)** bank

郵便局 **(yūbinkyoku)** post office

医院 **(iin)** doctor's surgery

営業中 **(eigyōchū)** open

閉店 **(heiten)** closed

案内 **(annai)** information

受け付 **(uketsuke)** reception

ホテル　**(hoteru*)** hotel

旅館　**(ryokan)** Japanese-style inn

喫茶店　**(kissaten)** coffee shop